Food Regulation and Trade

Toward a Safe and Open Global System

TIM JOSLING   DONNA ROBERTS   DAVID ORDEN

Food Regulation and Trade

Toward a Safe and Open Global System

INSTITUTE FOR INTERNATIONAL ECONOMICS
Washington, DC
March 2004

Tim Josling is emeritus professor at the Food Research Institute and senior fellow at the Stanford Institute for International Studies, Stanford University. He has held academic positions at Stanford, the University of Reading, and the London School of Economics and Political Science. He is the author of *Agricultural Trade Policy: Completing the Reform* (1998).

Donna Roberts is a senior economist at the Economic Research Service, US Department of Agriculture. She served as a delegate to the WTO's Committee on the Application of Sanitary and Phytosanitary Measures while on assignment at the US Trade Representative's Permanent Mission in Geneva from 1996 to 2002. In her current position, she continues her research on food regulation and trade.

David Orden is senior research fellow at the International Food Policy Research Institute and professor in the department of agricultural and applied economics, Virginia Polytechnic Institute and State University. He was visiting fellow at the University of New South Wales (1990–91) and visiting professor at Stanford University (1998–99). He is coauthor of *Policy Reform in American Agriculture: Analysis and Prognosis* (University of Chicago Press, 1999).

INSTITUTE FOR INTERNATIONAL
ECONOMICS
1750 Massachusetts Avenue, NW
Washington, DC 20036-1903
(202) 328-9000 FAX: (202) 659-3225
www.iie.com

Printing by Kirby Lithographic Company, Inc.
Typesetting by Sandra F. Watts

Printed in the United States of America
06 05 04   5 4 3 2 1

Library of Congress Cataloging-in-
Publication Data

Josling, Timothy Edward.
   Food regulation and trade : toward a safe and open global system / Timothy Josling, Donna Roberts, David Orden.
      p. cm.
   Includes bibliographical references and index.
      ISBN 0-88132-346-2
   1. Food adulteration and inspection—Government policy. 2. Food adulteration and inspection—Law and legislation.
   I. Roberts, Donna H.   II. Orden, David.   III. Institute for International Economics (U.S.)   IV. Title

HD   2003
9000.9   2002192247
.A1
J67
2004

Contents

Figures

Boxes

Preface

The discovery of a single animal with "mad cow disease" in a herd in the state of Washington in December 2003 put on hold US beef exports to two dozen countries despite assurances offered to consumers that the US food supply remained safe. This incident has reminded us yet again of the intimate linkages between health and safety regulations, consumer confidence, and trade.

Earlier in 2003, several African countries declined shipments of US food aid on the grounds that they might contain genetically modified corn. They feared that their farmers might plant some of the seeds and thus compromise the countries' food exports to the European Union, which has banned those imports. This vividly illustrated that the different US and EU positions on food biotechnology regulation can have significant repercussions on countries in Africa and Asia and on the nature of world agricultural markets.

Sorting out which technical regulations are justified on health grounds or to correct other market failures and which are protectionist measures in disguise is a constant challenge for the multilateral trade system. The Uruguay Round attempted to resolve this issue by mandating the use of science-based risk management in animal, plant, and human health regulations affecting trade. It also took steps to ensure that measures taken by countries to achieve other legitimate regulatory and standards-based objectives would be least trade distorting. These disciplines were to be enforced through the strengthened dispute settlement mechanism to prevent countries from misusing their measures.

Nine years later, we see that disputes over these measures have not gone away. In one persistent case, the European Union still has in place a ban on hormone-treated beef in dispute for two decades and now ruled illegal by the WTO. Many other national import regulations continue to be regarded by exporting countries as nontariff barriers to trade.

This book attempts to explain why these issues are so intractable and what can be done to improve the compatibility of national food regulations to achieve smoothly functioning global food markets. The authors assess the current state of domestic and international food regulation from the perspective of an increasingly integrated food system. They point out the crucial distinction between risk-based regulations and those that relate to other quality attributes. They note the trend toward defining standards in terms of the production method as opposed to the product composition and the implications thereof for increasing trade friction. They also emphasize the emerging partnership between public agencies and private firms in the provision and enforcement of regulations and standards and the desirable role for international rules and institutions in these matters.

From their broad analysis and interwoven case studies, the authors conclude that there is ample room for improving the performance of regulatory authorities in providing safe food and preventing the spread of animal and plant disease. International institutions can play a vital role in coordinating these efforts among developed and developing countries and in reducing uncertainty. By contrast, the role of governments in the regulation of quality should in most cases be limited to the prevention of misleading claims, and international rules should be focused on reducing transactions costs through other means rather than imposing uniform measures across disparate markets.

This book is a complement to previous Institute publications on agricultural trade, including Dale E. Hathaway's *Agriculture and the GATT: Rewriting the Rules* (1987), Hathaway and William Miner's *Reforming World Agricultural Trade* (1988), and Timothy Josling's *Agricultural Trade Policy: Completing the Reform* (1998). Agricultural trade reform goes hand in hand with the improvement of health and safety regulations for agriculture and food. In the Doha Round, even the extension of the system of "geographical indications" for wines and spirits to other food products such as cheese and ham has become entangled with the attempt to liberalize trade. As trade in processed foods and high-value products expands, more controversial issues will center on questions of safety and quality. This book is a guide to understanding these issues and resolving them in a manner compatible with open trade, hence ensuring the efficient provision of a diverse, healthy, and safe food supply.

The Institute for International Economics is a private nonprofit institution for the study and discussion of international economic policy. Its purpose is to analyze important issues in that area and to develop and communicate practical new approaches for dealing with them. The Institute is completely nonpartisan.

The Institute is funded largely by philanthropic foundations. Major institutional grants are now being received from the William M. Keck, Jr. Foundation and the Starr Foundation. A number of other foundations and private corporations contribute to the highly diversified financial resources of the Institute. About 18 percent of the Institute's resources in our latest fiscal year were provided by contributors outside the United States, including about 8 percent from Japan.

The Board of Directors bears overall responsibilities for the Institute and gives general guidance and approval to its research program, including the identification of topics that are likely to become important over the medium run (one to three years), and which should be addressed by the Institute. The director, working closely with the staff and outside Advisory Committee, is responsible for the development of particular projects and makes the final decision to publish an individual study.

The Institute hopes that its studies and other activities will contribute to building a stronger foundation for international economic policy around the world. We invite readers of these publications to let us know how they think we can best accomplish this objective.

C. FRED BERGSTEN
Director
January 2004

Acknowledgments

This book is the culmination of several years of collaboration among the three authors on the issues surrounding agricultural and food safety and quality regulations.

Our efforts began with the joint work by Donna Roberts and David Orden on the easing of a long-standing US ban on imports of avocados from Mexico and a worldwide assessment of technical barriers to US agricultural exports spearheaded by Roberts. Two National Research Initiative grants from the US Department of Agriculture (USDA) and additional financial support from the USDA Economic Research Service enabled all three of us to investigate and analyze the trade impacts of sanitary and phytosanitary (SPS) barriers. This led to a bulletin on this subject for the Economic Research Service, collaboration between Roberts and Tim Josling on a study of the beef hormone dispute, a collective study of SPS issues in the global poultry market, and various papers on the impact of SPS measures on developing countries. Communication was enhanced by a year that Orden spent at the Institute for International Studies at Stanford University working on building SPS barriers into trade models. We also thank the European Commission for supporting Orden's contributions in 2002 through a grant to the International Food Policy Research Institute.

In addition to our own joint efforts, we have each gained significantly from coauthorship with others on these issues: Josling with Lee Ann Patterson, Dirk Heumeuller, Peter Philips, and Ian Sheldon; Roberts with Laurian Unnevehr, Julie Caswell, Kate DeRemer, and Suzanne Thornsbury; and Orden with Richard Snape, Eduardo Romano, Clare Narrod, Joseph Glauber, and Everett Peterson. Roberts also gained much from discussions with colleagues at the US Permanent Mission to the World Trade Organization and other experts in Geneva during her six-year tour there. However much we try to absolve our many associates from responsibility, their influence is clearly in this volume.

Each of us also has had valuable research assistance in these projects, from students and others, and we would like to thank in particular Nishita Bakshi, Fuzhi Cheng, Takayoshi Yamagiwa, and Rachel Anderson for their efforts.

Authorship of this book is equally shared. Though chapters were drafted individually, in the process of editing they became common property. We have taken care not to burden the reader with any differences that remain in our own opinions. The cordiality of coauthorship survived even the stresses of a lengthy editing process, and we assume collective responsibility for the final product. Roberts writes in her own capacity, and the ideas here should not be assumed to represent those of her employer.

We would like to thank C. Fred Bergsten and his colleagues at the Institute for International Economics for their enthusiasm and support, which carried us through the various stages of the project. This volume is intended to fill one niche in the impressive list of publications on trade policy issues produced by this institution. We benefited from the helpful comments of the participants in an Institute seminar in May 2002 and particularly from detailed suggestions from Julie Caswell after that meeting.

We would like to acknowledge the very helpful and constructive comments of reviewers Dale Hathaway, Clare Narrod, Robert Paarlberg, Stefan Tangermann, Laurian Unnevehr, and John Wilson. None are to be blamed for our errors of omission or commission, but the text was improved considerably by their input.

Finally, we would like to acknowledge the patience of our families, who, as ever, provided moral support when publication deadlines imposed on other activities.

1

Food Regulation in an Open Economy

Consumers expect the world food system to provide them with a wide choice of products that are safe and nutritious and have other desirable qualities. In most countries, domestic food production and local delivery mechanisms go a long way toward achieving these goals. But, increasingly, imported goods are supplementing countries' domestic food supply. Through international trade, food choices are becoming more diverse, and foods are available at prices that are considerably lower than if each country could buy only from its own producers.

Because citizens universally hold their governments responsible for ensuring that foods procured both domestically and internationally meet certain expectations, complex regulatory regimes are in place for food markets. These regimes broadly succeed in providing a high level of safety and consumer satisfaction, at least for those people with adequate incomes to purchase through regulated channels. In short, the global food system generally works well.

There is, however, considerable room for improvement in international food regulation. The food system is susceptible to pests and diseases that can damage agricultural production at home or abroad. Unsafe crop and livestock production methods or failures in food processing and handling continue to cause some illness. These are the very conditions that food regulations can help to avoid. And yet regulatory measures are often perversely divergent among countries, and trade restrictions designed to favor domestic producers are often disguised as health and safety rules. Moreover, the factors affecting food regulation are constantly changing. New pathogens are emerging to challenge existing procedures, and new detection and eradication technologies are creating opportunities to update regulatory measures, prompting both trade opportunities and trade frictions. The increased movement of food products, animals, and people across borders adds to the pathways by which disease-causing organisms can spread, elevating the need for vigilance and control. Finally, evolving consumer preferences produce additional calls for regulations for both safety and quality attributes, in particular in wealthy countries. The result is that the national and international regulation of foods is under stress.

The provision of food safety, for example, presents public authorities with an interesting dilemma. Policies with this objective have to be both effective and unobtrusive. They have to be firmly overseen by public institutions and at the same time must extensively involve the private sector. They need to reflect national conditions and local preferences and at the same time be consistent with the realities of a global economy. Food safety regimes that work well have the confidence of the consumer. Indeed, even the occasional outbreak of food-borne illness will reflect on the success of the regulatory agencies in their role as watchdogs and reinforce the notion that the food system is under control. By contrast, food regulatory regimes that are dysfunctional attract media attention and consumer anxiety even when outbreaks of illness are not serious or life-threatening.

Regulation of the food supply is closely scrutinized in most countries by producer and consumer interest groups. Producers tend to focus on the costs of regulations, while some consumer groups focus on well-defined health issues—both the prevention of disease and illness and the promotion of better long-term nutritional habits. Other groups have taken an interest in how food is produced: whether farms are using environmentally sound practices, whether pesticides and other chemicals are being used, and how animals are being treated. These process-oriented groups often identify modern industrialized food production with negative social impacts and look positively toward an "alternative" agriculture. Genetically modified (GM) foods are a current source of controversy for these groups. The debate over GM regulation has centered on consumers' right to know how their foods are produced, as well as on whether genetic modifications of a kind difficult to attain by normal crossbreeding pose a risk to human health or to biodiversity, or violate ethical norms. Food regulation issues have thus become part of a broader social discourse on desirable industrial structures and the impact of technology on the quality of life.

Food regulations that affect trade are also critical for developing countries and their place in the global economy. These countries are playing a significant role in food trade, and increasingly in the high-value processed food trade. As exporters, they are finding higher value added a useful way of avoiding dependence on primary commodities; as importers, they are satisfying desires for modern service sectors such as supermarkets and convenience food outlets.

The broad regulatory challenge facing the governments of developing and developed countries alike is to design institutions and policies that ensure the wide availability of food products with attributes consumers seek without imposing undue regulatory burdens. But ensuring food safety and quality comes at a cost, and guarantees are not absolute. Thus regulatory decisions involve trade-offs among objectives, and are inevitably constrained by the availability of resources. Often these trade-offs and resource constraints are most apparent when developing countries are affected by the regulatory decisions of developed countries. Food regulations then become an issue in the North-South trade discourse.

The context for food regulation and global integration also has been transformed since the terrorist attacks on the World Trade Center and the Pentagon on September 11, 2001. Biosecurity has taken on new dimensions, and products that move across borders are treated more suspiciously. This situation has created uncertainty and transactions costs that impinge particularly on trade that could put domestic animal, plant, or human populations at risk. Thus efforts to integrate global agricultural and food markets face daunting new security as well as economic and political challenges.

For these many reasons, the issues surrounding food regulation have become important topics in both domestic and international policy discussions, and will remain so. Regulators are being asked increasingly to provide services related to safety and quality in food markets. As a result, the regulatory environment for agricultural and agroindustrial producers will likely become ever more complex in the coming years, even while reform initiatives aimed at reducing the number and rigidity of regulations in other sectors are under way.

Globalization of the Food Supply

The growing globalization of the food system over the last few decades is a remarkable economic development with wide-reaching consequences. What was once a set of national markets linked mainly by raw material trade from land-rich to land-scarce countries has become a loosely integrated global market with movements of capital, raw and semiprocessed goods, final products, and consumer retail services. The world trade in agricultural products is approaching $600 billion annually, with developed countries exporting slightly more than developing countries of that total and importing considerably more (see table 1.1). Bulk commodities of grains and oilseeds now make up only one-sixth of trade in agricultural products. Trade in the many diverse processed and high-value food products now exceeds 80 percent of global agricultural commerce, and continues to grow at twice the rate of the trade in primary products.

Table 1.1 Trade patterns in agricultural, forestry, and fishery products (billions of US dollars)

	Importer	
Exporter/products	Developed countries	Developing countries
Developed countries		
Bulk commodities	13.2	10.4
Processed intermediates	35.4	18.3
Produce and horticultural products	22.7	3.7
High-value processed products	90.1	33.1
Related agricultural products	50.2	26.5
Total	211.6	92.0
Developing countries		
Bulk commodities	37.1	36.4
Processed intermediates	27.1	29.1
Produce and horticultural products	15.7	12.1
High-value processed products	25.8	25.5
Related agricultural products	53.5	25.1
Total	159.3	128.0

Note: Bulk commodities include primarily grains and oilseeds; processed intermediates include oilseed meals, vegetable oils, animal feed, pet food, live animals, wool, and hides and skins; horticultural products include fresh fruits and vegetables; high-value processed products include roasted coffee, cocoa products, beverages, dairy products, eggs, meats, and processed fruits and vegetables; related agricultural products include seafood, distilled spirits, leather, fish, wood, yarn, thread, and leather.

Source: International Bilateral Agricultural Trade (IBAT) database (1997), developed by the Economic Research Service, US Department of Agriculture, from UNCTAD (United Nations Conference on Trade and Development) bilateral trade data.

Developing countries remain relatively more dependent than developed countries on trade in bulk commodities.

The growth in levels and diversity of agricultural trade presents a greater likelihood that conflicts will arise over food regulation. Yet there is no inherent reason why increased trade is inconsistent with achieving food safety and quality objectives. Quite the contrary, trade can contribute to the provision of a safe, high-quality, diverse food supply. Countries have wide latitude to set their own standards and apply regulations to ensure that foods, whether procured at home or abroad, meet those standards.[1] In some cases, common standards can be agreed on at an international

---

1. Standards establish product specifications for common and repeated use, and may be either mandatory or voluntary. In this book, the legal status of a standard is noted when the distinction is important.

level, thereby creating scope for exporters to achieve greater economies of scale in both production and certification. In other cases, national regulations will legitimately differ, but with transparency and nondiscrimination, producers should be able to take such differences into account and even benefit from them.

Unfortunately, the integration of global food regulation into a seamless web of national and multilateral measures remains an aspiration, not a reality. Trade tensions are on the rise, in part reflecting the rapid growth in the processed food trade and the development of sophisticated food supply chains. This growth has had the effect of highlighting the differences in national regulations. It also underscores the utility of strengthening the global regulatory framework to facilitate desirable food trade.

In a step toward better management of regulation-based trade conflicts, international rules related to regulatory decisions were strengthened in 1995 under the World Trade Organization (WTO). A globalized food system requires at minimum a consistent framework within which domestic regulations can be developed, even if those regulations are not entirely harmonious. At one level, this is a technical task. Domestic regulators can and do meet in bilateral, plurilateral, and multilateral forums to compare scientific evidence on hazards, to discuss regulatory differences arising from income differentials or cultural heterogeneity among countries, and to iron out arbitrary regulatory provisions that unnecessarily impede trade. Yet domestic bureaucratic entanglements complicate the task of avoiding incompatible regulations. In some instances, domestic regulatory agencies cling to past practices and standards, in part out of inertia and in part as a way of ensuring bureaucratic survival. Their task of devising technical regulations for a global market is complicated by the tendency at the political level for food issues to be widely cast as involving national sovereignty. National politicians are not keen to cede authority to outside agencies or other governments to regulate their domestic food supplies.

National food regulatory systems are also subject to the political pressures exerted by narrow interest groups. Indeed, the regulatory role of public authorities often is subverted to private ends—not to intentionally compromise public health or consumer choice, but to increase incomes to those firms and individuals who can benefit from some aspects of the regulations. Some vested interests exploit regulatory differences for the sake of furthering producer protection. Others push for a degree of harmonization that may be inappropriate, seeking reduced costs for commercial advantage. And some organized consumer and environmental groups divert regulations from the pursuit of national goals of food safety to favor other agendas.

Global agriculture is also riddled with national subsidies to farmers and trade barriers that protect farmers in some countries and discriminate against those in others. This situation perpetuates a widely criticized disarray in world agricultural production and generates substantial trade conflicts.[2] Since the inception of the General Agreement on Tariffs and Trade (GATT) in 1948, agriculture has been treated as a special case in trade rules and kept largely outside the liberalizing process for multilateral trade. Partly as a result of this exemption, the growth rate of agricultural trade, particularly trade of bulk commodities, has been less than that of trade in other goods. It was not until the GATT Uruguay Round negotiations of 1986–94 that governments began to address agricultural distortions with agreed on disciplines on domestic agricultural support, market access, and export subsidies. But only modest progress was achieved in reducing support and protection levels in the Uruguay Round. Ongoing conflicts over the remaining interventions and their effects have exacerbated efforts to resolve disputes about food regulations.

Despite these political realities, the case for coherence in food regulations is clear: the global food system can work better if domestic measures are disciplined to reduce the scope for trade conflicts. Technical trade barriers exist in most industries, but these measures are particularly instrumental in restricting the movement of primary and processed agricultural products. Regulatory progress will entail ensuring that the benefits stemming from open markets and international trade are not reduced by the misuse of various measures for protectionist purposes, and that conflicting regulatory instruments do not inadvertently impede trade. It will also entail ensuring that attention to trade issues does not undermine industry and public trust in food safety regulations or the satisfaction of the diverse preferences of consumers.

The movement toward strengthened global integration in agriculture and food is now at a crucial juncture. Agricultural policy reform and food-sector regulatory issues are key to the success of the WTO round of talks known as the Doha Development Agenda, launched in November 2001 and scheduled for completion in 2005 but likely to be delayed after failure to reach midterm agreement at meetings in Cancún in 2003. Developed countries agreed in the initial Doha negotiations to further economic integration by providing technical assistance to efforts to build up the regulatory capacity of developing countries and increase their participation in international standard-setting institutions. The agricultural negotiations in the Doha Round are aimed largely at reducing countries' protection levels and further restricting domestic agricultural support programs. But several proposals in the Doha agriculture negotiations urge wider latitude in the WTO rules for "nontrade concerns." Some dimensions of the proposed latitude could undercut progress toward ensuring

---

2. The authors have written elsewhere on distortions arising from domestic and trade policies for agriculture. See, for example, Josling (1998); Orden, Paarlberg, and Roe (1999); and Moyer and Josling (2002). OECD (2003) provides the latest annual estimate of the magnitude of these subsidies in developed countries.

that regulatory standards are not impediments to agricultural trade, in particular by citing elements of the food production process as reasons for excluding imports or for subsidizing domestic production based on particular technologies.

Objectives and Organization of This Book

This book assesses in broad terms the current state of regulation of the global food system and highlights avenues for progress toward more open agricultural trade with sustained or enhanced food safety and quality standards.

Objectives

In examining the status and prospects for food regulation and trade, this book addresses four basic questions:

- What is the nature of the food safety and quality issues that require, or appear to require, public regulation?

- How do countries address these various issues through domestic and international institutions, policies, and measures?

- What trade tensions arise among countries from the different regulatory decisions made by governments, and how might these tensions be reduced?

- How might the international regulatory framework be strengthened to make the safety and efficiency of the global food system more effective?

Organization

Chapters 2 and 3 describe the scope of food regulation and its effects on trade. Chapter 2 looks at the rationale for regulatory activities and characterizes the institutions through which national regulations are enacted and administered, together with the sets of regulations and directives produced by these decision bodies. Trade conflicts sometimes arise over broad issues such as the appropriate goals of regulation, but they occur more often over differences about specific regulatory policy instruments and requirements for verifying compliance with the applied measures. Chapter 2 also examines the economic impacts of regulatory interventions and the political economy of the food trade regulatory process and includes a framework for assessing whether there is regulatory "overprotection" or "underprotection."

Chapter 3 turns to the international institutions that have emerged to discipline national regulations with the objective of improving the functioning of the global food system. The chapter describes the relevant provisions of the GATT, the newer WTO agreements on sanitary and phytosanitary (SPS) measures and on other technical barriers to trade (TBT), and the components of the agreement dealing with the trade-related aspects of intellectual property (TRIPS).[3] The role of international standards organizations in the global food system is examined in this context. The chapter assesses how well the WTO has functioned in disciplining global food regulations since it came into force in 1995. This assessment encompasses the effects the WTO disciplines have had on regulatory decisions at the national, bilateral and regional levels; the notification of regulations and objections raised to these regulations in the SPS and TBT Committees of the WTO; and the trade conflicts over food regulations that have gone forward through the formal WTO dispute resolution process. The chapter concludes with a discussion of the food regulation issues that are on the WTO Doha Development Agenda and are the subject of ongoing negotiations.

Chapters 4–7 look in detail at a variety of current and potential food regulatory issues in order to further determine the nature of the trade problems they invoke, how they are related to national regulatory policies, and where the potential exists for improvements in the multilateral framework in which the national regulations operate. Several illustrative examples are elaborated in each chapter.

One key distinction among food regulation issues is that some involve threats to animal, plant, and human health and safety and some involve the nonhealth aspects of product quality and methods of production. More specifically, regulatory issues related to animal, plant, and human health and safety center on risk-reducing measures taken after advice from experts in the biological sciences; those related to the nonhealth aspects of product quality and production methods involve nonrisk-reducing or quality-related measures in which risk assessment usually plays a minor role. Risk-reducing measures are adopted to address market failures that fall into two categories. The first category comprises failures that arise primarily in production, in instances in which individual producer efforts are insufficient to stem the spread of an agricultural pest or disease. The second category is composed of failures that occur primarily at the point of purchase or consumption, when imperfect information reduces incentives for private firms to supply the levels of food safety that consumers desire. Some degree of public regulation in the area of animal, plant, and human health is widely recognized as a legitimate

---

3. *Sanitary* refers to human and animal health measures; *phytosanitary* refers only to plant health instruments. When a distinction between animal and human health issues is needed, the animal issues are referred to as "zoosanitary" measures.

function of government, although this consensus leaves ample room for disagreement about individual regulatory measures.

The regulation of food quality is also intended to remedy information failures—but of a different kind. Markets provide the private sector with many incentives to furnish the quality attributes sought by consumers. Yet, because some of the attributes that consumers are willing to pay for cannot be ascertained directly by them at the time of purchase, regulatory oversight of producers' claims is viewed as a responsibility of the public sector. Advocates of a larger role for government in the regulation of quality in the agricultural sector, as compared with the industrial sector, assert that because many food products carry no brands, the ability of reputational mechanisms to protect the integrity of market transactions is diminished. International food trade may compound this problem of establishing reputation and providing reliable information to consumers.

The risk-reducing regulations affecting trade are discussed in chapters 4 and 5. Chapter 4 looks at the control of animal and plant pests and diseases, including zoonotic diseases that can be transmitted from animals to humans. The coordination of national regulatory actions to address these hazards will often produce benefits, but trade tensions occur when countries differ in pest or disease incidence, set different regulatory standards, or utilize different control measures. Chapter 4 assesses the extent to which animal and plant pests and diseases have caused trade conflicts, and three examples are presented of recent regulatory decisions and their effects: for plant pests, the recent easing of a long-standing US ban on imports of avocados from Mexico, and for animal diseases, the challenges associated with management of foot-and-mouth disease (FMD), which is endemic in some countries and occurs in costly sporadic outbreaks in others, and the crisis in food regulation that has stemmed from bovine spongiform encephalopathy (BSE) or "mad cow disease," which has been associated so far with over 100 human fatalities in Great Britain.

Chapter 5 looks more closely at food safety and control of food-related human health hazards not directly tied to animal diseases. The food safety agencies of many countries have received major overhauls over the past decade, but mostly in response to domestic concerns rather than the international spread of illness or disease. Food safety issues lead to trade conflicts, but for reasons different than those associated with animal and plant hazards. This chapter examines regulations that seek to prevent illness from food-borne pathogens such as *Salmonella*, *E. coli*, and aflatoxins. Even more contentious are those food safety issues that relate not so much to the struggle of humans to control naturally occurring pathogens, but to the possible and perceived side effects of utilization of particular modern technologies and production processes. This chapter examines the long-standing dispute between the United States and the European Union over treating livestock with hormones to increase growth rates, and the possible implications for human health of antibiotics and other drugs administered to livestock in concentrated production systems.

Chapter 6 turns to the regulation of food quality, in particular through the provision of information to guide consumer choice. It describes alternative roles for the private and public sectors in creating, verifying, and enforcing quality standards and labeling. Examples discussed include the standards of identity that are needed to define products, but that can be turned into trade-distorting measures if misused to artificially distinguish between closely related domestic and foreign goods. Chapter 6 also looks at the regulation of geographic indications and country-of-origin labels to draw the distinction between information on locality of production that might improve consumer decisions and information that gives certain groups of producers the opportunity to exclude others from contesting particular markets. Finally, this chapter examines nutritional information, which, while benefiting consumers, could increase the transactions costs of trade among countries with different labeling systems.

The discussion of quality-oriented regulations highlights a second useful distinction for categorizing regulatory measures. This distinction rests on whether a measure is related to an attribute of the final product (a content attribute) or to a characteristic of the production process (a process attribute), including the location of production. Each kind of attribute can be important to, but not detectable by, consumers. Consumers cannot determine on their own, for example, whether orange juice has been enriched with calcium or whether coffee is shade-grown. When authorities choose to achieve an information or other public policy goal through regulations directed at content attributes, verification of the attribute can be achieved through testing. Regulations that instead target process attributes generally require a record-keeping system to verify ingredient or product sources. Whether regulations target content or process attributes is sometimes dictated by the ultimate regulatory goal, but in other instances it reflects the choices of regulatory authorities. Their choices will affect the parameters of the regulations that set out the breadth, depth, and precision of requirements to substantiate claims about food products and ingredients, which in turn will affect the costs and benefits of the measures imposed.

Several of the most pressing contemporary challenges to the food regulation system have arisen because the regulation of quality-related process attributes is at issue. The main feature of these challenges is that they raise the prospect of a proliferation of product differentiation based on the process of production, with associated complexities in verification of compliance with regulations and the potential for conflict among trading partners with different regulatory standards. Three of these issues are discussed in chapter 7. Paramount among these challenges is the regulation of genetically modified foods. The introduction of such food products— so far mainly corn and soybeans but also a growing number of other products—has brought to the forefront several issues: the rights or desires of consumers to be told about the technology behind the foods they buy, whether this right or desire is to be addressed through voluntary or mandatory content or process regulation, what tolerances will be associated with various product claims, and the burdens that different regulatory options will place on verification of compliance. Emerging conflicts over genetically modified foods raise risk-related issues as well as issues of consumer preferences and choice, both of which complicate the regulatory task and bring different coalitions of political forces to bear on decision-making institutions. The adoption and regulation of agricultural products derived from biotechnology has polarized countries, and is splitting much of the global food market into GM and non-GM systems. Other process attribute issues, though less contentious so far than genetically modified foods, are providing similar trade-related challenges. Two of these issues receive attention in chapter 7: the certification of organic food and other eco-labeling of food products, and the growing concern about animal welfare that is linked to intensive livestock production.

Chapter 8 synthesizes the experience with the different types of regulations in the context of the need for a safe and open global food system. Countries must protect producers and consumers from trade-related food-sector risks. They also must guard against new forms of protectionism that seek to redefine the global trade system from one of a mutually beneficial exchange of goods and services that satisfies diverse consumer preferences to one in which overly prescriptive regulation reduces the contestability of markets, raising prices and limiting choice for the consumers whom such measures are intended to serve. The goal should be a well-functioning regulatory framework that recognizes the benefits from public roles in securing food-related health, safety, and quality, but also recognizes that the private sector is often better placed than governments to respond to consumer preferences. This chapter concludes with a few recommendations for an agenda to improve the efficiency of domestic regulations and the multilateral governance framework in order to ensure a more effective and cohesive food system.

2

Trade-Related Regulations in the Global Food System

All governments regulate their food sectors extensively. These regulations are set within broader legal frameworks that provide judicial redress in cases of unexpected adverse effects from food production or consumption. Although general legal provisions are an important component of ensuring food safety and quality, the need for specific regulatory measures to buttress this legal framework is widely accepted.

Sound economic reasons exist for food regulations, but the regulatory process is also susceptible to political pressures from narrow interest groups. The result can be ill-advised regulatory measures and levels of protection. Trade frictions arise most frequently when importing countries are prevented by political considerations from implementing the regulatory decisions that emerge from technical rule-making processes. In these cases, exporters feel they are being affected adversely by regulations that restrict their market access for the economic benefit of import-competing domestic producers, or because of unjustified consumer pressures that constrain their ability to offer goods. Thus, although much of the regulation observed in the food sector rests on solid foundations, trade disputes occur when the purpose, severity, or instrumentation of regulations can be questioned.

This chapter sets the stage for analysis of trade-related regulations in the global food system by summarizing the economic rationales for such measures, characterizing regulatory institutions and classifying their outcomes, describing risk assessment and management choices, analyzing the economic effects of regulation on trade, and discussing the political economy of the regulatory overprotection or underprotection that often leads to trade frictions.

Economic Rationales for Food Regulation

A complex system of market, legal, fiscal, and regulatory measures governs the incentives for firms to supply food products that have the safety and quality attributes sought by consumers. Firms that misjudge consumer demand risk losing sales revenue, market share, and their business reputation or brand capital. A country's legal system reinforces the incentives provided by market forces: firms found responsible for contaminated food or consumer fraud may have to compensate plaintiffs seeking legal redress or pay punitive damages.

In many cases, market forces and legal remedies alone provide insufficient incentives for public health and environmental protection. As summarized in John Wilson and Keith Maskus (2002), the economic rationales for some form of government intervention in markets fall broadly into two categories: (1) achieving provision of public goods, and (2) facilitating production and exchange through various means of lowering transactions and information costs. These rationales are especially salient when market failures are associated with the production, processing, distribution, and consumption of food products. The spread of animal and plant diseases, outbreaks of food-borne illnesses, distribution of misleading food labels, or use of production practices that do not reflect contemporary norms may signal the need for corrective measures.

Providing Public Goods

When markets fail, fiscal incentives, such as subsidies or taxes to hasten adoption of new technologies, sometimes offer the best solution. However, mandatory regulatory measures may be needed when the risks associated with products are great, delayed, or imperfectly known, or when no efficient legal system is in place so that citizens find it impossible, costly, or slow to prosecute claims related to domestic or imported goods under product liability or consumer fraud laws. Private firms that violate regulations are subject not only to civil legal liability but also to government penalties, including fines, product recalls, plant closures, new import protocols, or loss of market access.

To the extent that regulations enhance the efficiency of the food sector, they are economically beneficial. Prudent policymakers will weigh the benefits associated with a regulatory action against the costs that it entails. Whatever decision criteria are employed, regulatory choices within countries are primarily national prerogatives, and national institutions occupy the central role in determining, implementing, and enforcing food-sector rules.

Consider, for example, the situation in which the public good provided is a low prevalence of a pest or disease that affects agricultural production. Control of an animal or plant health hazard often cannot be accomplished optimally by individual producers—destroying a diseased animal in one herd, for example, has positive consequences for other herds that will not be realized without government intervention to encourage eradication. Therefore, regulations may be required to achieve the greater production capacity that would result from fewer hazards to crops and livestock. Risk management is a product of activities pursued simultaneously by private agents involved in agricultural production and by related public regulatory agencies. The public agencies will undertake interventions and enforce regulations that determine the overall prevalence of a pest or disease, given private behavior. Private agents will choose their production activities after assessing the prevalence of the hazards they face. The optimal strategies therefore often emerge from joint public- and private-sector efforts to engage in pest and disease control.[1]

Additional complications arise when pests and diseases, by possibly spreading across international borders, threaten international trade opportunities. In such instances, coordination of regulatory policies among countries may be optimal, but often it is not achieved. As a result, quarantines and other restrictions are imposed at national borders, and additional requirements are imposed on production and handling processes within countries, as prerequisites to trade. Tensions persist in the global food system over some of these measures imposed by national governments to protect animal, plant, and human health.

Reducing Transactions Costs

Food regulation also can accomplish desirable objectives under the second rationale—facilitating production and exchange through reduced transactions costs. When information about health or quality attributes is unknown or asymmetrically distributed between producers and consumers, regulations can improve the functioning of markets. Economic theory distinguishes among the search, experience, and credence characteristics of a product—all of which can influence consumers' purchasing behavior (Darby and Karni 1973). Consumers can ascertain search characteristics, such as size of a fruit, through examination before purchase. An experience characteristic, such as how long a product's quality can be maintained or its shelf life, often cannot be determined until after purchase. Consumers accumulate information about the experience characteristics of a food product over time, although with attendant costs of learning. By contrast, consumers cannot determine the existence or extent of a credence characteristic, such as whether the product has pesticide residues or is genetically altered, even after repeated purchases and consumption.

---

1. Brown, Lynch, and Zilberman (2002) describe the social welfare maximization problem for plant pest control in agricultural production.

When food products have experience and credence characteristics, markets may fail to provide efficient price signals. For example, when provided with imperfect information, consumers may not pay for desired levels of safety or producers may not supply improved safety. In these situations, government regulations can improve market efficiency. Public intervention is justified economically when a food safety measure, such as legally mandated limits on pesticide residues, improves social welfare net of industry costs. Regulated grades, standards, and labeling are other tools available to governments to reduce the transactions costs that impede efficient production and exchange.

Geographical indications (GIs) that identify the producer or region of production are a somewhat unusual tool for remedying information failures in food markets. GIs are a form of intellectual property that has a potential value in the market that is jointly created by private-sector investments in production and marketing and the public laws and regulations that protect these investments. GIs are therefore club goods (excludable but not rival) which organized producers can use to privately appropriate the surplus generated by their application. Some producers have long used GIs, such as "Bordeaux," to command premium prices for their products in domestic and foreign markets. The explosion in global demand for distinctive wines, spirits, and food products over the past decade has heightened interest in their use and attention to their regulation (Maskus 2000).

Food Regulation and Trade

The majority of food regulations are social welfare–enhancing measures that may place legitimate restrictions on trade. Nonetheless, food regulations are increasingly appearing at the center of trade disputes. One difficulty for the global food system is that the incidence of risks or available market information can vary across countries. Thus the benefits of a regulation may exceed its costs in one country but not elsewhere. Another difficulty is that regulations may rest on comparisons of nonmarket benefits with market costs and therefore may be more susceptible than otherwise to challenge by trading partners. But perhaps the most significant problem for the global food system is that both the stringency of regulations and the provision of farm support and protection policies tend to increase among wealthier countries, complicating the political economy of the regulation of food.

Classification of Regulations

Classification of food regulations by their goals, attribute focus, and other dimensions will serve as an initial road map to an otherwise diffuse set of measures at the domestic and international levels. The instruments that make the regulations operative, as well as conformity assessment mechanisms, also can be classified according to their type. Indeed, such classifications provide policymakers and analysts with an organizational framework for discussing trade disputes and for negotiating international regulatory guidelines. They also act as a conceptual foundation for evaluating food regulations and as a guide to specification of economic models to gauge the trade and welfare effects of these measures.

First it is helpful to distinguish between the national and international institutions through which regulations are promulgated and administered and the sets of regulations and directives produced by these decision-making bodies.

Regulatory Institutions

Food regulatory institutions comprise the legislative and executive bodies that formulate laws and directives related to the food sector; the judicial systems by which those laws are adjudicated and enforced; and the administrative agencies that are responsible for implementing the regulatory mandates imposed by laws and executive decisions. National food regulatory institutions have characteristics that reflect the political circumstances and other factors specific to a country. Regulatory institutions therefore differ substantially among countries.

Systematic differences among institutional structures of countries may be reflected in differences in regulatory outcomes. In turn, systematic differences among the outcomes of the regulatory institutions of a given country also may occur as control over institutions shifts among domestic political parties or in response to evolving public expectations. Thus food regulatory institutions can be described in terms of their structure and prevailing philosophy during a particular period of time, though nations can and do make changes in these institutions. Because of national sovereignty, domestic regulatory institutions are themselves rarely the subject of international trade conflicts. International regulatory institutions, including their operating procedures and even philosophical orientation, are more commonly the subject of dispute among nations.

Dimensions of Food Regulations

The substantive output of food regulatory institutions is manifest in the large collections of laws and directives that embody, or lead to, food regulations. A classification of such regulations along four basic dimensions exemplifies the range of options open to countries (see table 2.1). The classification variables are goals, attribute focus, breadth (across

Table 2.1   Classification scheme for food regulations

Dimension	Classification
Goals	*Risk-reducing.* Regulations that ensure an acceptable level of animal, plant, or human health or safety
	Quality. Regulations that provide differentiation of goods based on content and process attributes not directly related to health or safety
Attribute focus	*Content attributes.* Regulations that target material aspects of the product
	Process attributes. Regulations that target the processes by which a product is produced, processed, handled, or distributed
Breadth	*Vertical.* Regulations specific to a single product or closely related products in one or more stages of the marketing chain
	Horizontal. Regulations applied across products that are not necessarily closely related
Scope	*Uniform.* Regulations that apply equally to products of domestic and foreign origin
	Specific. Regulations that apply only to imported products, often only of certain origins

products), and scope (among domestic and foreign goods). Each of these variables distinguishes regulations in some way that can be significant in gauging the impacts of regulatory decisions on international trade.

Goals of Regulations

The classification of regulations by their goals is clearly relevant to the task of evaluating their success. Goals also play a role in identifying the trade rules under which a regulation can be challenged. An important distinction, as noted earlier, is between risk-reducing measures and those aimed at providing the quality or product differentiation that is of interest to consumers but has little to do with risks to health or safety. This distinction is important when considering the significance of risk assessment, risk management, and risk communication in regulatory decision making. As noted, risk-reducing measures are subject to a substantial amount of scientific advice. The public good element provided is a degree of collective security to domestic producers, processors, and consumers. Quality-related regulations, by contrast, are adopted by governments to provide consumers with the information they need to make informed decisions.

Trade difficulties over regulations can become particularly intractable when two goals are addressed by one measure. This is the case in the current dispute over genetically modified foods, where some countries cite food safety and environmental risks in justifying regulations that reflects national food quality preferences related to methods of production. Such linkages of goals are often associated with new technologies: tensions within societies on the desirability of adopting new production and processing techniques can spill over into regulations designated as safety guarantees. Domestic interest groups opposed to the technology would have an incentive to make this link so that they could form coalitions and raise the visibility of the issue on the domestic political agenda. Fusion of goals in the articulation of regulatory measures puts a particular strain on international trade relations and often brings charges of covert protectionism.

Attribute Focus of Regulations

The second way in which to classify food regulations—whether the regulation focuses on a content or process attribute of the product—was also mentioned in chapter 1. Regulations that target content attributes include those that establish requirements for existence or quantity. Examples include requirements for fortification of enriched grain products with folic acid or for a minimum butterfat content for products labeled "ice cream." Measures that target process attributes might indicate the source or origin of the product, such as mandatory country-of-origin labeling, or method of production or processing, such as a requirement for shrimp to be harvested using turtle excluder devices (TEDs).

Regulations that target process attributes are especially prone to controversy. Many consumers value information about the methods used in producing their food, and well-designed regulations can improve the functioning of markets. So, too, can other regulations adopted to help farmers to differentiate their products. These measures target production methods to facilitate the creation of value added at the farm level. Regulations with a process attribute focus, such as organic standards, can establish the means for producers to successfully adopt a higher-profit, higher-cost, consumer-oriented business model that emphasizes product quality and diversity—a potentially attractive alternative to the low-cost, high-volume model required for bulk commodities. Policymakers may intend that such regulations create market-oriented mechanisms to relieve some downward pressures on producer incomes. But such regulations may not improve market performance if they become barriers to trade and their design creates the opportunity for some favored producers to exclude others from the domestic (or foreign) marketplace.

Even those process attribute regulations that arise primarily in response to consumer rather than producer interests can lead to greater trade frictions if the requirements for verifying compliance are viewed as overly prescriptive. Competitive food suppliers usually have private (voluntary) tracking systems and standards in place in response to market and legal incentives. The objectives of these private systems are to improve supply-side management through monitoring production flows and retail activity, to facilitate the development of highly differentiated products for niche markets, and to pinpoint product quality defects (Golan, Krissoff, et al. 2003). Mandatory regulations that increase the required breadth, precision, or depth of a firm's tracking system may increase the reliability of quality claims and therefore benefit attribute-conscious consumers. These regulatory regimes may also benefit some firms if increased consumer confidence leads to increased product purchases (Unnevehr and Nelson 2002). But both domestic firms and a country's trading partners may object to traceability and other regulations when they substantially increase verification costs in instances in which it seems unlikely that consumers would be willing to pay a sufficient premium for the regulated attribute.

Breadth of Regulations

The breadth of coverage among products is a third useful way in which to classify food regulations. The basic choice is between "vertical" regulations, which apply to a single product or closely related products at one or more stages of production and processing, and "horizontal" regulations, which apply across many products that are not necessarily closely related.

Most countries employ a mixture of vertical and horizontal regulations in their food sector, and the distinction is used widely in discussions of the EU body of regulations and directives. Vertical regulations tend to be used when a particular subsector has unique problems or conditions. Horizontal regulations are more feasible if the regulatory issues are general, or if the subsector is widely dispersed.

The choice has implications for the type of measures imposed and the ease of their operation in an open economy. Vertical regulations have certain advantages for the industry concerned, such as creating scale economies or barriers to entry, and tend to be developed with the help of such interests. Horizontal regulations are often more attractive to consumer and environmental groups—for them, the wider breadth is an advantage—and where the industry view is less cohesive.

Both vertical and horizontal regulations can pose challenges in international trade. For vertical regulations, which affect different levels of the production, marketing, and distribution of a product, problems may be associated with the various stages being undertaken in different countries. For horizontal regulations, their application to many products is likely to cause trade tensions unless equivalent regulations are in place among trading partners.

Scope of Regulations

The scope of food regulations refers to whether their application depends on where a product originates. Many food regulations apply to goods from all sources, domestic and foreign—a feature that distinguishes these measures from standard trade policy instruments. Regulations that apply to domestic and foreign goods can be termed "uniform." Still other regulatory measures are applied only to imported goods. Frequently, regulations are directed only at products from certain countries and are therefore termed "specific." These measures are used to mitigate different levels of risk posed by imports from different sources. An importing country may use a variety of regulatory measures to mitigate the risks associated with importing one product from different locations, which inherently raises the prospect of trade disputes arising from claims of discrimination.

The scope of a regulatory measure has implications for who will bear the cost of its imposition. Uniform regulations generally affect the final delivery costs of goods for domestic as well as foreign producers. Domestic interests may nonetheless lobby for socially suboptimal measures that raise their own unit costs if such regulations limit competition (Hoeckman and Leidy 1993). The incentives for such behavior vary with the number and relative size of firms, the production technologies, and the type of good (Thilmany and Barrett 1996). Specific regulations have more potential to segment international markets, fundamentally altering the nature of competition. They may transform a "small" country into a "large" country in international markets or create market power for individual firms (Sumner and Lee 1997).

Instruments Used in Food Regulations

Although some international disputes are best understood in terms of the dimensions of regulations just described, often these disputes revolve around specific policy instruments. An increasing number of instruments are available to governments for implementing food regulations (OECD 1997). This range of instruments can be conveniently divided into quantitative restrictions, technical standards, and informational remedies (see box 2.1).

Quantitative Restrictions

Of the instruments used to implement food regulations, quantitative restrictions, including import bans, are the most explicitly trade-limiting. These restrictions are most appropriate when the risks or uncertainties posed by a hazard are great and alternative measures for effectively reducing the risk to negligible levels are technically infeasible. Such cases

Box 2.1   Trade-based food regulatory instruments

Quantitative restrictions	→	Spatial (national and regional) bans on imports
		Temporal restrictions (quarantine periods and seasonal access)
		Export prohibitions
Technical specifications	→	Product standards
		Process standards
Informational remedies	→	Mandatory disclosure
		Controls on voluntary claims

arise, for example, when current monitoring and detection technology cannot distinguish between imports of hazardous and nonhazardous products, or when effective treatments or eradication programs do not exist. Import bans are most frequently used to protect livestock, crops, and native species of flora and fauna from foreign pests and diseases.

Total import bans are controversial, but not all import bans entirely prohibit trade of a product from a particular source. Partial bans, such as seasonal or regional bans that do not completely preclude entry of a given product from the exporting country, also are used extensively to protect animal and plant health. Typically, these measures are used when regulatory authorities more fully understand the risk factors, and when a more narrowly targeted ban can effectively reduce the risks to acceptable levels. For example, regulatory authorities can safely implement a seasonal ban that allows imports of certain horticultural products from an exporting country for part of the year if they have detailed knowledge about the effects of climatological factors on the biology of the identified quarantine pests and understand how the host status of the commodity might vary over the growing season. Trade controversies arise when partial bans based ostensibly on technical considerations turn out to preclude all of the otherwise feasible trade opportunities.

Technical Standards

Technical standards stipulate conditions that have to be met to gain access to a particular market. Product standards might specify the nature of the product itself (e.g., size, weight, or chemical composition), or content attributes such as absence of particular diseases and microorganisms. By contrast, process standards stipulate use of certain production, processing, handling, or distribution technologies. As noted earlier, sometimes the goal of a regulation dictates whether a product or process standard is applied, but often this is a choice of regulatory authorities.

Economic theory generally suggests the desirability of product over process standards when feasible, because product standards allow latitude for firms to meet a regulatory goal at the least cost. At times, however, process standards are more efficient because of technical factors or verification cost considerations (Antle 1996). For example, the sequential application of required production methods designed to reduce progressively the likelihood of a certain disease or pest in the final product (known as a "systems approach" to risk management) may be preferable to extensive testing that involves destruction of the final product. Similarly, a process standard designed to reduce microbial contamination in food might be a superior regulatory tool to setting specific product standards, given the expense of microbiological tests and the recurrent nature of the pathogen hazard (MacDonald and Crutchfield 1996, Unnevehr and Jensen 1999).

In principle, any firm in any country willing to expend resources to meet the specified technical standard can export a product to a country setting that standard. But, in practice, technical standards shift comparative costs among producers, and some firms may be prevented from meeting the standard by the absence of satisfactory verification services. Thus, although technical standards appear to be less disruptive of trade than quantitative restrictions, the effect can be very similar. A standard that cannot be reached or can be reached only at a prohibitive cost is equivalent to a ban on imports. It is an empirical question whether technical standards are more trade-restrictive than partial bans. Exporting firms may find that the costs of complying with a foreign standard are prohibitive if it is stringent or varies significantly from a domestic or international standard. Standards can also be written in ways that favor domestic producers—for example, by requiring use of an input more widely available in the home country than in potential exporting countries.[2] It is true, however, that many technical standard regulations affecting trade are uniform and so affect costs for domestic as well as foreign producers.

Informational Remedies

When market failures stem from informational failures, informational remedies may be preferred over other measures. Informational regulations fall into two categories: (1) mandatory disclosure requirements, and (2) controls on voluntary claims. When combined with credible certification institutions, these instruments can transform the experience or credence characteristics of a food product into searchable characteristics, for example when orange juice is labeled "calcium enriched." In theory, the purchasing patterns

---

2. A well-known example is Italy's "pasta purity" regulation, which allowed only products made entirely with durum wheat (grown throughout southern Italy but found in few other areas in Europe) to be marketed under the generic term *pasta*.

of well-informed consumers will then be sufficient incentive for producers to provide the range of quality for which consumers are willing to pay without further government intervention.

Informational remedies have generally been viewed as the least onerous form of government regulation. Alan Sykes (1995) points out, however, that if requirements vary from market to market, manufacturers must incur not only the costs of producing different labels but also the possibly substantial costs of maintaining distinct inventories for each market. Recent initiatives to require additional labeling, particularly for process attributes, can raise verification costs for food manufacturers and simultaneously affect consumer demand. The potentially large market effects that some of these labeling regulations could have, particularly those for genetically modified foods, have made the adoption of mandatory labeling regimes particularly controversial.

Conformity Assessment

Conformity assessment is verification of compliance or equivalence with a food regulation. The requirements for assessing conformity with a measure have two dimensions: (1) specification of the means used to verify compliance or equivalence with a measure,[3] and (2) designation of who is authorized to make the assessment. Authority can be vested in private suppliers' declarations; private, third-party agents; or public (regulatory agency) third parties.

Issues related to conformity assessment are increasingly at the forefront of regulatory debates because of the growing reliance on process standards in the regulation of animal and plant health and food safety. Even among developed countries with high levels of regulatory capacity, different views on the appropriate roles for the private and public sector in conformity assessment have given rise to trade disputes. For developing countries, conformity assessment requirements are often a significant impediment to trade, even when trading partners agree on who will provide various verification services. Inevitably, more administrative discretion is involved in the enforcement of process standards than product standards, so judgments about the capability and integrity of verification services in the exporting country figure importantly in decisions to allow trade. It is not surprising that judgments about such matters often differ between importers and exporters, particularly those from developing countries.

Debate over conformity assessment has also intensified because of the growing number of food quality regulations that target process attributes. The use of private, third-party certification services in the global food

---

3. This dimension was discussed earlier with respect to the policy instrument chosen to achieve the regulatory goal and the attribute focus of the regulation.

system has grown in recent years because of the large increase in private standards (Caswell, Bredahl, and Hooker 1998). Even so, governments often require public-sector verification of compliance with food quality, as well as food safety, regulations. By contrast, a supplier's declaration of conformity with standards usually suffices for trade in industrial products, particularly in countries with a sound legal infrastructure (WTO 2000c). When use of private services is constrained by regulatory regimes that require public-sector provision of verification services, imports are effectively prohibited from countries that lack adequate public regulatory infrastructure, even if individual foreign firms can meet importers' standards.

Risk Analysis and Appropriate Degrees of Caution

At the heart of many disputes over risk-related food regulations are different interpretations of the role of risk assessment or disagreements on the extent to which scientific evidence provides a sufficient basis for risk management decisions. Not surprising, the countries exporting agricultural products have sought to enshrine scientific evidence as a basis for food regulations. But the science associated with risk analysis often leaves room for substantial uncertainty over the incidence of risk and the effectiveness of proposed management strategies. This uncertainty poses problems for those authorities who ultimately are responsible for the consequences of regulatory decisions. Tension runs high between the governments of exporting countries, which prefer that regulations be based on "objective" criteria to minimize the scope for domestic political manipulation, and the governments of importing countries, which know that they will be held accountable if science "has it wrong" or if low-probability, high-consequence adverse events occur. Further room for dissension among countries emerges because agricultural exporters often have strict import regulations in their own food sectors, aimed at ensuring that pests and diseases do not enter and diminish their production capacity or interfere with their access to foreign markets. These strict regulations by exporters can cause problems in a complex trading world where commercial opportunities for intrasectoral trade exist in many markets. The imposition of strict regulations makes it difficult for exporters to exercise credible leadership toward regulatory actions abroad that they would favor.

Disputes over appropriate levels of risk avoidance recently came to a head in discussions among countries of the "precautionary principle" of risk management.[4] The precautionary principle guides political and

4. Patterson and Josling (2001) have described the evolution of this concept, based on the German sociolegal tradition, as it gained policy recognition in the 1980s with the rapid development of environmental laws.

regulatory action toward strict measures intended as ecological or health safeguards (even in advance of scientific proof or need), and places the onus of proof on those who propose change. This principle can be characterized as a conservative approach to risk management in which regulation anticipates harm that has not already been documented for a given category of products. It does not take into consideration the relative costs and benefits of regulation to industry and the public, including the benefits forgone by delayed approval.

Critics of the precautionary principle as a basis for regulatory decision making for the food system argue that although caution is necessary, it is impossible to eliminate all risks from scientific advances or commerce. The precautionary principle could distort regulatory priorities, stifle important life-enhancing research and industrial competitiveness by creating unnecessary bureaucratic delays or precluding the development of some products, and be used to justify protectionist measures. Critics of the precautionary principle prefer a "preventive" approach that responds to "scientifically proven adverse impacts that have arisen in earlier generations of products" (Tait and Levidow 1992, 221). A "pre-market clearance" approach to regulation, in which new products and processes are screened to ensure they do not give rise to recognized hazards, is considered consistent with adequate risk prevention. Advocates of the preventive approach favor case-by-case and step-by-step procedures, in which different steps in research and production processes are examined according to the specific risks involved in each step and new regulations are based on demonstrated harmfulness. In this way, science and market development can proceed, and in the process accumulated knowledge will help to clarify what risks actually exist. This approach still introduces approval delays as compared with a regime of unregulated science and technology adoption, but it provides more flexibility than a regime based on the precautionary principle.

Trade Effects of Food Regulations

Assessment of the efficiency of regulations in an integrated food system requires estimation of the economic impacts of regulatory measures. It is clear that trade is affected by technical regulations. But less clear is the magnitude of these effects on prices and quantities in markets or on the welfare gains from trade. Complying with regulations entails direct costs that are difficult to ascertain.[5] When a regulation is uniform in scope, the net economic and trade effects can be dominated by the regulation's effects on the costs of domestic firms. Even in these cases, the effects of the regulation on domestic and foreign producers can differ. When the

---

5. Roberts, Josling, and Orden (1999) discuss more fully the issues raised in this section.

scope of a regulation is specific, it has inherently differential impacts on one or more exporters.

Considerably more information is needed to assess the effects of the various food regulations than is needed to assess the impacts of standard tariffs and nontechnical, quantitative trade restrictions. When the cost differentials between domestic and foreign suppliers are reasonably well known, the "tariff equivalent" of a regulation can be defined as the tariff that would reduce imports by the same amount, but the equivalence should be qualified. Tariffs yield government revenue, whereas regulations impose compliance costs that use up real resources, often at home and abroad.

An additional complexity in evaluating the impacts of food regulations is that, unlike other trade barriers, they have indirect as well as direct effects in markets. Regulations that seek to limit the domestic pervasiveness or prevent the importation of an animal or plant pest or disease-causing organism will typically have an impact on the domestic supply of the products that would be vulnerable to those risks. Such a regulation is conveniently thought to be a means of avoiding an adverse shift in the domestic supply function—a shift stemming from either infection or infestation or the cost of remedial treatment of the affected animals or crops. The regulation translates into decreased imports (or increased exports) in the regulating country. However, even when the regulation applies only to imports it may be misleading to call its effects a trade "distortion," because it could represent the most efficient way of dealing with the state of nature presented by the existence of a hazard.

Many food-sector regulations affect the demand rather than the supply of the product in the importing country. A ban on imports of a food that would pose a health threat can prevent a market collapse caused by eroding confidence in the safety of supply. Likewise, consumer confidence in experience and credence characteristics of foods may be difficult to establish for imported products. If consumers are uncertain whether a food purchase will be of sufficient quality, an alternative product might be purchased instead. In this situation, regulations enhance consumers' voluntary food choices by improving the information on which to base decisions. In either food safety or food quality cases, domestic market demand is affected, and trade without regulation might lead to a net loss in welfare.

The impact of a food regulation on trade thus stems from the direct cost of compliance incurred by domestic suppliers, the indirect impacts of the regulation in question on domestic supply and demand, and its impacts on related foreign excess supplies. The incidence of this cost will depend on market structure and the combination of elasticities of supply and demand. And it will depend on the scope of the regulation.

For an importing country, the imposition of a specific regulation on one source of a traded good may have little net effect if costs from other sources are not affected, but the impact on bilateral trade is likely to be pronounced. The net trade effect on the exporter depends on whether other importers place similar restrictions on the exports in question. If all importing countries restrain the product of a single exporting country through technical regulations, the exporting country would suffer the maximum trade effect. When all supplying countries are similarly restrained, the impact on each supplier is lessened, but it still can be significant.

The propensity for a specific import regulation to cause a trade conflict thus depends to a certain extent on the specificity of the restriction among exporters and the extent to which other importers follow suit. All of this suggests that technical regulations affecting trade are not amenable to simple multilateral reduction negotiations.

Science and Economics in Risk-Reducing Regulations

Quantitative analysis of the effects of food regulation takes into account the circumstances that would prevail in the absence of regulations. Without such information, it is impossible to know to what extent food regulations act as trade barriers, which measures most impede trade, and how best to modify existing regulations to reduce any negative impacts. Such detailed knowledge is sometimes available; at other times, it is not.[6] But a few generalizations can be made on the interface between the science of risk assessment and management and the economic and trade analysis related to risk-reducing regulations.

The regulatory procedures of most countries require that risk-related decision making be based on sequential analysis: first, determine that there is essentially no or minimal risk associated with a proposed regulation, and, second, under that premise, assess its economic impacts. When risk-related decisions are made in this sequential manner, economic considerations become secondary as food regulations are promulgated by agencies depending on the scientific evidence. Under this approach, emphasis is placed on risk reduction rather than on a comprehensive analysis that takes risks and economic costs and benefits into account simultaneously (James and Anderson 1998, Roberts 2000). When the mandate of regulatory authorities to protect the domestic economy from negative sanitary and phytosanitary risks from trade is stated in strong terms, as it often is, then import bans and other severe quarantine measures emerge quite naturally as policy outcomes. A product ban is a high-level intervention to address a risk from imports, but a ban does eliminate the risk to the extent that it stems from legally sanctioned trade.

---

6. Krissoff, Bohman, and Caswell (2002) and Maskus and Wilson (2001) provide some quantitative studies of the impact of regulations on trade, as do later chapters in this volume.

Figure 2.1 Regulatory underprotection and overprotection

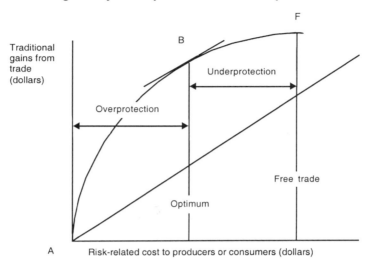

As the global food system becomes more integrated, trade gains ought to enter more fully into the calculus of regulatory agencies. They should incorporate scientific assessments and trade policy analysis in the design of good regulations. Economic analysis of trade should take into account the sensitivity of domestic costs to regulations and the extent to which consumer demand is supported by trust in regulatory decisions. As described earlier in this chapter, trade analysis that views all food regulations simply as "nontariff barriers" is as likely to be as misleading as scientific analysis that considers zero incidence of a risk as necessarily the socially optimal policy.

Richard Snape and David Orden (2001) illustrate these considerations in a simple diagram that forms the basis for figure 2.1. The vertical axis represents the expected traditional gain from trade arising from imports of a product into a particular country. The horizontal axis represents the (monetized) expected cost of the hazard linked with imports. Regulations that achieve trade with coordinates above the 45° line, when the direct and indirect effects on domestic supply and demand are taken into account, are deemed to have passed a benefit-cost test as desirable policy. Snape and Orden contrast this decision criterion with a primarily risk-based rule, which would preclude imports with high benefits relative to costs if they fall to the right of a vertical line representing the cutoff level of acceptable risk. This situation would entail rejecting trade in some cases where the benefit-cost ratio is above one and accepting trade in others (that satisfy the risk-based rule) where the ratio is less than one.

The analysis is extended in figure 2.1 by tracing a risks/benefits trade-off frontier between domestic risk costs and trade benefits for a range of import protocols. Ignoring benefits in setting regulations can lead to situations in which "too little" trade takes place because the risks are counted but the rewards are ignored. Conversely, if the risks are ignored or discounted relative to the benefits from imports, then "too much" trade occurs. The first situation can arise from mandates within domestic regulatory institutions to base decisions on risk avoidance. Too little protection from risks can occur if authorities either are unaware of the risks associated with trade or are persuaded by commercial interests to downplay their impact.

The risks/benefits trade-off frontier shown in figure 2.1 allows for the specification of an optimal level of protection where the benefits net of risks are the greatest. The curve ABF maps the trade gains and the risk-related costs to producers (or to consumers) from no trade gains and no risk at point A (autarchy) to the maximum trade gain and maximum risk with unregulated free trade (F). Various shapes are possible for the risks/benefits trade-off frontier as import levels rise, but it will generally be concave, as illustrated, because small amounts of trade will tend to produce large economic gains but pose limited risks, whereas the risks may continue to mount with trade even when most of the trade gains have been realized.[7] The optimal point is B, where at the margin the gains to trade (as conventionally measured) just balance the expected loss from the consequences of the importation of the pest or disease. By contrast, the most conservative protocol (point A) would eliminate trade, leading to a lower level of welfare than necessary as trade gains are passed up. The most permissive import protocol (point F) would allow free trade, but again this would not be optimal with a concave trade-off frontier, because the marginal costs of disease prevention or the consequences of pest infestation offset the marginal gains from trade beyond some level of imports.

The simple model of the risks/benefits trade-off in figure 2.1 allows "overprotection" to be defined as a situation in which a relaxation of the regulation would be socially beneficial and "underprotection" as a situation in which more restrictive import protocols would increase expected net social benefits. Measuring the functions involved accurately and calculating the social optimum are a challenge for empirical work, but in principle the concepts of overprotection and underprotection have a precise social meaning.

The integration of risk and economic analysis suggested here can be extended further to account for effects beyond the impacts of import

---

7. If both benefits and costs depend linearly on the level of trade, then the ABF frontier will be linear as well, and free trade will be optimal if gains from each unit of trade exceed costs. When the ABF curve is convex, net benefits (traditional gains less risk-related costs) fall from A to B and then rise as trade expands toward F. This again gives a corner solution, where no trade has to be directly compared with free trade because no intervening situation is better.

regulations on domestic supply and demand. Consider the case in which an exporting country introduces effective controls over the pest in question. The trade-off curve in figure 2.1 shifts to the left as risks are reduced for each level of trade. The optimum level of imports will also change as benefits from the action of the exporter accrue as an increase in the gains from trade combined with less risk to domestic producers or consumers. If the imposition of an international standard reduces the general risk from imports, the importer could gain considerably from being able to adjust trade to a level where the gains are greater. Thus the optimal policy for a country can only be defined in relation to the policies of other countries and to the existence of effective standards that reduce the riskiness of imports.

Capture of Regulations by Producers or Consumers

One explanation for overprotection by strict import regulations is regulatory "capture" by producer interests who effectively lobby for regulations stronger than are warranted by a full calculation of costs and benefits. The result is protection of domestic producers at the expense of domestic consumers. The regulations that countries have adopted for controlling the spread of animal and plant diseases rely largely on scientific information channeled through national agencies. Pressure on these agencies by those with rent-seeking ambitions has long been recognized as a problem for the trade system.[8] Typically, such situations involve the excessive use of import bans or quarantine restrictions, ostensibly to keep out animal and plant diseases and food-borne pathogens. When domestic producers can influence import regulations and their implementation, then overprotection is likely to be the result, and both consumers and foreign producers lose. The trade system has not been able to provide the full benefits of comparative advantage.

Underprotection can also be a political economy problem. Pressure from overseas interests or importing firms may lead to too much trade in certain products. When exotic pests can come in with trade, the regulatory infrastructure may lag behind the need for vigilance against pathogens. This lag may be of particular importance in some developing countries with limited regulatory capacity, leading at times to underprotection with high costs to domestic agricultural producers in some cases.

---

8. In a case strangely parallel to the current dispute over the sale of hormone-treated beef from the United States into the European Union, during the tenure of Chancellor Otto Bismarck (1871–90) Germany for many years banned imports of US pork. US pork producers were convinced, apparently with some justification, that the German regulations were unduly restrictive—see Snyder (1945).

Regulations addressing safety of the food supply are subject as well to another type of political pressure. Lack of reliable consumer information can lead to the capture of the regulatory process by consumer-oriented public interest groups. This capture can at times lead to overprotection, if the natural caution of regulators or unfounded public fears are turned into excessive regulation in response to pressure from organized consumer lobbyists. Exporters with safe food to supply can then be shut out of markets. The costs also are borne by those consumers who have to pay a higher price than necessary. Domestic producers may gain from this overprotection, but they can also lose in these situations if the excessively strict import protocol has a counterpart in excessive domestic regulations.

Food regulations that apply process standards are particularly subject to political economy capture. Although such regulations can be distorted to reflect producer interests, their capture by consumer and other groups with various agendas may pose the greater challenge. Much of the onus of sustaining an integrated global food system rests on the independence and credibility of the domestic institutions that implement regulations. If governments allow their food regulatory agencies to be politicized to support narrow interest group agendas, their decisions become susceptible to challenge as unnecessary restraints on trade.

Welfare-Enhancing Regulation of Food Trade

Increased trade is not inconsistent with food safety and quality objectives. Quite the contrary, trade can contribute to the provision of a safe, high-quality food supply. Yet trade tensions arise from different regulatory regimes, and such conflicts appear to be increasing. To avoid a clash between trade, safety, and consumer rights concerns, to the detriment of each, it is important to explore the causes of these tensions.

Trade conflicts over risk-related measures can arise from genuine disagreements about scientific evidence. Sometimes the science is not in place, requiring interim judgments that may be challenged by other countries. More often, the disagreement is over scientific evidence supporting the positions of different governments. Other trade issues arise from an asymmetry of accountability between domestic and foreign suppliers in which foreign suppliers are less directly liable for the unanticipated negative consequences of their products. These issues are found in many areas of international trade, but they are particularly sensitive in the food sector.

A different set of issues arises over quality attributes. Sometimes producers seek recognition of their product identity as a property right, leading to conflict with suppliers of close substitutes. Consumers differ in their levels of demand for information and for standards about food products. Regulatory institutions differ in reliance on mandatory versus voluntary provision of assurances about content and process attributes. From each situation, international trade conflicts easily emerge.

The complexity of the systems of regulations related to the safety and quality of agricultural and food products poses a substantial challenge for trade analysis, negotiations, and dispute resolution. Classification of the differences among national regulatory institutions and their substantive outcomes serves as an initial road map to a dense regulatory maze.

The regulations imposed through various instruments have both direct effects on trade and indirect effects that result from induced shifts in underlying supply and demand. Optimal policies can be described conceptually, but are often difficult to ascertain empirically, and regulatory decision making is subject to political pressure that often results in over-protection for the benefit of influential domestic groups. These considerations underlie the efforts made to strengthen international regulatory oversight and to incorporate comprehensive trade rules into international agreements. The goal is to ensure that agricultural and food regulations do not impede welfare-enhancing trade, and, at the same time, do give countries wide latitude to set their health, safety, and quality standards.

3

Global Food Regulatory Framework

Global governance of food regulation was enhanced with the adoption of new and revised agreements at the conclusion of the Uruguay Round of multilateral negotiations in 1994. These agreements were viewed as critical to prevent governments from resorting to regulatory compensation to appease domestic interests as the Uruguay Round Agreement on Agriculture (URAA) began to put limits on agricultural trade barriers and subsidies. This chapter reviews these agreements, together with other elements of the multilateral governance framework for food regulations. It also evaluates what has been learned and what challenges lie ahead after six years of reporting, consultations, and dispute settlement about such regulations within the WTO.

Multilateral Governance of Food Regulation

The Uruguay Round agreements strengthened the GATT articles, agreements, and case law that had built up to govern the use of technical barriers to trade over the previous 50 years.[1] The negotiators of the original

---

1. Overall, the Uruguay Round negotiations produced the Final Act, signed in Marrakesh in 1994; the Marrakesh Agreement Establishing the World Trade Organization (or WTO agreement), which serves as an umbrella agreement; the General Agreement on Tariffs and Trade 1994 (known as GATT 1994, which includes the text of the original 1947 GATT articles and subsequent amendments); 16 agreements on goods, services, intellectual property, dispute settlement, and a trade policy review mechanism; and various plurilateral agreements, decisions, and declarations.

GATT treaty recognized the need to subject domestic regulations to international scrutiny so that the strategic application of technical measures by countries would not subvert the commercial opportunities created by lower tariffs and other trade policy reforms. The original GATT treaty set forth various rules designed to limit such abuses. Two GATT articles set out basic prohibitions: Article XI.1 broadly disallows quantitative restrictions, and Article III requires "national treatment" for "like products" to prohibit countries from applying discriminatory internal taxes and regulations to imports. The prohibitions defined by these articles are qualified by GATT Article XX, which recognizes the sovereign right of governments to adopt restrictions on trade if necessary to achieve legitimate policy objectives such as health and safety or conservation of exhaustible natural resources. Subject to the consensus-based approval by all Contracting Parties, a country could request a GATT panel to review a trade complaint. If the panel ruled against the respondent, and the ruling was adopted by consensus, that country could be required to revise its measure, offer compensating trade concessions, or suffer authorized retaliation in the form of higher tariffs on its exports.

The original GATT rules were augmented in the 1973–79 Tokyo Round negotiations, which produced the Agreement on Technical Barriers to Trade (often called the Standards Code). The Standards Code established obligations to ensure that mandatory regulations, voluntary standards, and conformity assessment procedures were not prepared, adopted, or applied to create unnecessary obstacles to trade. These multilateral rules disciplined the use of some protectionist policies.[2] However, neither the original GATT nor the Standards Code was able to stem disruptions of trade in international markets caused by a proliferation of apparently protectionist technical restrictions (Motaal 2002). Moreover, several prominent disagreements over regulations, especially food regulations, remained unresolved in the 1980s.

Three flaws in the pre–Uruguay Round legal infrastructure blunted the effectiveness of the disciplines on technical measures: (1) lack of a single integrated rule system, (2) the GATT's consensus-based dispute settlement process, and (3) ambiguity in the Standard Code's rules for regulations that established requirements for process and production methods (PPMs). Not all Contracting Parties to the GATT had signed the Standards Code, or indeed the other Tokyo Round codes, giving rise to a system sometimes referred to as "GATT à la carte." This system effectively precluded some standards-related disputes from being brought before a GATT panel for resolution. But even if two countries had signed

---

2. The 1986 Japanese ski standards dispute is one such example. In this case, American and European exporters successfully argued that evidence did not support a Japanese claim that imported skis could not function safely on Japanese snow. The case was settled in formal consultations before reaching a panel (Sykes 1995).

the Standards Code, the consensus-based GATT dispute settlement process allowed either country to block a panel report, or even to deny a request to convene a panel. The third loophole was created by the Standards Code itself, which only disciplined measures that "lay down characteristics of a product such as levels of quality, performance, safety or dimensions." The Standards Code omitted any explicit reference to PPMs in its key provisions, an omission that contributed to the high-profile standoff between the European Union[3] and the United States over the European Union's ban on hormone-treated beef.[4] This unresolved dispute was viewed as one of the more visible failures of the pre–Uruguay Round legal disciplines (Stanton 1997).

To remedy these defects, multilateral disciplines on the use of technical measures were revised, expanded, and strengthened in the Uruguay Round. The Punta del Este Ministerial Declaration launching the negotiations in 1986 stated that the objective was to create disciplines that would minimize the "adverse effects that sanitary and phytosanitary regulations and barriers can have on trade in agriculture." The negotiations therefore produced a new Agreement on the Application of Sanitary and Phytosanitary Measures (SPS agreement), which set out rules for measures that target certain enumerated hazards to animal, plant, and human life and health. The Standards Code was also revised, reappearing as the WTO Technical Barriers to Trade Agreement (TBT agreement). A new Agreement on Trade-Related Aspects of Intellectual Property Rights (TRIPS agreement) imposed obligations to provide minimum protection to a range of intellectual property rights, including geographical indications (GIs) of commercial identity for agricultural products and food. The GATT continued in force as well. Thus the Uruguay Round increased the scope and complexity of the legal infrastructure for food-sector technical regulations and standards, as illustrated in figure 3.1.

---

3. For a mixture of historical and legal reasons, the European Union is known as the European Communities at the WTO. The responsibility for trade policy rests predominantly with the "first pillar" of the European Union (the second and third pillars deal with foreign and security policy and with justice and home affairs, respectively). The first pillar includes the institutions that govern the economic aspects of the European Union and is based on the same treaty provisions that were established at the time of the founding of the European Communities. Hence, official WTO documents usually reference "the EC," and we therefore use this acronym when citing official WTO documents. However, we follow normal practice by using the term European Union, or EU, to reference the political entity of the 25 member countries. Technically, these member states are also WTO members in their own right, as is the European Union, though they act as one member in WTO matters. (For more information, see "The European Communities and the WTO" at www.wto.org/english/thewto_e/countries_e/european_communities_e.htm.)

4. This omission established the basis for the EU rejection of the US request to establish a technical experts group to evaluate the scientific basis for the hormone ban. See Josling, Roberts, and Hassan (1999) for a complete account of the legal stalemate in the hormones dispute under the GATT agreements.

Figure 3.1 GATT/WTO legal infrastructure for food regulations and standards

Before the Uruguay Round

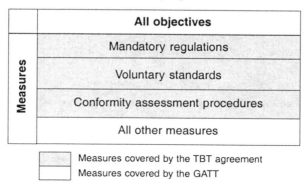

	All objectives
Measures	Mandatory regulations
	Voluntary standards
	Conformity assessment procedures
	All other measures

☐ (shaded) Measures covered by the TBT agreement
☐ Measures covered by the GATT

After the Uruguay Round

	Objectives		
	Protection of animal, plant, and human life and health within the territory of the member	Other technical objectives	Protection of intellectual property
Measures	All measures	Mandatory regulations	
			Geographical indications
		Voluntary standards	
		Conformity assessment procedures	
		All other measures	

☐ SPS agreement ☐ GATT 1994
☐ TBT agreement ☐ TRIPS agreement

The new dispute settlement rules also adopted in the Uruguay Round are critical to the effectiveness of the various WTO agreements. Under the single integrated rules system of the WTO Understanding on Rules and Procedures Governing the Settlement of Disputes (Dispute Settlement Understanding, or DSU), a single country can no longer block a request for review by a dispute panel or prevent the adoption of a panel's report by the WTO's dispute settlement body.

DSU procedures include formal consultations between the parties to a dispute, followed by examination of the dispute by a WTO panel and review of the panel's decision by the WTO Appellate Body if requested by the parties. If the disputed measure is found to violate WTO provisions, the parties to the dispute may request arbitration to determine a "reasonable period of time" for the respondent to change its policy or, if it does not, to determine the amount of compensation or retaliation due to the complainant (usually in the form of tariff adjustments on other products).

Taken together, the new agreements disciplining technical regulations and standards and the new dispute settlement procedures have spurred more requests for international panels to review food-related measures that restrict trade. This increase has, in turn, heightened the profile of these measures and encouraged closer scrutiny of food regulations by national governments and by WTO committees charged with furthering the implementation of the agreements.

Outside of the GATT/WTO framework, governments have also negotiated multilateral environmental agreements (MEAs), which, in some instances, include mandatory trade provisions, such as the Convention on International Trade in Endangered Species of Wild Fauna and Flora (CITES) and the Convention on Biological Diversity (CBD). To the extent that these MEAs require or authorize trade restrictions among signatories, they can be viewed as a waiver of any GATT obligations that might otherwise prohibit such measures. However, they are potentially in conflict with trade rules to the extent that they authorize otherwise GATT/WTO-illegal trade restrictions against WTO members who are not parties to the MEA (Hudec 1996).

To implement fully its technical agreements, the WTO relies on multilateral standards organizations and also draws on the expertise of other intergovernmental scientific bodies such as the World Health Organization (WHO). Together, the WTO, the multilateral standards and scientific organizations, and, to a lesser extent, the MEAs, along with their principles, rules, standards, and enforcement mechanisms, make up the multilateral governance framework for food regulation. This framework is reinforced by a network of bilateral, regional, and plurilateral trade agreements, which have come to play a role in global food regulation as well. These latter agreements provide the multilateral system with both challenges and opportunities to try out cooperative solutions in a context in which cooperation may come easier.[5]

---

5. Perhaps the prime example of a bilateral agreement on food regulatory issues is that between Australia and New Zealand. Food safety is regulated jointly through the Australia New Zealand Food Authority (ANZFA), and standards are administered through the Australia New Zealand Food Standards Council (ANZFSC). At the other end of the spectrum of bilateral approaches to food regulations is the attempt to use the transatlantic

The SPS Agreement

The SPS agreement was negotiated on the premise that domestic sanitary and phytosanitary standards based on international norms could reduce trade conflicts and lower transactions costs and that requiring scientific justification for standards that deviated from such norms would make it more difficult for countries to shelter domestic industries behind restrictive health and safety regulations. The SPS agreement maintains a delicate balance between the rights of member countries to determine their health and safety standards and their obligations to other countries as they seek to achieve those national goals.

Basic Provisions

The SPS agreement sets out disciplines for measures that are applied to protect plant, animal, and human health and life within the territory of the importing country from certain enumerated hazards, including pests, disease, and disease-causing or disease-carrying organisms, as well as additives, contaminants, and toxins that might be found in food, beverages, or feedstuffs.[6]

The agreement reiterates the GATT commitments but also sets out additional principles to minimize unnecessary obstacles to trade. They are:

- **Harmonization** (Article 3). Member countries are urged (but not required) to adopt international standards. A country that adopts the standards of designated international standards organizations is presumed to be in compliance with its WTO commitments.

- **Science-based risk management** (Articles 2 and 5). SPS measures must be based on scientific principles and sufficient scientific evidence; more

---

partnership between the United States and the European Union to resolve differences and increase comity, which has had limited effect—see the discussion of this partnership later in this chapter, and also see Pollack and Shaffer (2001) and Patterson and Josling (2001) for accounts of attempts to solve trade differences arising from regulatory conflicts at a transatlantic level.

Among the more ambitious regional initiatives in the area of food regulations is the Asia Pacific Economic Cooperation (APEC) process (Johnson 1996, Wilson 1995). APEC debated establishing an APEC Food System, which would have included both food safety and trade liberalization instruments. The trade liberalization aspects of the plan have been put on hold, along with other aspects of the APEC program for individual and collective market access improvements, but the food safety part of the program has yielded a framework, the APEC Food Mutual Recognition Agreement, that could facilitate trade in foodstuffs in the Asia Pacific region. Whether this is the start of more substantial cooperation in food regulations remains to be seen.

6. The complete definition is set out in Annex A of the SPS agreement.

particularly, measures must be based on a risk assessment. Measures should be chosen so as to minimize distortions to trade, and be no more trade-restrictive than necessary to achieve a country's "appropriate level of protection." Member countries are to avoid variation in the levels of health protection provided by their measures if the variation creates a disguised restriction on trade. Countries may adopt provisional measures to avoid risks, but they must seek information and carry out a risk assessment to justify permanent use of a trade-restricting measure.

- **Equivalence** (Article 4). A WTO member must accept that the SPS measures of another country are equivalent to its own if it is objectively demonstrated that the other country's measures achieve the member's appropriate level of protection, even if the measures themselves differ.

- **Regionalization** (Article 6). A country is required to allow imports from subnational regions abroad that are free or nearly free of pests or disease.

The obligations of member countries under the SPS agreement are qualified by recognition of national sovereignty. Article 3 of the agreement ensures that any country may choose a measure that differs from the international standard to achieve its appropriate level of protection as long as it complies with the other rules. Thus the SPS agreement takes into account that individual nations may be unwilling to subscribe to uniform standards for all hazards. Implicitly, this principle recognizes that it would not be optimal for them to do so in all cases.

In addition to setting out the rights and obligations of WTO members, the SPS agreement establishes new information exchange and enforcement mechanisms. To maintain transparency about applied measures, members are required to notify their regulations to the WTO and to provide trading partners with an inquiry point. A permanent SPS Committee meets three to four times a year to oversee implementation of the agreement and discuss contentious SPS measures on a continuing basis. The SPS agreement receives additional support through the resolution of conflicts under the rules of the DSU.

Relevant International Standards Organizations

The SPS agreement identifies three intergovernmental standards organizations to help achieve its objectives: L'Office International des Epizooties (OIE) for measures related to animal health and zoonoses affecting both animal and human health, the International Plant Protection Convention (IPPC) for plant health measures, and the Codex Alimentarius Commission (Codex) for food safety measures. These international organizations are given prominence through recognition of the standards they set as a basis for presumed compliance with the agreement. These three scientific bodies also provide channels for technical discussions of inconsistencies and differences among national regulations.

The OIE, IPPC, and Codex differ considerably in their composition and role. The OIE, whose headquarters is in Paris, was established in 1924. It is not affiliated with the United Nations. Its member states finance and run the OIE through an international committee of delegates from those states, a central bureau acts as the executive body, and commissions serve as the deliberative organs. The main commissions are those dealing with epizootic diseases, fish diseases, and standards. OIE issues an International Animal Health Code and an International Aquatic Animal Health Code. The commissions periodically update the codes, discuss protection strategies, and prepare manuals. The OIE also includes working groups and regional offices, as well as a network of laboratories that collaborate with the OIE in testing and certification.

The International Plant Protection Convention was established in 1952 with the objective of ensuring "effective common action to prevent the spread and introduction of pests and parasites affecting plants and plant products and to promote control measures." It is administered by a secretariat attached to the UN Food and Agriculture Organization (FAO) in Rome. Revisions to the convention agreed on in 1979 came into force in 1991. A further revision of the convention was adopted by the FAO Conference in 1997 and aligns the IPPC with the provisions of the SPS agreement (Victor 1998). The latest convention provides for the use of phytosanitary measures to protect the natural environment as well as commercial crops from invasive species. The convention is a treaty that obligates the signatories (currently 110 countries) to take certain steps to guard against the spread of plant pests and diseases. Countries must put in place adequate checks and certification and disinfectant procedures, and they must publish information about such procedures (OECD 1999). The IPPC encourages countries to use the least trade-restrictive policies to protect plant health, avoid unnecessary delays, and be transparent in their use of restrictions.

The Codex Alimentarius Commission was established by the FAO and WHO in 1962 to implement a joint food standards program and to create the Codex Alimentarius, a set of general and commodity-specific standards, guidelines, and recommended codes of practice designed to protect the health of consumers and to ensure fair trade practices (Codex 1999b).[7] The various Codex texts are intended to "guide and promote

---

7. The Codex Alimentarius Europaeus was established earlier, in 1958, to achieve more consistent methods of food testing among the countries in the European Communities. It was merged with a joint WHO and FAO standards committee on milk standards and reorganized as the Codex Alimentarius Commission (Victor 1998).

the development, implementation and harmonization of definitions and requirements covering food products with a view to facilitating international trade." Proposed norms navigate a complex eight-step process from their introduction to their ultimate approval. Member countries are not required to adopt Codex standards. The existence of international standards, however, has helped those countries that wish to use these standards either as a requirement for imports or as a template for their own regulations.

At present, 165 countries are represented on the Codex, which has an executive committee of 10 members and a small secretariat in Rome. The major work of the Codex is carried out by various subsidiary committees that negotiate the texts and discuss specific problems. Nine of these committees function horizontally, dealing with cross-cutting issues such as labeling or additives, and 16 others are vertical, dealing with specific commodities. Five regional committees focus on issues related to geographic areas.

For much of its existence, the Codex has been regarded as a technical organization that operates at an epistemic level, "largely unaffected by national political interests as well as national and international law" (Veggeland and Borgen 2002, 9). Committees were dominated by scientific experts who worked closely with bodies such as the Joint FAO/WHO Expert Committee on Food Additives (JECFA) and the Joint FAO/WHO Meeting on Pesticide Residues (JMPR). Now, however, because of the heightened legal status of its standards under the SPS agreement and its wide coverage in the area of food standards, the work of the Codex bodies has become especially sensitive. As a result, the prevailing judgment is that of the three standard-setting institutions referenced in the SPS agreement, the SPS agreement has politicized decision making within Codex more than in the other standards organizations. Four specific instances are often cited to support this conclusion: (1) the two-year debate over the 1995 Codex "Statements of Principle," (2) the 1995 vote on Codex beef hormone standards, (3) the 1997 vote on Codex mineral water standards, and (4) the failure of Codex to adopt JECFA's recommended standard for recombinant bovine somatotropin (rbST), a synthetically produced version of a naturally occurring hormone intended to increase milk production.

---

8. In the debate over the Codex Statement of Principles (formally, the "Statement of Principles Concerning the Role of Science in the Codex Decision-Making Process and the Extent to Which Other Factors Are Taken into Account"), the United States and European Union sought to propagate decision criteria that favored their domestic agricultural policy regimes. The United States and its allies argued that food safety standards should rest solely on scientific evidence, while Europe and its allies sought to introduce a "need" criterion, which held that productivity-enhancing food technologies threatened the livelihoods of economically marginal farmers and were not "needed" in the face of excess global capacity. A compromise resulted in a statement that Codex standards "shall be

In the first matter, compromise language was eventually negotiated.[8] In the second and third matters, the standards for hormone-treated beef (favoring producers in North America, Japan, Australia, New Zealand, and Korea, among others) and mineral water (favoring European producers) were approved by slim majorities rather than by consensus. In the fourth matter, the Codex voted to hold the draft standard for rbST at the last step of the eight-step approval process rather than adopt it as an international standard—an outcome favored by countries that had banned the domestic use of rbST for a variety of reasons unrelated to human health, including consumer concerns, animal welfare concerns, and concerns about the impact of increased milk production on small dairy farmers (Codex 1999a).[9] More recent controversies addressed in the WTO, such as the regulation of genetically modified foods, now routinely spill over into Codex deliberations.

Implementation of the SPS Agreement

The obligations under the SPS agreement address aspects of national regulations that could create trade disputes. Experience has accumulated within the WTO and the standard-setting organizations from which the implementation of the agreement can be evaluated. While hard to quantify, it is apparent that the SPS agreement has generated broad-based regulatory review by many WTO members, both major agricultural exporters and importers, as they determine whether they and their trading partners are complying with obligations. Evidence suggests that regulatory authorities are either unilaterally modifying regulations or voluntarily modifying regulations after technical exchanges (Roberts 1998). To give just two examples of accelerated schedules for making long-standing measures consistent with the obligations in the SPS agreement: in 1997 Japan agreed to rescind its 46-year ban on several varieties of tomatoes grown in the United States after weighing scientific research indicating that they were not afflicted with tobacco blue mold disease, and in 1999 the United States ended a 20-year dispute with four European countries by agreeing

---

based on the principle of sound scientific analysis and evidence," but, where appropriate, Codex will consider "other legitimate factors" in protecting consumer health and promoting fair trade practices (Codex 2001a). Subsequent efforts by Codex to translate these principles into more specific guidance have achieved some progress, but fundamental differences in approaches to risk management are still evident (Codex 2001b).

9. The United States maintained that JECFA's scientific evaluation should be the only determining factor for the adoption of the rbST standard, and that on the basis of this evaluation the standard should be adopted. Germany (speaking on behalf of the European Union) stated that adoption of the standard "would not be appropriate" (Codex 1999a).

to allow imports of rhododendrons in growing media under a new phytosanitary protocol. More systematic reports, while far from comprehensive, reinforce the anecdotal evidence of a demonstration effect from the SPS agreement. The United States and Australia, respectively, report resolution of 338 and 240 SPS cases in bilateral negotiations over five years (USDA's *SPS Accomplishment Reports* 1996–2000 and *World Food Chemical News* 2001a). Enacting regulatory changes that allow greater market access has become easier now that the SPS agreement assures policymakers that their trading partners must conform to the same science-based principles. The requirements have also prodded authorities to revisit regulations whose longevity could be attributed to simple inertia rather than overt protectionism.

Progress toward realization of the four principles under the SPS agreement—harmonization, science-based risk management, equivalence, and regionalization—also reflects how well the framework of the SPS agreement and supporting institutions has addressed agriculture and food regulatory issues.

Harmonization

The SPS agreement's endorsement of harmonization stems from repeated complaints by exporters that compliance with divergent SPS measures substantially increases the transactions costs of trade. Firms that ship products to several different markets stand to gain if harmonization results in lower production and certification costs on a per unit basis. Harmonization also can benefit consumers—an outcome more likely if the regulatory heterogeneity arises from differences in chance events, informational differences, or interest group capture. Harmonization is less likely to be appropriate if differences in income, taste, and risk are the primary sources of variation in national regulations.

The impact of harmonization on trade appears to be constrained as much by the lack of specific international standards as by normative considerations under the SPS agreement. Of the SPS measures notified to the WTO by members during 1995 to 2002, a majority stated that no international standard existed for the measure. The character of international standards as a public good leads to an expectation of underinvestment in their creation. This underinvestment may lead not only to too few international standards but also to too many outmoded standards, which may account in part for the low adoption rate for those standards that do exist. Over the first four years of the SPS agreement (1995–99), partial or full acceptance of international standards as a percentage of total notified measures was highest for the lower-middle-income countries at 38 percent; followed by high-income countries, 22 percent; lower-income countries, 20 percent; and upper-middle-income countries, 17 percent (Roberts, Orden, and Josling 1999).

The generality of recent international standards also is important in assessing their impact on trade and trade disputes. Over the past decade, international standards organizations have allocated more of their resources to developing meta-standards that identify common approaches to risk identification, assessment, and management than to specific international standards per se. Exporters' anticipated gains from international meta-standards may be smaller than from specific international standards because adherence to the same general guidelines leaves scope for countries to develop different regulatory regimes to manage risks. For example, even countries that adopted the Codex's 1997 "General Principles of Food Hygiene" have had substantive differences in their requirements for reducing microbial risks, as the European Union's decision to ban imports of US poultry meat in 1997 illustrates (Becker 1999). Thus in recent years international standards organizations have contributed more to the trade system by setting out scientific approaches to regulation than by promulgating standards that are identical across countries, implying that the benefits from international standards have accrued more to consumers than exporters.

Science-Based Risk Management

The requirement to base regulations on scientific risk assessment clearly reduces the latitude for disingenuous use of SPS regulatory interventions. In each of the four SPS disputes to reach the WTO Appellate Body since the SPS agreement came into effect, the regulations at issue were judged to violate this requirement.[10] However, the impact of the science-based risk management requirements of the SPS agreement within the WTO extends beyond formal dispute settlement results. The explicit obligation to base measures on science has led to the resolution of many issues in Geneva before they advance to dispute settlement. In particular, food safety measures that discriminate among sources of supply attract close scrutiny, and sometimes appear to lack scientific rationale. For example, an exemption to a ban on sauces containing benzoic acid that Australia had granted to New Zealand during their transition to a common food standards system was replaced with a tolerance level for all imports in response to a Philippine complaint in the SPS Committee. Disagreements over less overtly discriminatory measures have been resolved by means of updated risk assessments. For example, a scientific review led Korea to amend its new food code to exempt poultry meat destined for further processing and cooking from its new zero tolerance standard for *Listeria*, thereby allowing imports of Thai frozen chicken to resume (WTO 2002f).

---

10. The four cases—EC-Hormones, brought by the United States and Canada; Australia-Salmon, brought by Canada; and Japan–Varietal Testing and Japan-Apples, both brought by the United States—are discussed later in this chapter.

Although the obligation to base measures on risk assessments can often avert trade disputes, it cannot always do so, sometimes because the relevant risk assessments are not available to inform regulatory responses to new hazards. "Emergency" measures have accounted for 17 percent of the total SPS measures notified to the WTO (OECD 2002). Because such measures are generally very trade-restrictive, they often give rise to complaints if importers fail to modify these policies as new evidence emerges.[11] For example, the European Union had to repeatedly petition Argentine regulators before they modified trade restrictions on Belgian chocolate, German milk powder, and Swedish cacao oil butter—long after other countries had lifted bans on these products upon learning that the OIE and the WHO had reaffirmed that existing scientific data did not indicate that dairy products are BSE vectors.

Risk assessments also do not avert disagreements over measures that reflect extremely conservative approaches to mitigating scientifically verified risks. The national sovereignty principle of the SPS agreement entitles countries to adopt measures that achieve their chosen levels of protection, subject to the requirement that measures be no more trade-restrictive than necessary to achieve these levels. In seeking enabling legislation for undertaking WTO obligations, the US Statement of Administrative Action to Congress asserted that this provision, along with other language in the agreement, "explicitly affirms the rights of each government to choose its levels of protection including a 'zero risk' level if it so chooses" (President of the United States 1994). The national sovereignty principle thus provides leeway for countries to adopt measures that achieve incremental reductions in risk regardless of the costs to either their domestic producers and consumers or their trading partners.[12] Conservative measures may be maintained under the agreement even when these measures fail to increase domestic welfare. To cite but one recent example, New Zealand decided to maintain a ban on imports of bone-in poultry cuts from the United States based on an assessment that shipments posed a risk of three introductions of infectious bursal disease in noncommercial (i.e., backyard) chicken flocks per 100 importation years (New Zealand Ministry of Agriculture and Forestry 2000).[13] Such policies may be scientifically

---

11. Annex B of the SPS agreement requires a country to publish a new regulation in advance of its entry into force "except in urgent circumstances." The procedures for notifying the WTO of these emergency regulations is set out in the SPS Committee's "Recommended Notification Procedures" (WTO 1996).

12. In other words, requiring evidence of some risk precludes application of SPS regulations only in cases that are shown to lie on the vertical axis in figure 2.1, while otherwise allowing countries to choose their level of risk aversion.

13. The OIE regards infectious bursal disease as a hazard "of socio-economic and/or public health importance within countries" (List B) but finds that it lacks "the potential for very serious and rapid spread, irrespective of national borders," and is not a disease "of serious socio-economic or public health consequence" (List A). See chapter 4 for further discussion of the OIE's recommended risk management practices for List A and List B diseases.

justifiable, but nonetheless fail benefit-cost tests by ignoring the benefits of imports to domestic consumers. Such measures are likely to be seen as unreasonable by exporters.

The SPS agreement provides little elaboration of risk management principles to guide resolution of disputes other than the requirement to minimize trade effects for chosen levels of risk reduction. Negotiators of the agreement judged it inappropriate for the WTO to be more prescriptive about risk management, seeing the standards organizations as the better forum for the development of templates for regulatory practices. Guidance has been provided by the OIE, IPPC, and Codex, and internationally recognized standards and procedures may further narrow the scope for trade disagreements.[14] But it is unrealistic to expect that these principles will eliminate disputes over the best course of action to take in regulation, given the scientific evidence. Science is descriptive, not prescriptive. A risk management decision will therefore always require a choice among different policy options, each with different costs and benefits. Options that severely limit market access to achieve extremely incremental health or safety benefits are likely to be contentious, even if based on science.

Equivalence

Article 4 of the SPS agreement requires each WTO member to accept another member's measures as equivalent to its own if the exporting country can demonstrate that its measures achieve the importing country's desired level of SPS protection. This provision recognizes that regulatory flexibility allows countries to allocate scarce resources efficiently rather than identically. The SPS agreement also seeks to promote trade by requiring members, upon request, to enter into consultations for bilateral and multilateral agreements on the equivalence of their measures.

Equivalence determinations mostly involve process standards, because countries are more easily able to compare product standards that stipulate the observable or testable attributes of goods. An enormous number—and arguably a growing proportion—of food safety SPS measures are process standards, as discussed in depth in chapter 5. The SPS equivalence obligation therefore has the potential to yield significant benefits in international markets for products such as cheeses, meats, fresh produce, and seafood—that is, those products for which process standards are the main instruments used to manage microbial risks.

There is no systematic accounting of negotiations of equivalence

---

14. The Codex's "Working Principles for Risk Analysis" and the Codex "Statement of Principles" noted earlier are two examples of risk management guidance promulgated by an international standards organization for the benefit of its members. The adoption by the Codex reflects a strong desire on the part of member countries to achieve a consensus on some aspects of risk management policy, but these documents have not yet reconciled disagreements over some fundamentals such as the role of precaution and "other legitimate factors" in regulatory decision making.

arrangements to date, but their use is not common in international food trade, despite the conceptual appeal.[15] The administrative burden of equivalence determinations is often significant, involving evaluation of infrastructure, overall program design and implementation, and specific technical requirements. For example, a framework agreement signed by the United States and the European Union in July 1999 to recognize equivalence of some SPS measures for selected animal products[16] required six years of occasionally high-profile negotiations that extended to details such as the color of wall paint in food-processing facilities. Under this agreement, the exporting country must continue to comply with the importing country's measures that are not judged to be equivalent, including several that regulate food and feed additives and animal drug residues. Both the European Union and the United States also recognize the equivalence of some measures for selected meat and dairy products from Australia, Canada, and New Zealand. However, numerous regulatory differences remain in contention, even between countries generally recognized as having rigorous regulatory standards that are rigorously enforced.

Often, differences between countries hinge not only on the equivalence of different process standards themselves but also on how conformance with different standards is ascertained. For example, differences over government and industry roles in certification have held up EU recognition of the equivalence of the US production and inspection systems for food-grade gelatin. Exports from the United States to the European Union have been suspended since June 2000, when the European Commission's new BSE-related regulations came into force. The European Commission has indicated that most US gelatin safety measures are equivalent to corresponding EU measures. However, the European Union has been unwilling to import US gelatin until there is more oversight by the US Food and Drug Administration (FDA) of industry self-certification of compliance with the two "non-equivalent" measures (WTO 2002f).

Given the problems that developed countries have had with equivalence arrangements, developing countries have questioned whether this provision of the SPS agreement will provide many export opportunities for them (WTO 1998c). Some equivalence agreements exist between developing and developed countries, especially for seafood products.[17] However,

---

15. Although the SPS Committee has urged members to submit information on their bilateral equivalence arrangements, few have done so (WTO 2001b). Gascoine (1999) discusses reasons for limited early use of equivalence in international food trade.

16. The agreement applies to approximately $1 billion in EU exports of dairy products, fish, and meat to the United States, and to a similar value in US exports of fish, hides, and pet food to Western Europe.

17. The European Union, for example, states that 62 countries have been recognized as implementing an equivalent system of inspection and certification for fishery products, and another 41 await equivalence evaluations but can currently export fishery products to individual EU member states on the basis of bilateral agreements (WTO 2002d).

developing countries, echoing the claims of developed countries, have argued that often compliance with domestic measures rather than equivalence of alternative measures is required by importing countries. Even developing countries that have had substantial success as agricultural exporters, such as Brazil, Mexico, and Thailand, have gone on record to note the difficulties in gaining recognition of equivalence (WTO 1999e, 2001d).

Globally, the limited access to developed-country markets for poultry meat illustrates both the potential and challenge of equivalence. Of the 148 WTO member countries (as of September 2003), only 15 are eligible to export fresh, chilled, or frozen poultry meat to the European Union; only 4 can export to the United States; only 1 can ship to Canada; and none are allowed to export to Australia.[18]

Because of a recent decision by the SPS Committee to increase the transparency of equivalence arrangements, a more systematic assessment of the impact of equivalence on global food trade will eventually be possible.[19] Transparency may further the objective of increasing regulatory flexibility, but significant constraints remain nonetheless. First, significant time and resources can be required for equivalence determinations, as the bilateral framework agreement between the United States and the European Union illustrates. According to the United States, the potential for equivalence may be limited because the actual trade benefits often do not justify the administrative burden (WTO 2000a).[20] Second, after recognizing the equivalence of an alternative regulatory regime, national regulators may have to offer the same alternative to domestic producers, requiring in turn new or revised domestic regulations. Finally, if national regulations are specified in legislation, there is little scope for regulators to consider other options without new legislative authority.[21]

---

18. In addition to the four countries (Canada, Great Britain, France, and Israel) that are permitted to export fresh, frozen, or chilled poultry to the United States, some plants in northern Mexico can reexport US-origin poultry meat to the United States after minimal processing.

19. In 2001 the committee revised its recommended procedures to provide for the notification of equivalence of SPS measures and finalized the notification format in June 2002. In its Decision on the Implementation of Article 4, the committee noted that equivalence could be accepted for a specific measure or measures related to a certain product or categories of products, or on a systemwide basis (WTO 2001a).

20. The United States also has cautioned that equivalence does not imply mutual recognition. Under the equivalence provisions of the SPS agreement, market access is contingent on a scientific determination that an exporter's alternative measure achieves the level of SPS protection required by the importer, not on the reciprocity of such determinations.

21. For example, the US Egg Products Inspection Act of 1970 requires continuous inspection of processed eggs by government inspectors, a standard that is currently met by only one other country (Canada).

Regionalization

The regionalization provision of the SPS agreement is an integral part of a science-based approach to regulating trade, because differences in levels of risks do not always correspond to national political boundaries. Regionalization allows countries to export products from areas where animal or plant health risks are considered negligible, thereby benefiting consumers without jeopardizing the agricultural resource base in the importing country. Chile's decision to allow imports of fresh melons and watermelons from all US production areas except Hawaii is one example of a regional approach to mitigating pest risks (WTO 2000b). By ensuring that geographic eradication or reduced incidence of hazards leads to trade gains, regionalization also provides incentives for additional investments in control measures. Over time, this SPS provision is likely to be of growing importance in international agricultural markets.

As with equivalence, agricultural producers in developing countries face more challenges than developed-country producers in capitalizing on the regionalization provisions, because exports will generally depend on adequate public-sector investments in laboratory, inspection, monitoring, and certification infrastructure. And national regulations will not always be effective: transborder pest or disease controls may be required where there are insufficient natural barriers or where animals, including wildlife, move freely across borders. It is therefore likely that creating or strengthening implementation of regional sanitary and phytosanitary measures across as well as within countries will often be necessary to realize fully the gains from trade. Coordination of this sort requires substantial institutional capabilities (see the discussion of control of FMD in chapter 4).

The TBT Agreement

The TBT agreement sets out rules for mandatory regulations, voluntary standards, and conformity assessment procedures that are not covered by the SPS agreement.[22] Like the SPS agreement, the TBT agreement acknowledges the right of countries to develop product requirements as well as procedures to assess compliance with those requirements. However, it attempts to ensure that the preparation, adoption, and application of these measures do not create unnecessary obstacles to trade. The TBT agreement is becoming increasingly important in global food markets as governments promulgate more regulations and standards in response

---

22. Article 1.5 of the TBT agreement states that "the provisions of this Agreement do not apply to sanitary and phytosanitary measures as defined in Annex A of the Agreement on the Application of Sanitary and Phytosanitary Measures."

to growing consumer demands for products with specific quality attributes or for information about those attributes.

Basic Provisions

While technical regulations and conformity assessment procedures are covered in the main body of the TBT agreement, standards are covered in the Code of Good Practice for the Preparation, Adoption and Application of Standards (Code of Good Practice) set out in Annex 3 of the agreement. The substantive disciplines of the TBT agreement begin with a list of legitimate objectives for which regulations may be developed. These provisions also delineate the types of evidence that can be used to judge whether the required measures are necessary to fulfilling those objectives:

> Such legitimate objectives are, inter alia: national security requirements; the prevention of deceptive practices; protection of human health or safety, animal or plant life or health, or the environment. In assessing such risks, relevant elements of consideration are, inter alia: available scientific and technical information, related processing technology or intended end-uses of products.

The agreement then sets out key principles for adherence by WTO members. Article 2 of the TBT agreement stipulates that members

- must not discriminate against imported like products from other WTO members;
- must not adopt measures that are more trade-restrictive than necessary to fulfill a legitimate objective;
- must monitor and review measures to address changes in circumstances and objectives;
- must base measures on international standards when available and where appropriate;
- must give positive consideration to recognizing other members' measures as equivalent to their own, even if different, provided that they are satisfied that another country's measures adequately fulfill the objectives of their own regulations; and
- must base measures, where appropriate, on product performance requirements rather than design or descriptive characteristics.

The TBT agreement also requires each country to ensure that its central government standardizing bodies adhere to the Code of Good Practice, which endorses most of the principles found in the TBT agreement itself. WTO members also are to take reasonable measures to ensure that other governmental and nongovernmental standards organizations within their territories accept and comply with the code.[23]

In addition to these disciplines, the TBT agreement sets out information exchange and enforcement mechanisms that are very similar to those established under the SPS agreement. These mechanisms include notification procedures and inquiry points for informing other WTO members of changes in TBT measures, a TBT committee to discuss issues on a continuing basis, and use of WTO dispute resolution mechanisms for resolving conflicts between countries in a timely manner.

Related Standards Organizations

The TBT agreement, unlike the SPS agreement, does not reference specific international standards organizations. Instead, the WTO recognizes the international standards of all of those organizations that adhere to the principles established by the TBT Committee in the Decision of the Committee on Principles for the Development of International Standards, Guides, and Recommendations (WTO 2000c). These principles include transparency, openness, impartiality and consensus, effectiveness and relevance, coherency, and attention to the needs of developing countries.[24]

A diffuse set of public and private organizations promulgate international food standards, either as a principal or as an ancillary undertaking. These organizations include regional institutions such as the United Nations Economic Commission for Europe (UN/ECE); plurilateral institutions such as the Organization for Economic Cooperation and Development (OECD), which operates the Scheme for the Application of International Standards for Fruits and Vegetables and recently has taken responsibility for plurilateral dialogue on the regulation of biotechnology; and multilateral institutions such as the International Dairy Federation (IDF) and the International Organization for Standardization (ISO).

---

23. All nongovernmental as well as governmental standardizing organizations are invited to accept the code and abide by its provisions. Motaal (2002) notes that because most of the organizations that develop standards are nongovernmental, the code was created to bring their work under the purview of the TBT agreement.

24. Not all international organizations that address food regulations meet the criteria laid out by the TBT Committee. The WHO, for example, has not always adopted its standards on the basis of consensus, and other organizations do not provide an opportunity to comment on proposals being considered by WTO countries that are not members of the standards organization. These institutions may nonetheless influence the development of international standards recognized as such by the WTO. For example, the WHO is well positioned to convene expert scientific panels on issues of emerging importance, such as biotechnology and microbial resistance, and to distribute their findings even if the findings are not in accordance with the views of the entire WHO membership.

Public and private institutions often collaborate in the development of international standards. For example, the IDF, a private organization, is the source of draft standards for milk products in the intergovernmental Codex Committee for Dairy Products. Several state and provincial governments have similarly contributed to the development of eco-labeling standards that have been adopted by the ISO, another private organization. In most instances, the international standards themselves are voluntary; when mandatory, only members of the organization are obliged to comply. However, as reference points for the global food system, either by incorporation into national regulations or through voluntary contracts of private firms, such standards have the potential to affect trade significantly.

The Codex, responsible for promulgating standards to promote fair food trade practices as well as to improve food safety, is the foremost multilateral institution in the governance framework for food quality measures. The very first Codex standard (for canned tomatoes) was related to its fair trade mandate rather than food safety. Over the past few years, the Codex has drafted, finalized, or amended international standards or guidelines for quantitative declarations of ingredients, nutrition labeling, health claims, country-of-origin labeling, organic production and labeling, and labeling of genetically modified foods (Codex 2001c). Bodies such as the Codex Committee on Food Labeling have become battlegrounds at the center of some of the most prominent disputes over food regulation within the global trading system.

Implementation of the TBT Agreement

In the implementation of the TBT agreement, the appropriate use of labels for agricultural and food products to signal quality attributes has been one of the most contentious issues among countries. Proposed requirements for country-of-origin labeling for perishable foods, eco-labeling of forestry products, traditional expressions for wine and spirits, labeling for genetically modified products, and other labeling regimes draw objections from members at almost every meeting of the TBT Committee (WTO 2002c). Disagreements over these proposals arise to some extent from uncertainty over the TBT agreement's rules for labeling what have been called "non-product-related process and production methods" (npr-PPMs), regulations that target process attributes not materially evident in the end product. Much of this uncertainty stems from the agreement's definition of a technical regulation. Annex 1 of the TBT agreement defines a technical regulation as a

> [d]ocument which lays down product characteristics or their related processes and production methods, including the applicable administrative provisions, with which compliance is mandatory. It may also include or deal exclusively with terminology, symbols, packaging, marketing, or labeling requirements as they apply to a product, process or production method.

In the view of some WTO members, the ambiguous language used in this definition has called into question the applicability of Article 2 requirements to npr-PPMs. The first sentence refers only to product characteristics or their "related" PPMs. The second sentence, which explicitly mentions labeling, refers to "products" and PPMs without qualification. The lack of a specific reference to npr-PPMs in the definition could be taken to suggest that such measures are not bound by the rules in the TBT agreement per se, although other GATT disciplines might apply. Instead, some countries have taken the lack of explicit mention of npr-PPMs in the definition to imply that such measures are simply not allowed. Other countries have disagreed with this interpretation, arguing that such measures should be, and are, disciplined by the TBT agreement; otherwise, many important regulations—in particular, many of the emerging quality-related process attribute regulations—would be outside its scope (WTO 2001f, 2001g). This unresolved debate poses a serious challenge for the governance of food regulations. The npr-PPMs, or process standards addressing process attributes, are growing in importance in domestic and international food markets (see the more in-depth discussion in chapter 7).

Should a complaint over a labeling regime for an npr-PPM advance to a WTO panel, one factor likely to be relevant is whether the measure discriminated against an imported like product in violation of Article 2 of the TBT agreement. Several GATT/WTO dispute panels have analyzed "likeness" under GATT Article III.4 rules for national treatment, but the meaning of like products under the TBT agreement has not been interpreted by a panel or the Appellate Body. The Appellate Body's first opportunity to examine the meaning of "likeness" under GATT Article III was provided by the European Union's appeal of the panel report in the Canada-EU asbestos dispute in 2001 (WTO 2001c). For this determination of likeness, the judges based their analysis on four criteria that were slightly modified from earlier GATT reports: (1) the physical properties of the products, (2) the extent to which the products are capable of serving the same or similar end uses, (3) the extent to which consumers perceive and treat the products as alternative means of performing particular functions in order to satisfy a particular want or demand, and (4) the tariff classification of the products.[25]

Because of the varying interpretations of the definitions and articles in the agreement, the TBT Committee agreed in 2001 to begin a series of informal meetings to discuss uncertainties about the legitimacy of various

---

25. The Report of the Working Party on Border Tax Adjustments (BISD 18S/97, adopted December 2, 1970) outlined the initial approach for analyzing "likeness." Based on the first three criteria, this approach has been followed and developed since by several panels and the Appellate Body. The fourth criterion, tariff classification, was not mentioned in this report, but was included by subsequent panels.

labeling policies (WTO 2001g). If countries are unable to agree on a common understanding of the rights and obligations set out in the TBT agreement, the remaining ambiguities may have to be resolved via formal WTO dispute resolution. Although the dispute settlement process may lead to resolution in specific cases, the outcomes would have less generality and less legitimacy than rules produced by deliberate debate among all WTO members.

The TRIPS Agreement

The TRIPS agreement obligates countries to provide "effective and appropriate means for the enforcement of trade-related intellectual property rights" for each type of intellectual property that it covers. The three main kinds of intellectual property instruments are copyright for artistic and literary works; patents and similar devices for inventions, industrial designs, and trade secrets; and trademarks, signs, and geographical indications for commercial identification.

The provisions of the TRIPS agreement of particular importance to global food trade are the international rules for protection of GIs.[26] Although GIs are used for industrial products, such as Silicon Valley microchips, most are used to aid in the marketing of agricultural products. Countries differ considerably in the way their laws handle GIs. Some countries have specific GI laws. Others use trademark law, consumer protection law, marketing law, or common law, or some combination of these. Some countries have formal lists of registered geographical indications. Others do not, preferring to rely on court case histories (based on criteria such as consumer protection) to identify where problems have arisen and been resolved. Although it does not harmonize these national regulations, the TRIPS agreement does establish criteria that domestic regulations must meet. The objective is to avoid trade conflicts that inevitably arise if different countries have different coverage and use incompatible instruments for protection of intellectual property.

Basic Provisions

The TRIPS agreement sets forth the negotiated definition of a GI and provides two different levels of protection for this type of trademark. GIs are defined as "indications which identify a good as originating in the territory of a Member, or a region or locality in that territory, where

---

26. TRIPS protection for new plant varieties (though not necessarily by patents) and for innovations in microbiology also is important to the world food system, but these forms of intellectual property are beyond the purview of this book. See Watal (2000) for a discussion of these issues.

a given quality, reputation or other characteristic of the good is essentially attributable to its geographic origin."

Article 22 of the TRIPS agreement offers protection for GIs for all goods, requiring countries to provide the legal means for private interests to prevent the use of a designation that is misleading or constitutes unfair competition. GIs for products protected under US law include "Idaho" for potatoes and "Washington State" for apples. Examples of foreign GIs that are protected in the United States are "Roquefort" (for cheeses), "Darjeeling" (for tea), and "Swiss" (for chocolate).

The TRIPS agreement provides additional protection for GIs that identify wines and spirits. Article 23 stipulates that any use by a third party of a wine or spirit GI belonging to another is prohibited—consumer protection or unfair competition does not have to be demonstrated. Moreover, the use of terms including kind, type, style, or imitation in tandem with a wine or spirit GI is prohibited.

Article 24 of the TRIPS agreement sets out two exceptions to the general rules. Countries are not required to extend protection to a GI if the term is the generic name for the product in the importing country. The United States can therefore continue to permit the use of "chablis," "champagne," and "Swiss cheese" as synonyms for white wine, sparkling wine, and Emmenthal-style cheese, because they have been recognized as generic terms under US trademark law.

The second exception is found in Article 24's grandfather provisions for existing product names. An importing country is not required to protect a GI if a trademark was in use in that country before the TRIPS agreement came into effect or before the GI was protected in its country of origin. Protection for existing names for wines and spirits is narrower under the grandfather provisions. Names for these products must have been in continuous use in the importing country for at least 10 years before conclusion of the Uruguay Round to exempt the importing country from its obligation to protect a GI that uses the same product identifier.

Related Governance Institution for GIs

The TRIPS agreement specifically references the World Intellectual Property Organization (WIPO), based in Geneva, as the relevant international body for GIs. The WIPO administers various international agreements that deal partly or entirely with the protection of geographical indications, such as the Lisbon Agreement for the Protection of Appellations of Origin and Their International Registration. The WIPO's Standing Committee on the Law of Trademarks, Industrial Designs and Geographical Indications, composed of representatives of member states and interested organizations, considers new initiatives for the international protection of GIs.

Implementation of the TRIPS Agreement

The TRIPS agreement's wide accommodation of national differences in protection of GIs narrows the scope for successful legal challenges. Thus few complaints about this form of intellectual property have surfaced under the Uruguay Round rules, and only one formal dispute over GIs has emerged over the 1995–2002 period.[27]

This record belies, however, the level of discord over the administration and enforcement of GIs in the world food system. The TRIPS agreement calls for negotiations on two aspects of GI protection, although it does not say when these negotiations should take place, or when they should end. Article 23 calls for negotiations on the establishment of a multilateral centralized registry system for GIs for wines and spirits, and Article 24 requires negotiations aimed at extending the higher level of protection Article 23 accords to wines and spirits to other products. Countries differ widely in their positions in these negotiations.

One set of proposals for the central registry sees the system as essentially a database: Members would report the GIs for wines and spirits that they protect, and other members would take the information into consideration when making a decision about protection under their own systems. Another group of countries have proposed that participating countries be obliged to protect the GIs listed on the central registry, subject to certain conditions. Similarly, WTO members differ widely on extending Article 23 protection to other products. These differences stem from, among other things, diverse interpretations of which product identifiers can be considered GIs and are therefore eligible for protection.

Disagreement even extends to the appropriate WTO venue for negotiations on strengthened GI protection for products other than wine and spirits. The Doha Ministerial Declaration refers to these negotiations as one of many "implementation issues" that "shall be addressed as a matter of priority by the relevant WTO bodies." These bodies are then to report back to the Trade Negotiating Committee, which oversees the multilateral trade talks. Some countries have concluded that this language establishes a mandate for GI extension negotiations as part of the "single undertaking" of the Doha Round, but others see only an obligation to continue discussions in the TRIPS Council, the WTO body that oversees implementation of the agreement. Frustrated proponents of GI extension have thus explicitly linked progress on this issue to the Doha negotiations on agriculture. Proposals for expanding GI protection have been submitted to the agriculture negotiations, casting GI protection as a question of market access for agricultural products (Roberts, Unnevehr, et al. 2001).

---

27. The formal dispute (DS 174 in table 3.2) involves a US objection to the breadth of GI protection for a Czech Republic beer. It has led to the cancellation of two trademarks of the Anheuser-Busch company in four European countries.

Any assessment of whether strengthening protection for GIs will improve the global food system must consider several issues. Property right holders will benefit if new rules reduce the transactions costs of globally marketing differentiated products. Consumers also may benefit if new rules lead to lower search costs and curbs on misleading claims. However, producers and consumers in some countries may be disadvantaged if repatriation of GIs results in the loss of generic identifiers that consumers have come to associate with a style rather than the origin of a product, such as Dijon mustard. Developing countries that do not produce wine and spirits must weigh whether the benefits of strengthened rules for GI for products of interest to them, such as tea and rice, are greater than increased enforcement costs for protection of domestic and foreign GIs in their home market. These issues are examined at greater length in chapter 6.

Enforcement of the Multilateral Disciplines

The quantitative impact of food regulations on trade and welfare is largely unknown, primarily because systematic information on the regulations themselves is lacking and methods of economic assessment are underdeveloped (Beghin and Bureau 2001, Maskus and Wilson 2001). However, the evidence suggests that disagreements over these measures have become more important over time. This raises the question of whether the mechanisms set up in the WTO have made it easier to solve trade conflicts over technical regulations. Two avenues can be identified within the WTO through which it has had an impact. First, the WTO has provided a forum, primarily through the SPS and TBT Committees, in which members can informally discuss technical barriers to trade and resolve questions or disputes over existing regulations or new measures that have been notified to the WTO. Second, in a small number of cases, formal disputes have been launched under the DSU.

SPS and TBT Notifications and Counter-notifications

The WTO's notification requirements are the cornerstone of the transparency provisions that are intended to facilitate decentralized policing by trading partners to ensure compliance with the substantive provisions of the SPS and TBT agreements. All of the major agricultural exporting and importing countries now routinely notify the WTO of proposed measures.

In fact, between 1995 and 2001 members submitted more than 2,400 SPS notifications to the WTO, far more than submitted under prior GATT obligations.[28] As might be expected given its wider scope, countries have submitted many more notifications under the TBT agreement than the SPS agreement. Between 1995 and 2001, the WTO recorded nearly 4,100 TBT notifications (WTO 2002e). Although agriculture's share of worldwide merchandise trade is about 10 percent (and it accounts for a much smaller share of the economies of developed countries that submitted the majority of TBT notifications), about 800, or 20 percent, of the TBT notifications referenced agricultural products (USDA 2002).

Each notification indicates, among other things, what the proposed measure is, the product or products to which it is applied, whether it is based on an international standard, and when it is expected to come into force. Although the notifications are essentially "regulator to regulator" communications, and more could be done to clarify how these measures might affect trade, the notification process has increased the transparency of national regulatory decisions. This increased transparency contributes to the smooth functioning of the world trading system by facilitating both compliance and complaints by trading partners. Compliance is aided when advance notice of new or modified measures gives firms an opportunity to change production methods to meet new import requirements, thereby minimizing the disruptions to trade flows of such changes. Notifications also give trading partners an opportunity to raise questions or objections to proposed measures in the relevant committee before they are adopted as regulations. In all cases, trading partners can continue to raise objections to measures viewed as violating WTO obligations.[29]

WTO members have taken advantage of this process, registering 187 complaints (or "counter-notifications") in the SPS Committee between 1995 and 2001 (see table 3.1).[30] In the SPS Committee, counter-notifications have been spread among goals related to animal, plant, and human health. A large number of complaints have concerned the regulation of transmissible spongiform encephalopathies (TSEs), which include bovine spongiform encephalopathy (BSE). TSE measures alone accounted

---

28. Between 1980 and 1990, countries notified the WTO of only 168 measures to prevent risks to public health and safety under the Standards Code, and fewer than half of those notifications concerned SPS regulations (GATT 1990–91).

29. Emergency measures are "notified" after the fact, but they are still subject to the scrutiny of trading partners while they remain in effect.

30. Other WTO committees have formally adopted the term *counter-notifications* to reference complaints or requests for further information. Although the SPS and TBT Committees have not done so, the term is used here to help distinguish the complaints raised in these committees from those that proceed to formal dispute settlement. The complaints are variously recorded under "information from members," "specific trade concerns," and "other business" in the minutes of the SPS Committee meetings (G/SPS/R series) and under "administration and implementation of the agreement" in the minutes of the TBT Committee (G/TBT/M series). These sources are drawn on throughout this analysis.

**Table 3.1   Number of complaints about regulations (counter-
notifications) brought before the WTO's SPS
Committee, 1995–2001**

| | Regulatory goal of contested measure | | | | | |
Complaints by	Plant health	Animal health	TSEs[a]	Human health	Other[b]	Total
Developed countries against						
Other developed countries	12	3	23	19	1	58
Developing countries	12	6	15	16	1	50
Multiple countries	0	1	0	0	0	1
Subtotal	24	10	38	35	2	109
Developing countries against						
Developed countries	11	12	10	20	1	54
Other developing countries	7	9	2	3	1	22
Multiple countries	0	2	0	0	0	2
Subtotal	18	23	12	23	2	78
Total	42	33	50	58	4	187

a. Transmissible spongiform encephalopathies, including BSE.
b. Includes complaints about administrative issues and horizontal regulations that reference human, animal, and plant health as objectives.

Source: Authors' tabulation from WTO (2002h).

for more than a fourth of the complaints raised in the SPS Committee since 1995, indicating that BSE has significantly disrupted international trade.[31] The BSE case, which has been an important test for the global health system, is examined in chapter 4.

Developed countries were most often the source as well as the target of counter-notifications that identified SPS regulations as unjustified trade impediments. Measures falling in the TSE and human health categories accounted for more than two-thirds of developed-country complaints. These measures also accounted for nearly three-fourths of the complaints raised against developed countries. The complaints against developed countries by other developed countries (42) outnumbered those by developing countries (30) in these categories, suggesting that access to the

---

31. The large number of trade disputes is related to the reluctance of countries to relax emergency import restrictions in the light of the human health consequences, the lack of established precedent for many of the health measures put into place, and the fact that cattle, the vector of BSE, provide so many food and industrial products, including meat and milk for human consumption, gelatin for pharmaceutical purposes, semen for breeding, and other by-products used in cosmetics and commercial animal feed, among other things.

same scientific information and technologies still leaves ample scope for disagreement over food safety measures among trading partners with similar per capita incomes.

Whether developing countries have been able to participate effectively in the activities of the various committees has been a concern of the WTO. The incidence of counter-notifications sheds some light on this important institutional question. Developing countries have accounted for just over 40 percent of the counter-notifications, or slightly less than their share of global food trade. A slight majority of the developing country counter-notifications targeted animal and plant health measures.

Contention over labeling in implementation of the TBT agreement has been reflected in labeling requirements being among the principal targets of counter-notifications raised in the TBT Committee. The committee recorded 117 complaints related to 38 labeling regulations in its meetings between 1995 and October 2002 (WTO 2002g). In 2000, during the last formal review of the operation and implementation of the TBT agreement, the committee reiterated that labeling regulations must be consistent with WTO rules in view of the number of disagreements over these measures (WTO 2000c). The large majority of the counter-notifications referenced labeling requirements for agricultural products (102), and the remainder were directed at regulations for industrial products (10) or both agricultural and industrial products (5).

The proposed labeling regimes have drawn objections for various reasons. One reason is that exporters believe compliance costs will be high, even if there are no anticipated impacts on demand. This objection most often applies to labeling that importers require for customs enforcement of other border policies such as tariffs and tariff rate quotas (TRQs).[32] Egypt's proposed regulation requiring the name of the country of origin to be woven into each end of a bolt of cloth falls into this category. Other objections to labeling regimes are related to the regimes' expected market effects. Objections to some proposals, such as the country-of-origin labeling requirements proposed by the United States and Japan for foodstuffs, reflect this concern. Other labeling regimes raise concerns because exporters fear both higher supply costs and significant effects on demand. In this category are the highly controversial notifications of mandatory labeling regimes for genetically modified products by Australia, Brazil, Chile, the European Union, and New Zealand, which collectively were the target of 15 TBT counter-notifications (see chapter 7).

Proposed regimes for labeling process attributes (npr-PPMs), whether mandatory or voluntary, also have been especially controversial. Examples

---

32. Under the Agreement on Agriculture, TRQs limit the quantity of agricultural imports eligible for a low tariff.

are the voluntary labeling scheme for dolphin-safe tuna proposed by the United States, the mandatory eco-labeling of timber proposed by the Netherlands, and the voluntary labeling of industrial and agricultural products using socially responsible production methods proposed by Belgium. Together, these regimes have accounted for 23 counter-notifications from both developed and developing countries.

WTO Dispute Settlement Cases

Between 1995 and 2002, WTO member countries made 32 formal requests for consultations related to food regulation trade barriers under the DSU. These complaints, which are summarized in table 3.2, account for 11 percent of the total formal DSU complaints for all products under all agreements over this time period.[33] Nineteen of these complaints reference animal or plant health measures, with the balance referencing food safety measures (six), labeling measures (four), environmental measures (two), and geographical indications (one). Formal complaints related to food regulations exhibit the same pattern observed for counter-notifications—developed countries are both the petitioner and respondent in the majority of cases, but not in every case. More recently, over the four years 1999 to 2002, developing countries initiated more complaints (six) than developed countries (five).

Seven complaints related to food system regulation reached a WTO panel ruling and the Appellate Body. Five of these complaints involved SPS measures, and all of them concerned regulations found to have no rationale in terms of risk reduction. In the first complaint (DS 18), Canada challenged Australia's ban on salmon imports imposed ostensibly to prevent the spread of disease in recreational and commercial fish stocks. In separate complaints (DS 26 and DS 48) heard by the same WTO panel, the United States and Canada challenged the scientific basis for the EU ban on growth hormones in beef production. In the fourth complaint (DS 76), the United States challenged Japan's testing requirements regarding treatment effectiveness for all new varieties of selected horticultural products. In the most recent SPS case to go to the Appellate Body (DS 245), the United States challenged Japan's strict phytosanitary regime for imported apples to prevent entry of diseases such as fire blight.

The measures at issue in these cases were imposed by developed countries. In each case, the panel and Appellate Body ruled for the complainants (exporters) on at least some grounds, so these disputed cases have shown

---

33. It also is notable that 70 percent of the complaints that have cited violations of the TBT agreement over this same period were related to food regulations. Only eight complaints referenced other sectors, including textiles, petrochemicals, and pharmaceuticals.

Table 3.2 WTO disputes over regulation of agricultural product safety and quality, 1995–2002

Dispute number	Petitioner(s)	Respondent	Issue	Agreement(s) referenced in dispute proceedings	Status (through September 2003)
1995					
DS 3	United States	Korea	Measures concerning testing and inspection of agricultural products	GATT, SPS, TBT, URAA	Consultations
DS 5	United States	Korea	Measures concerning shelf life requirements	GATT, SPS, TBT, URAA	Settled
DS 7	Canada	European Communities[a]	Trade description of scallops	GATT, TBT	Settled
DS 12	Peru	European Communities	Trade description of scallops	GATT, TBT	Settled
DS 14	Chile	European Communities	Trade description of scallops	GATT, TBT	Settled
DS 18	Canada	Australia	Measures affecting importation of salmon	GATT, SPS	Panel and Appellate Body ruled against Australia
DS 20	Canada	Korea	Measures concerning bottled water	GATT, SPS, TBT	Settled
DS 21	United States	Australia	Measures affecting importation of salmon	GATT, SPS	Settled
1996					
DS 26	United States	European Communities	Measures affecting meat and meat products (hormones)	GATT, SPS, TBT, URAA	Panel and Appellate Body ruled against EC

(table continues next page)

Table 3.2 *(Continued)*

Dispute number	Petitioner(s)	Respondent	Issue	Agreement(s) referenced in dispute proceedings	Status (through September 2003)
DS 41	United States	Korea	Measures concerning the testing and inspection of agricultural products	GATT, SPS, TBT, URAA	Consultations
DS 48	Canada	European Communities	Measures affecting meat and meat products (hormones)	GATT, SPS, TBT, URAA	Panel and Appellate Body ruled against EC
DS 58	India, Malaysia, Pakistan, Thailand	United States	Import prohibition on certain shrimp and shrimp products	GATT	Panel and Appellate Body ruled against the United States
DS 61	Philippines	United States	Import prohibition on certain shrimp and shrimp products	GATT, TBT	Consultations
DS 72	New Zealand	European Communities	Measures on butter products	GATT, TBT, import licensing	Settled
1997 DS 76	United States	Japan	Measures affecting agricultural products (varietal testing requirements)	GATT, SPS, URAA	Panel and Appellate Body ruled against Japan
DS 96	European Communities	India	Quantitative restrictions on imports of agricultural, textile, and industrial products	GATT, SPS, URAA	Settled

(table continues next page)

Dispute number	Petitioner(s)	Respondent	Issue	Agreement(s) referenced in dispute proceedings	Status (through September 2003)
DS 100	European Communities	United States	Poultry requirements	GATT, SPS, TBT	Consultations
1998					
DS 133	Switzerland	Slovakia	Dairy product imports and transit of cattle (BSE restrictions)	GATT, SPS, import licensing	Consultations
DS 134	India	European Communities	Restrictions on rice	GATT, customs valuation, import licensing, SPS, TBT, URAA	Consultations
DS 137	Canada	European Communities	Measures affecting imports of wood of conifers	GATT, SPS, TBT	Consultations
DS 144	Canada	United States	Certain measures affecting imports of cattle, swine, and grain	GATT, SPS, TBT, URAA	Consultations
1999					
DS 174	United States	European Communities	Protection of trademarks and geographical indications for agricultural products and foodstuffs	TRIPS	United States has requested a panel to hear its complaints
2000					
DS 203	United States	Mexico	Measures affecting trade in live swine	GATT, SPS, TBT, URAA	Consultations

(table continues next page)

Table 3.2 *(Continued)*

Dispute number	Petitioner(s)	Respondent	Issue	Agreement(s) referenced in dispute proceedings	Status (through September 2003)
DS 205	Thailand	Egypt	Import prohibition on canned tuna with genetically modified soy oil	GATT, SPS	Consultations
2001					
DS 210	United States	Belgium	Administration of measures establishing customs duties for rice	GATT, TBT, URAA, Customs Valuation Agreement	Settled
DS 231	Peru	European Communities	Trade description of sardines	GATT, TBT	Panel and Appellate Body ruled against EC
DS 237	Ecuador	Turkey	Certain import procedures for fresh fruit	GATT, GATS, SPS, import licensing procedures, URAA	Settled
2002					
DS 245	United States	Japan	Measures affecting importation of apples	GATT, SPS, URAA	Panel and Appellate Body ruled against Japan
DS 256	Hungary	Turkey	Import ban on pet food	GATT, SPS, URAA	Consultations
DS 263	Argentina	European Communities	Measures affecting imports of wine	GATT, TBT	Consultations

(table continues next page)

Table 3.2 WTO disputes over regulation of agricultural product safety and quality, 1995–2002 *(Continued)*

Dispute number	Petitioner(s)	Respondent	Issue	Agreement(s) referenced in dispute proceedings	Status (through September 2003)
DS 270	Philippines	Australia	Importation of fruits and vegetables	GATT, SPS, import licensing	Under review by panel
DS 271	Philippines	Australia	Certain measures affecting importation of fresh pineapple	GATT, SPS	Consultations

a. See chapter 3, footnote 3.

Source: WTO (2003a).

that the measures of countries with advanced scientific establishments are not immune to challenge.

The two other cases that reached WTO panels and the Appellate Body involved developing-country complainants and pertained to provisions of WTO law dealing with environmental measures (DS 58 filed against the United States by India, Malaysia, Pakistan, and Thailand) and with restrictive identity labeling (DS 231 filed against the European Union by Peru).

In addition to these seven complaints, 25 formal WTO complaints were filed against food-sector regulations during 1995–2002. Two of these complaints have proceeded to WTO panels though not to the Appellate Body as of December 2003: the Philippines complaint against Australian quarantine measures for fresh fruits and vegetables (DS 270) and the US complaint against the EU regime for protection of GIs (DS 174).[34] Ten complaints were settled prior to a panel hearing or the release of a panel report. Thirteen cases related to the regulation of food are technically still pending, although WTO reports indicate that trade has resumed in some instances (WTO 2002h, 2002f). One of these cases involved Egypt's restrictions on Thai tuna packed in soybean oil, which is the first case related to genetically modified food to come before the WTO.

---

34. The US request for a panel to hear its complaint against the EU GI measures was submitted to the WTO in August 2003. The complaint against Australia's quarantine measures is still under review by a WTO panel.

Rulings about SPS Measures

The formal dispute rulings reveal how different articles of the SPS agreement can be used to evaluate the legitimacy of a measure. The outcome of these cases is summarized in table 3.3.

The bellwether test of the disciplines of the SPS agreement was the challenge by the United States and Canada of the scientific basis for the European Union's ban on growth hormones in beef production, discussed further in chapter 5. The European Union's defense of its measure rested on its claims that the international standards for these hormones did not meet its public health goals and that the ban represented a precautionary approach to managing uncertain risks. The WTO panel concluded, and the Appellate Body upheld the decision, that the European Union's ban violated the provisions of the SPS agreement (McNiel 1998, Roberts 1998). Both the panel and the Appellate Body affirmed the right of WTO members to establish a level of consumer protection higher than the level set by international health standards. The ban was nonetheless judged to be in violation of the SPS agreement, because, in violation of Articles 3.3 and 5.1, it was not backed by an objective risk assessment. The panel and judges also rejected the European Union's use of the precautionary principle in its legal defense, because no explicit reference to this principle appears in the SPS agreement. Article 5.7 of the agreement recognizes a conditional precautionary principle, which allows countries to provisionally adopt measures "on the basis of available pertinent information" while seeking additional information "necessary for a more objective assessment of risk." However, the European Union could not defend its permanent ban by reference to this provision.

The panel also ruled that the EU ban violated Article 5.5, which requires countries to avoid variation in the levels of health protection provided by its SPS measures, if such variation results in discrimination or creates a disguised restriction on trade. The Appellate Body overturned this panel finding. The judges concurred with the panel that EU policies on the use of growth-promoting substances in animals were "arbitrary and unjustifiable" because the European Union allowed their use in pork. However, they disagreed that the ban was "a disguised restriction on trade," perhaps in deference to the fact that the ban arose from public anxieties that emerged in the late 1970s and early 1980s after widely publicized reports of illegal veterinary drug use in Italy and France. Although the Appellate Body was willing to acknowledge that the ban was originally motivated by "consumer concerns" rather than protectionism, the overall outcome of the case suggests that the WTO will rule against measures based on popular misconceptions of risks as well as more overtly discriminatory measures.

In the salmon case, the Appellate Body concurred with Canada that Australia's 1975 ban on imports of fresh, chilled, or frozen (eviscerated)

Table 3.3 Decisions in the four SPS cases heard by WTO panels and the Appellate Body

SPS provision violated	European Communities:[a] Hormones—As judged by		Australia: Salmon—As judged by		Japan: Varietal testing—As judged by		Japan: Apples—As judged by	
	Panel	Appellate body	Panel[b]	Appellate body	Panel	Appellate body	Panel	Appellate body
Article 2.2. Measures must be based on scientific principles and must not be maintained without sufficient scientific evidence.			X	X	X	X	X	X
Article 2.3. Members must ensure that SPS measures do not arbitrarily or unjustifiably discriminate between members where identical or similar conditions prevail.			X	X				
Article 3.1. Members shall base their SPS measures on international standards, where they exist, except as otherwise provided for in Article 3.3.	X							
Article 3.3. Members may adopt SPS measures which result in a higher level of SPS protection than would be achieved by measures based on the relevant international standards, if in accordance with the requirements under Article 5.	X	X						

Article 5.1. Measures must be based on a risk assessment.	X	X	X		X	X	X
Article 5.5. Members shall avoid distinctions in levels of SPS protection if such distinctions result in discrimination or a disguised restriction on trade.	X		X				
Article 5.6. Measures must be not more trade-restrictive than required.				X		X	
Article 5.7. Members can adopt measures on a provisional basis when scientific evidence is insufficient, but must seek additional information to conduct a risk assessment.	X		X	X	X		X
Article 7 and Annex B. Measures must be transparent.					X		X

a. See chapter 3, footnote 3.

b. The original panel, at the request of Canada, reviewed the revised measures adopted by Australia after the Appellate Body's ruling. The panel judged that the revised measures were not in compliance with Australia's obligations under Articles 2.2, 5.1, and 5.6 of the SPS agreement. It also ruled that Tasmania's continuing ban on Canadian salmon imports was in violation of Articles 2.2 and 5.1. Australia has since revised its measures to Canada's satisfaction; the Tasmanian ban is still in place.

salmon from the Northern Hemisphere was inconsistent with the legal obligations set forth in the SPS agreement. The Appellate Body ruled that the report used by Australia to inform its policy decision did not constitute a risk assessment because it did not evaluate the likelihood of entry, establishment, and spread of diseases, nor did it evaluate the potential consequences of these diseases. The Appellate Body agreed with the panel finding that the report contained "general and vague statements of mere possibility of adverse effects occurring; statements which constitute neither a quantitative nor a qualitative assessment of probability." The Appellate Body also concurred with Canada that the ban provided a level of environmental protection that was arbitrarily higher than that provided by other Australian SPS measures, because Australia allows imports of other fish that are potential vectors for the same, or even more virulent, diseases.

The third SPS case to reach the Appellate Body was the varietal testing dispute. At issue were Japanese requirements to test whether methyl bromide treatments effectively exterminate codling moths on each new variety of fruit and walnuts imported into that country. The United States argued that such requirements restricted US exports (the cost of the required trials discouraged exporters from marketing new hybrids in Japan) and were unscientific because Japan could produce no evidence to support the claim that variety is a causal factor of variation in extermination efficacy. The panel and Appellate Body ruled that Japan's phytosanitary measures were not based on a risk assessment or on sufficient scientific evidence, because evidence presented during the proceedings indicated that testing each product, rather than each variety of each product, was sufficient. Japan's argument that the measure was provisional was not accepted since it had been in place for 48 years. Even if the measure had been accepted as provisional, the Japanese requirement for data from an exporter did not fulfill the obligation under Article 5.7 to seek additional information to complete a risk assessment. Finally, the panel and the Appellate Body found that, in violation of Article 7, the measure was not transparent, because it failed to meet the conditions for publication set out in an annex of the SPS agreement.

In the most recent SPS case to reach the Appellate Body, the United States brought its complaint against Japanese requirements for imported apples (including chlorine dip, cold treatment, and orchard inspections by Japanese phytosanitary authorities) to the WTO for resolution. A WTO panel concurred with the United States that these measures violated the SPS agreement, primarily because there was no scientific basis for the requirements. The WTO Appellate Body upheld the panel's findings in November 2003. Most other countries accept the US phytosanitary regime (which includes good commercial production practices, grading and sorting, and visual inspection for pests) as adequate for mitigating the risk of diseases and pests affecting apples, such as fire blight and coddling moth.

The effectiveness of the DSU rulings, as measured by the changes made to importers' policies after a successful challenge, has been mixed. To date, the salmon and varietal testing cases have successfully concluded with changes in the importing country's measures. Japan and the United States are still negotiating a mutually acceptable settlement in the apples case. In the hormones case, the European Union did not fulfill its obligation to bring its measure into compliance with the SPS agreement by a May 1999 deadline, stating that it needed more time to complete risk assessments. The WTO consequently authorized the United States and Canada to increase tariffs on US$128.1 million of EU exports until the European Union complied with the ruling or provided compensation for the ban by lowering other trade barriers. The parties continue to discuss options, such as increased market access for hormone-free beef and labeling, but the case has not yet been settled. Both the ban and the retaliatory tariffs remain in place.

The rulings in these four SPS disputes provide important case law. The four formal WTO rulings on SPS regulations set precedents on the requirement for risk assessment, consistent risk management, the limits on adoption of measures on a provisional basis, and transparency. The outcome of the hormones dispute also raises questions about the capacity of the WTO to resolve disputes about food regulations when intense national political sensitivities are involved.

Rulings about TBT and GATT Articles

The remaining two formal disputes related to food regulations pertain to other provisions of WTO law. The first WTO panel report to examine the compliance of a food regulation (or indeed any regulation) with the TBT agreement involved Peru's complaint against the European Union's regulation of the labeling of sardines (DS 231), which is discussed in detail in chapter 6. The panel found that the EU regulation, which restricted use of the term *sardines* to one species found off the coasts of Europe and Morocco, was in violation of Article 2.4 of the TBT agreement, which requires countries to use international standards except when "ineffective or inappropriate" to "the fulfilment of the legitimate objectives pursued." The panel found that a Codex labeling standard for sardines was both effective and appropriate for meeting the European Union's three stated objectives of market transparency, consumer protection, and fair competition. This case provides some guidance about the status of international standards under the TBT agreement.

The other case, the shrimp/turtle dispute, could have significant implications for food regulations that affect trade, though somewhat less direct. It involved an environmental measure related to food trade. In 1996 India, Malaysia, Pakistan, and Thailand brought a case (DS 58) against US restrictions (Section 609 of Public Law 101-162) on shrimp caught without turtle excluder devices (TEDs) designed to reduce accidental deaths of sea turtles in shrimp trawler nets. The WTO panel and Appellate Body agreed that the objective of the US law was legitimate under Article XX(g) of the GATT, which allows trade restrictions to protect exhaustible natural resources, but faulted the implementation of the policy, which had resulted in arbitrary and unjustifiable discrimination against the complainants in violation of Article XX's preamble. Two years later, on the grounds that the United States had not appropriately implemented the recommendations of the WTO, Malaysia requested that the matter be referred once again to the original panel, as provided for by the DSU. In particular, Malaysia objected to the fact that the United States had chosen to bring its policies into compliance by providing foreign suppliers with TED technology rather than by lifting its import prohibition on shrimp from countries that had not adopted the same conservation policy. The panel and the Appellate Body agreed, however, that US implementation of the rulings and recommendations in the initial case was justified under Article XX(g) of the GATT, noting the ongoing and serious "good faith" efforts of the United States to reach a multilateral agreement with the complainants.

The shrimp/turtle case is one of those in GATT/WTO jurisprudence that calls into question the "product-process doctrine" that was first applied in the 1991 Tuna-Dolphin decision.[35] The effect of this legal doctrine was to make it prima facie GATT illegal for governments to adopt trade-restrictive taxes or regulations based on how the product was produced, unless the production method (such as unsanitary food processing) materially affected the product. Thus regulations prohibiting the sale of imported goods based on how they were produced—even if the same regulations applied to domestic products—would violate GATT Articles III or XI, unless justified under one of the public policy exceptions of GATT Article XX.

The legal reasoning of the shrimp/turtle decision suggests that Article XX exceptions can be available to permit governments to regulate products on the basis of the process by which they were produced. However, it is unclear whether the scope of the Article XX exception validated by the shrimp/turtle decision will extend beyond environmental measures, or even how much precedent this case set. Consequently, some legal scholars have concluded that the product-process doctrine remains a potential "lethal threat" to regulations with a process attribute focus (Hudec 2001).

---

35. In this dispute, the panel ruled that a US import ban on tuna harvested in ways harmful to dolphins violated either GATT Article III.4 (which requires that the imported product "be accorded treatment no less favorable than that accorded to like products of national origin") or Article XI (which prohibits quantitative restrictions on imports), depending on the characterization of the law. The panel went on to rule that neither of these two GATT violations was excused under GATT Article XX, and thus that the tuna embargo was prohibited by GATT law.

The Doha Development Agenda Negotiations

Despite the intention of the Uruguay Round to provide a durable multi-lateral framework to discipline the use of food safety and quality regulations, proposals submitted by countries both leading up to and after the Doha Ministerial Conference in November 2001 indicate that a remarkable divergence of views has emerged about this framework. Developing-country proposals signal frustration with the increasingly exigent standards faced by their exports, the new obligations to justify their own regulatory regimes, or both. They worry that without more progress on meeting these challenges, their participation in international trade will be further marginalized. The proposals of some developed countries, however, would likely increase the challenges faced by developing countries. These developed countries argue that the adequacy of current WTO rules has been called into question by new production technologies, new disease outbreaks, and new demands for regulations that are responsive to consumer concerns. They call for modification of WTO rules to give governments more latitude in regulating risks and product differentiation. This approach is advanced as an enlightened strategy for the entry of agriculture into the "century of quality, not quantity."

WTO members agreed at the Doha Ministerial Conference to take concrete steps to improve implementation of the current agreements in order to address some of the issues and concerns of developing countries (WTO 2001e).[36] These steps include initiatives under both the SPS and TBT agreements that came into effect at the Doha Ministerial Conference. Specifically, greater technical and financial assistance is to be provided to developing countries to help them to fulfill their own obligations under these agreements, to increase their participation in the international standards organizations, and to enable them to comply with new SPS and TBT measures in export markets.[37] In addition, countries are committed to developing a program to advance implementation of the equivalence obligation under the SPS agreement. WTO members also will give developing countries more time to comply with their measures—a form of WTO special and differential treatment—as long as staggered implementation allows the importing country to realize its appropriate level of protection.[38]

---

36. In May 2000 the WTO initiated "implementation negotiations" to address the needs of developing countries after the Seattle Ministerial Conference failed to launch a new round of trade negotiations (WTO 2001e).

37. In September 2002 the World Bank (WB) and the WTO launched an initiative to link aid to trade opportunities to help in the fight against poverty. The joint WB/WTO initiative included a fund called the Standards and Trade Development Facility.

38. Other issues on which no agreement could be reached were referred back to subsidiary WTO bodies (e.g., the SPS and TBT Committees), which will discuss them further and report back to the committee overseeing all trade negotiations in this round.

Beyond these specific initiatives, the Doha Declaration commits WTO members to further negotiations on some issues related to food regulation through several different venues. Most important, the declaration confirms that nontrade concerns will be part of the negotiations on agriculture, in addition to the three Uruguay Round pillars of market access restrictions, export subsidies, and domestic support measures resulting from national farm policies. In the Uruguay Round, countries identified food security and rural development as nontrade concerns that required specific exemptions from the rules set out in the Agreement on Agriculture. In the Doha Round, some developed countries have identified food safety, food labeling, and animal welfare as additional nontrade concerns meriting special treatment. They have proposed modification of rules set out in the agriculture agreement and in other agreements as they apply to agricultural products. Specifically, these countries advocate subsidies for meeting animal welfare standards and increased protection for geographical indications for products other than wines and spirits, explicit recognition of the legitimacy of the precautionary principle, and mandatory labeling of npr-PPMs. Some developing countries have supported these proposals, but most see them as running counter to their interests in the agriculture negotiations by increasing the difficulty of gaining access to developed-country markets and diverting attention from the core agenda of lowering other barriers to trade.

The Doha Declaration also calls for negotiations on trade and the environment that may have implications for the governance of food regulation. The trade and environment negotiation group will address how WTO rules are to apply to WTO members that also are parties to environmental agreements. These negotiations are widely perceived to be a means of clarifying the WTO status of trade measures that might be taken under any of the multilateral environmental agreements, but in particular the Biosafety Protocol of 2000 (also called the Cartagena Protocol), which authorizes use of the precautionary principle in risk management.[39] The Doha Declaration also asks the WTO's Trade and Environment Committee to continue its work on environmental labeling.

In short, although no country has formally proposed reopening the SPS or TBT agreement during the Doha Round of trade negotiations, the WTO is immersed in issues that will further define the global food regulatory governance regime. In view of the many uncertainties about these negotiations, the next chapter turns to more detailed examination of the global regulation of agricultural and food products.

---

39. The Doha Declaration is careful to note that the negotiations shall not prejudice the WTO rights of any member that is not a party to the MEA in question, and that the outcome shall not add to, diminish, or alter the balance of rights and obligations of members under existing WTO agreements, in particular the SPS agreement. The Biosafety Protocol is discussed in chapter 7.

4

Control of Animal and Plant Pests and Diseases

The success of modern agriculture is in large part a story of accomplishments in the long endeavor of humans to control nature, including through efforts to protect the health and vitality of domesticated animals and plants. This is not a struggle that can be won in any permanent sense. Ever-evolving hosts of invasive species and infectious organisms afflict domestic animals and cultivated plants, as well as wildlife and natural fauna. Some of these pests and diseases affect only a particular species; others pose multiple threats. Identification, management, containment, and, in some cases, elimination of these hazards remain global challenges.

Migration of pests and transmission of diseases of animals and plants across international borders occur through natural events, including geographic movements of the pests, roaming of animal populations, and conveyance by migratory birds. Other transmissions occur with the movements of people and commercial products. Each of these threats requires countervailing actions, but it is trade in animal products and crops that leads to most international regulatory measures.

This chapter examines SPS regulations related to animal and plant pests and diseases and their impacts on the trade system. The first section of this chapter gives a brief overview of the prevalence of animal and plant pests and diseases and of the international systems for reporting outbreaks and eradication efforts. The second section assesses the extent to which the presence of animal and plant pests and diseases in some places, but not in others, has caused international trade conflicts. The three examples of regulatory challenges described in the third section illustrate in greater depth both the potential for regulatory innovations consistent with an open global food system and the ongoing challenges of management and control of transmissible agricultural pest and disease hazards.

Animal and Plant Pests and Diseases and Their Control

The multilateral framework of disciplines on regulations in the areas of animal and plant pests and diseases requires a risk assessment approach. It allows countries to defer to harmonized international standards set by L'Office International des Epizooties (OIE) and the International Plant Protection Convention (IPPC) should they choose to do so. If countries decide to exceed those guidelines with higher domestic standards, their decisions must be based on a scientific risk assessment, as discussed in chapter 3.

The OIE has developed standards for regulation of the principal livestock and poultry diseases. Its International Animal Health Code includes sections on import risk analysis, certification, import/export procedures, diagnostic tests, transport, and accredited testing institutions. Transmissible animal diseases are classified. List A comprises the 15 most harmful diseases that have "the potential for very serious and rapid spread, irrespective of national borders, and which are of serious socio-economic or public health consequence." List B is composed of nearly 70 additional diseases of cattle, sheep and goats, swine, poultry, and multiple species that are "considered to be of socio-economic and/or public health importance within countries." Outbreaks of the List A diseases must be reported to the OIE by its member nations. International coordination of the response to these outbreaks is designed to inhibit the spread of infections across borders and to encourage energetic eradication measures. A ban on exports of products that are potential risk vectors from a country or region afflicted with a List A disease by a country that is free of that disease is widely accepted as a justifiable mitigation measure. Similar measures can be applied to List B diseases, depending on the circumstances.

The reports to the OIE of disease outbreaks often have a geographic pattern. For example, OIE reports for four List A diseases show that more than 13,000 outbreaks of foot-and-mouth disease (FMD) were reported in 2001 (OIE 2003c). These outbreaks occurred primarily in Asia, South America, and Europe, with a few scattered cases in Africa. Outbreaks within each region were often located in one or two countries. For example, outbreaks in India and Nepal accounted for almost 80 percent of the total Asian number. Similarly, Argentina and Uruguay in South America and the United Kingdom in Europe reported outbreaks that accounted for over 90 percent of regional totals. Outbreaks of a disease of sheep and goats (*peste des petits*) were concentrated in Asia, mostly in Nepal, India, Iran, and Oman. Classic swine fever was reported primarily in Europe, Asia, and the Caribbean, with a few outbreaks in South, Central, and North America. Over 2,400 outbreaks of Newcastle disease of poultry were reported. Newcastle disease was most common in Asia and Africa, again with some reported outbreaks in South and North America. Mexico was the only North American country that reported any of the four diseases (classic swine fever and Newcastle) in 2001. None of the outbreaks of these four diseases during the year occurred in Oceania. This geographic concentration of animal diseases among continents, within continents, and within countries plays an important role in disease control. Geographical boundaries have become proxies for incidence and infestation in some cases, while in others it becomes possible to relax certain restrictions from areas that are disease free.

The IPPC and nine regional affiliates Regional Plant Protection Conventions (RPPCs) provide the international coordination for control of plant pests and diseases. The IPPC maintains information on quarantine pests through an FAO global plant pest and information system. This database is more extensive than that of the OIE, given the greater number and types of hosts and pests for commercial plant species than for animals, the adaptability of many pests to multiple hosts, and their ability to naturalize and affect different ecological and agricultural systems. The IPPC database provides information on 9,000 host plants and 11,000 plant pests. Categories of plant pests include, but are not limited to, viruses, fungi, bacteria, nematodes, insects, weeds, phytoplasma, and parasites. Regional affiliates of the IPPC and individual countries maintain even more detailed site-specific databases of quarantine pests.[1]

The objective of the IPPC is to protect countries from importing plant pests and to facilitate trade through dissemination of information and effective control technologies. The quality of protective measures depends on the capacity and willingness of the regulatory agencies of member countries to detect and identify pest species on imported or exported plant products. Plant protection is a specialized field in which experts tend to focus on a particular plant or group of plants and the relevant pest species. Effective risk analysis requires knowledge of pest life cycles, modes of attack on the plant host, method of dispersal, mobility of the pest at different life stages, alternate hosts, disease symptoms, and damage potential. Dormancy and pesticide resistance increase the complexity of implementing control or eradication programs for plant pests. Evaluation and monitoring systems require sophisticated equipment to detect the

---

1. The most advanced regional identification system is maintained by the European Plant Protection Organization (EPPO). Its A1 list comprises pests that may be a threat to the EPPO countries but are not yet present in the region. The A2 list is made up of pests that are present in the EPPO region but are not widely distributed and are being officially controlled. On the A1 list are about 175 pests for which the EPPO recommends quarantine. On the A2 list are about 90 pests for which EPPO recommends that quarantine measures be evaluated on a country- and case-specific basis.

presence of pests at the microscopic level. Thus, although knowledge of pest risks is essential to the success of plant protection measures, and the IPPC provides a forum in which countries can share technical information, effective controls depend on regulatory decision making and the availability of resources to implement regulations within countries.

Trade Issues Related to Agricultural Pests and Diseases

Differences in the incidences of pests and diseases and in regulatory capacities among countries constitute a broad justification for border measures that reduce sanitary and phytosanitary transmission risks. In some situations, the need for such measures, or the credibility of the specific regulatory instrument utilized, is open to question. But it is not easy to determine how often SPS regulations that restrict imports unnecessarily distort trade. Although the WTO SPS Committee provides one forum for doing so, there is no single, comprehensive database on disputed measures. Nonetheless, investigators have accumulated substantial evidence in recent years about the questionable trade barriers that have been justified by assertions of risks from animal and plant pests or diseases.

Completion of the WTO agreements in 1995 provided the impetus for one US survey to investigate these issues. After collecting and analyzing extensive data, investigators identified which foreign technical regulations faced by US agricultural exports in mid-1996 were potentially subject to challenge under the new SPS or TBT disciplines.[2] The criteria used in determining which regulations were potentially subject to challenge were lack of scientific justification for a measure, reliance on excessively trade-restrictive means of mitigating acknowledged risks, application of regulations in an apparently discriminatory manner, and other substantive and procedural issues related to the disciplines of the WTO agreements. The set of technical barriers identified included policy instruments of differing degrees of trade restrictiveness—among them import bans, mandatory product and process standards, and informational remedies such as labeling requirements.

The survey identified 185 technical barriers addressing animal and plant

---

2. Roberts and DeRemer (1997) describe the survey design, pretesting, and implementation, and report some descriptive survey results; also see Thornsbury (1998) and Thornsbury et al. (1999). Technical barriers applied to imports by the United States were not within the purview of the survey, nor were technical barriers applied to non-US products by other countries. Still, the survey provides one of the most complete assessments of the technical barriers faced by agricultural exports of one country on a cross-sectional basis at a fixed moment in time. Since 1996, regulatory and trade agencies of numerous countries have initiated annual reports of SPS disputes that have arisen or been resolved. Web pages such as www.agriculturelaw.com provide another dynamic glimpse, though not a systematic accounting, of emerging disputes and their outcomes through news clippings accumulated daily.

health risks to commercial production as of questionable merit. These barriers were imposed by 61 countries and two regional trading blocs, and were estimated to limit US exports by $2.1 billion.[3] Only 31 of the measures were directed at protecting animal health, demonstrating that the United States has benefited from being recognized as free of many quarantine diseases. Most of the questionable barriers were directed at phytosanitary objectives. Out of 154 phytosanitary measures, 60 were partial or total product bans. Another 50 were based on process standards. Over half of the estimated trade effect of questionable animal and plant measures ($1.2 billion) arose from the process standard regulations. Often, these were requirements for treatments of exports against potential pests that were viewed as unnecessarily restrictive given domestic and foreign growing conditions.

At the multilateral level, the counter-notifications summarized in table 3.1 (along with the few disputes that have gone to formal settlement procedures) are further evidence of contentious regulatory measures. This record is widely informative about trade disputes over SPS regulations among countries, but it is incomplete because various disputed cases are resolved through other avenues. Even for those cases raised in the SPS Committee, the final outcome between the disputing parties will be recorded only if they choose to report that outcome at a committee meeting. The WTO Secretariat has urged countries to do so, but with only limited success.

The 42 counter-notifications related to plant health shown in table 3.1 span a diverse range of commodities and pest or disease hazards. Most of these disputes center on the regulatory measures of a single country (or the European Union) affecting imports of a specific commodity from one or a few specific exporters (WTO 2002f). Complaints that measures are not based on a risk assessment or impose excessive or unnecessary risk-avoidance procedures are common, along with complaints that countries are not acting in accordance with IPPC standards or recommendations. In several instances, countries objected that the regulations to which they were subject were not equivalent to the requirements faced by other exporters representing a similar or greater risk. And several complaints asserted that measures enacted by national judicial or subnational legislative bodies were inconsistent with the SPS agreement. Only

---

3. An additional 117 measures identified addressed other concerns, primarily the food safety and quality issues discussed in chapters 5 and 6. The total estimated impact of the 302 questionable barriers on trade was nearly $5 billion. Of this total trade worth, almost $3.7 billion, equivalent to more than 5 percent of the total value of US agricultural exports in 1996, stemmed from either prohibited entry (by 107 barriers blocking an estimated $700 million in trade) or less stringent measures that limited market expansion but did not completely block access (164 barriers constraining trade valued at an estimated $3 billion). An additional $1.2 billion in existing trade faced proposed new restrictions that were being considered by a foreign government.

a few complaints suggested that measures were imposed for commercial reasons, in flagrant violation of the requirement that they be related to SPS concerns.

Among the 33 counter-notifications related to a variety of animal health regulations, most concerned the imposition of measures by an importer that were deemed excessive by the exporting country given the level of risk present. Complainants pointed out often that measures did not conform with the standards and guidelines of the OIE. In particular, when new disease threats emerge, the WTO can play a substantial role in acting as a venue for discussions of measures and of modifications sought in domestic regulations, as discussed in chapter 3 in relation to the 50 counter-notifications related to transmissible spongiform encephalopathies (TSEs) and as described in more detail in this chapter.

Animal and Plant Regulations in Practice

In addressing international transmission of sanitary and phytosanitary risks, regulators face diverse challenges from known and newly emerging sources. This section illustrates risk assessment and management issues in three cases: the negotiations that have resulted in partial access for Mexican avocados into the United States, a case viewed as a bellwether of dispute resolution among North American Free Trade Agreement (NAFTA) countries; the continual problems posed by endemic infestations and sporadic outbreaks of FMD; and regulatory management of BSE as a serious new cattle disease in the United Kingdom in the 1980s and as a dangerous zoonosis once it was linked in 1996 to the fatal human variant Creutzfeldt-Jakob disease (vCJD).

Partial Easing of US Avocado Import Restrictions

One approach to easing technical trade restrictions is to shift from import bans to less restrictive instruments of pest control. The key to the less restrictive alternative is often a systems approach to risk management, whereby a set of process standards are specified that reduce the externality risk associated with trade of a commodity. Adoption of systems approaches is firmly anchored in Article 5.6 of the WTO SPS agreement, which requires members to ensure that their measures "are not more trade-restrictive than required to achieve their appropriate level of sanitary or phytosanitary protection."

In 1997 and 2001 a ban against importing Mexican avocados into the United States was partially lifted. This case is an example of application of a systems approach to a situation that had become mired in political and scientific controversy. The circumstances and solution shed light on both the economics and politics of pest infestation disputes, and demonstrate that a restrictive SPS measure can be at least partially relaxed through appropriate process standards when there is mutual commitment to negotiations.

The ban on imports of Mexican "Hass" avocados was initiated in 1914 when there were no known controls (chemical or natural predators) for certain host-specific avocado pests prevalent in Mexico but not present in the United States. After pesticides and cultural practices were developed, the Mexican state of Michoacán began to establish an industry centered on approved, export-oriented avocado orchards. Mexican quarantine authorities then argued that the Michoacán avocado export protocols provided adequate protection against pest risks of concern to the United States. Mexico contended that the US ban could not be justified on a risk basis but was maintained to protect the incomes of US avocado producers. The US avocado industry, concentrated in southern California and represented by the California Avocado Commission, bitterly opposed opening the US domestic market to Mexican avocados. The commission acknowledged that it received domestic prices above those of Mexican exports, but asserted that it feared pest infestations associated with trade, not competition, in the marketplace.

Regulators at the US Department of Agriculture (USDA) were caught in the middle of this controversy. Twice during the 1970s, the USDA took the preliminary steps needed to ease the avocado import ban, but both times the decision was not carried through.[4]

The issue then lay unresolved until NAFTA negotiations gave Mexico an opportunity to raise its concerns again. After four years of procedural negotiations, data collection, and joint analysis, the USDA proposed a rule in July 1995 to allow imports of Mexican avocados grown and processed under conditions specified by a systems approach to pest risk management.

The proposed systems approach included preharvest, harvest, packing, transport, and shipping measures designed to reduce pest risks. The USDA limited distribution of imports to the northeastern United States, in order to avoid geographic proximity with regions susceptible to pests, and to four winter months when the risk of establishment of pests was mitigated by adverse weather. The USDA asserted that its proposed approach would provide domestic growers with adequate sanitary protection. With the proposed systems approach in place, the USDA estimated the probability of a seed pest or fruit fly outbreak would be less than once every 1 million years, and a stem weevil outbreak might occur on average once every 11,402 years. A recent USDA assessment of percentages of pest risk reduction produced by specific measures under its systems approach is shown in table 4.1.

---

4. See Roberts and Orden (1996) for a detailed analytic chronology of the avocado dispute.

Table 4.1   Risk reduction under a systems approach to Mexican avocado imports (percent)

		Pests of quarantine concern				
Risk mitigation measure	Fruit flies (*Anastrepha* spp.)	Small avocado seed weevils (*Conotrachelis aguacatae*)	Avocado stem weevil (*Copturus aguacatae*)	Large avocado seed weevil (*Heilipus lauri*)	Avocado seed moth (*Stenoma catenifer*)	Hitch-hikers and other pests
Field surveys	40-60	95-99	80-95	95-99	95-99	40-75
Trapping and field treatments	55-75	0	0	0	0	3-20
Field sanitation	75-95	15-35	70-90	15-35	15-35	20-40
Host resistance	95-99	0	0	0	0	0
Postharvest safeguards	60-90	0	0	0	0	40-60
Packing house inspection and fruit cutting	25-40	50-75	40-60	50-75	50-75	30-50
Port-of-arrival inspection	50-70	50-70	50-70	50-75	50-75	60-80
Winter shipping only	60-90	0	0	0	0	50-75
Limited US distribution	95-99	95-99	90-99	95-99	95-99	75-95

Source: USDA (2001b).

Because of the geographic and seasonal restrictions in USDA's 1995 proposed avocado import rule, partial easing of the ban opened less than 5 percent of the US market to Mexico. Even this partial access was opposed by the California Avocado Commission, which had closely monitored the deliberations from the outset of the NAFTA negotiations. The commission recommended that Mexico be allowed to export avocados only under stringent conditions that would effectively have precluded trade for the foreseeable future.[5]

---

5. The commission proposed the following conditions: (1) Mexico would establish pest-free zones; or (2) the imported avocados would be treated with a pesticide that would ensure, with a very high degree of probability, that exotic pests were eliminated; or (3) additional scientific research would unequivocally establish that Hass avocados were not

In a benefit-cost analysis that took uncertainty about pest infestation into account, David Orden and Eduardo Romano (1996) divided the US avocado market into the two submarkets proposed by the USDA—the northeastern winter market and the national aggregate for all other regions and seasons. In the northeastern winter market, the domestic price was assumed to fall to the price level of exports from Mexico when trade was allowed. For the rest of the United States, an equilibrium price was determined by domestic supply and aggregated demand.[6]

If no pest infestation occurred, the winter season price in the northeastern region fell by 35 percent and consumption increased with the proposed partial easing of the avocado import ban. The domestic price for the remaining aggregated US market fell by 1.3 percent, because domestic avocados displaced from the northeastern winter market were absorbed through expanded consumption elsewhere and through slightly reduced domestic production. Orden and Romano estimated that domestic avocado growers would lose nearly $2.4 million, but avocado consumers would benefit, resulting in a net national welfare gain of $2.5 million, mostly due to the lower price in the Northeast. By contrast, full liberalization of trade (which was not considered by the USDA in 1995) was estimated to depress domestic avocado production by as much as 50 percent after full adjustment to lower prices and to raise consumer surplus by nearly $90 million nationwide.

Orden and Romano also looked at the economic effects of the proposed avocado rule if trade produced a pest infestation in the United States, causing higher domestic production costs and lower yields. In the worst-case scenario, partial easing of the import ban reduced availability of avocados outside the northeastern winter market because of lower domestic output and pushed up the equilibrium domestic price by 30 percent to the disadvantage of consumers. The domestic price increase partly offset the effects on producers of higher costs and damage to yields, but their net loss was $14.7 million, almost seven times as large as from partial easing of the ban when no pest infestation occurred. Partial easing of the avocado quarantine would not be sound phytosanitary or economic policy under these circumstances, but a much higher probability

---

hosts of pests injurious to avocados and other fruits and vegetables grown in the United States. The first condition, establishing and maintaining a pest-free zone, required substantial eradication, monitoring, and quarantine enforcement costs well beyond the perimeters of commercial export groves in Mexico. Although it might eventually prove feasible technically, such an approach was regarded as uneconomical by Mexican officials, who believed that pest risks were already negligible. On the second condition, all parties agreed that no adequate postharvest treatment was available. On the third condition, results of fruit fly host status research had indicated that fruit flies will attack Hass avocados shortly after they have been harvested, so this condition also could not be met.

6. See Orden and Romano (1996); Romano (1998); and Orden, Narrod, and Glauber (2001) for more detailed descriptions of the analysis.

of pest infestation than was estimated by the USDA was required to produce an expectation of negative net welfare effects. For full trade liberalization, even under the worst-case pest infestation, there was a positive benefit-cost outcome, because consumer gains throughout the country from lower prices of imports more than offset the domestic producer losses.

With minimal pest risks estimated by the USDA, it issued in February 1997 a final rule for limited importation of avocados from Mexico under the systems approach (USDA 1997a), despite ongoing and strenuous opposition by the California Avocado Commission.[7]

Since 1997, no pest infestations traceable to avocado imports have been detected, and the wholesale prices of avocados imported from Mexico have averaged about 25 percent less than those for domestic avocados. Shipments of California avocados to the northeastern winter market have largely been displaced by imports from Mexico: California shipments fell from an annual average of 7.7 million pounds during 1986–94 to just 1.0 million pounds during 1999–2000. Imports from Mexico have averaged over 23 million pounds over the 1998–99 through 2001–02 shipping seasons, well above the displaced California shipments.

The large quantity of Mexican imports since 1997 suggests that one effect of the easing of the quarantine has been expanded consumer demand because of the improved quality and seasonal availability of avocados. To the extent that demand has expanded, partial easing of the ban has provided consumers and Mexican producers with benefits at little cost to domestic producers. Avocados from Mexico have also served to stabilize the market in the face of weather-related variability in the domestic supply.

Based on its partial success in opening avocado trade in 1997, Mexico requested expanded geographic and seasonal access to the US market in September 1999. The USDA acted more quickly on this request than on the initial rule. An amended rule in November 2001 added access for avocados from Mexico to a west-central region and lengthened the shipping season allowed to six winter months. The 2001 ruling doubled the proportion of the US market to which Mexico gained access, to about 10 percent. This decision encountered less public opposition by the domestic industry than the initial easing of the quarantine, but the USDA did deny a petition by the California Avocado Commission not to expand

---

7. Intense opposition from the commission was effective in blocking change to the quarantine in time for the 1995–96 and 1996–97 winter shipping seasons. The commission attempted to circumscribe USDA authority through an amendment to the USDA's congressional appropriations legislation and threatened legal action to block lifting of the ban. It also placed full-page advertisements in several national newspapers to bolster its case. Against the backdrop of a hangman's noose, one of these ads claimed that the "USDA is about to sign the death warrant for a billion dollar American industry" (*The Washington Post*, March 11, 1996, A16).

Mexican access. Later, the commission filed suit to have the USDA rule overturned.[8]

The issuance of the 1997 and 2001 USDA regulations allowing avocados from Mexico into parts of the United States is an example of adoption, in the face of substantial domestic industry opposition, of a systems approach to risk mitigation that is less trade-distorting than a complete import ban. Further progress toward trade liberalization may be possible under the precedent set by these two rules.

Under the systems approach in the USDA's 2001 rule, the seasonal restriction, "winter shipping only," was estimated to reduce risk for just two types of pests by 50 to 90 percent, which is a relatively small effect compared with that produced by other measures (see table 4.1). Eliminating the seasonal restrictions on shipments of Mexican avocados to the northeastern and west-central regions would again more than double the proportion of the US market accessible to Mexico and might be relatively easy to justify. Achieving additional regional access—to the southeastern, southwestern, and Pacific markets—appeared more problematic. Limited geographic distribution was credited with reducing some pest risks by as much as 99 percent. Nonetheless, in June 2003 USDA regulators published for public comment a new risk assessment that concluded it would be safe to allow Mexican avocados into all 50 states throughout the year (USDA 2003). In its 2003 risk assessment, the USDA concluded that pest monitoring and fruit inspection procedures, together with natural impediments to pest establishment in the United States, led to essentially zero risk from avocado-specific pests, and that new research established that commercially produced Mexican avocados were not a host for fruit flies that could pose more general risks to US crops.

With the two existing USDA rules still subject to court challenge, the scope for Mexican access to the US market will remain constrained to certain parts of the country unless the USDA succeeds in making its proposed case that other measures in the systems approach to avocado imports from Mexico provide sufficient pest risk protection without the geographic or seasonal restrictions. The avocado dispute illustrates how difficult it is to make progress on trade expansion when complex risk issues are involved and a politically strong domestic industry is affected by the decision. It also illustrates the potential that exists for easing trade restrictions through use of science-based least-trade-distorting regulations.

Management of Endemic FMD

The control of FMD is an example of both the broader dimensions of the global management of pests and diseases and their economic and trade

---

8. The commission's suit was still pending in November 2003.

effects. FMD is an OIE List A disease that is endemic to many developing countries in Africa, Southeast Asia, and the Middle East, and to some countries in South America. Although no region in the world can be considered immune to an outbreak of this disease, Australia and New Zealand have never had a known case, the United States has been FMD-free since 1928, and most of Europe has been free of the disease in recent years. FMD has been eradicated from parts of Latin America, but Argentina, Brazil, and Uruguay fought new disease outbreaks in 2002 even though they had been recognized as FMD-free, or close to it. Unexpected FMD outbreaks occurred in Taiwan in 1997 and the United Kingdom in 2001, demonstrating the risks from this disease for every country, not just developing countries.

FMD is a vesicular disease that affects more than 70 species of domesticated and wild cloven-hoofed mammals.[9] Characterized by the formation of blisters and erosions, the disease causes decreased production of meat and milk, but it is rarely fatal to infected animals. The virus proliferates rapidly even under adverse conditions. It spreads mainly through airborne transmission (even over large distances), but also can be introduced into geographic regions where it was unknown through contaminated animal products, including meat and milk; through movement of human beings, vehicles, and domesticated or wild animals and birds; and through many other mechanisms (OIE 2003b).

In the event of a new FMD outbreak, the OIE recommends emergency measures that include "stamping out" the disease and restrictions on animal movements. A stamping out policy calls for immediate slaughter of affected and in-contact susceptible animals on affected farms, sanitary procedures for disposal of carcasses, and disinfection of premises. These steps are accompanied by a quarantine period in which the movement of animals is controlled. An even more severe control policy calls for stamping out by the slaughter of contact herds on nearby farms (Garner and Lack 1995). These disease control policies can be accompanied by emergency vaccination, often in a ring around the circumference of infected areas (AVIS 2003). Emergency ring vaccinations are an option in part because of the environmental risks attached to disposal of large numbers of slaughtered animals (Barnett, Samuel, and Statham 2001). Emergency vaccination might also be used in special cases, such as when endangered animals and rare species would otherwise have to be destroyed. Long-term protection against FMD can be achieved with routine vaccinations. The European Union banned the routine use of vaccines in 1991, but the practice is still utilized in some developing countries.

---

9. The possibility that the FMD virus will mutate and become a significant human zoonosis is viewed as remote given the rarity of the disease in human beings after centuries of close contact with infected animals (Brown 2001).

Because global eradication of FMD is impracticable, international monitoring and control measures are necessary. In a country with sporadic or infrequent FMD outbreaks, reestablishing disease-free status without vaccination requires no outbreak, no vaccinations, and no entry of imported vaccinated animals for at least 12 months. If a country pursues a policy of routine annual vaccinations, FMD-free status with vaccinations can be achieved by means of no outbreak of FMD for at least 24 months, a vaccination program in compliance with OIE standards, and an effective system of surveillance and regulatory control measures.

The 1997 FMD outbreak in Taiwan had significant commercial effects (USDA 1997b). Before this outbreak, Taiwan was the world's third-largest pork exporter; about one-third of its national production was sold overseas, almost exclusively to Japan. The FMD virus was transmitted to Taiwan from abroad, possibly from China by means of smuggling induced by higher Taiwanese pork prices.

In March 1997 the government announced a self-imposed ban on pork exports after detection of FMD on nearly 30 farms. Within three months, over 6,000 farms, containing more than 1 million hogs, were infected. Nearly 4 million of the country's 11 million hogs were slaughtered to bring the disease under control, and the direct financial losses were estimated at $378.6 million. Taiwan also initiated a vaccination program. By June 1997 it appeared that the epidemic was under control, but FMD reappeared in December 1997, and continued to be detected sporadically until April 1999. Taiwan seems unlikely to regain its status as a leading exporter of pork after these FMD outbreaks (Huang 2000).

A second unexpected outbreak of FMD occurred in the United Kingdom in 2001, after the country had been free of the disease since 1968. The 2001 outbreak was probably caused by the movements of animals across international borders (DEFRA 2003, Samuel and Knowles 2001). In less than two weeks the disease assumed epidemic proportions; movements of undetected sick animals were causing widespread geographic dispersion.

The United Kingdom chose to stamp out the disease through herd slaughter and other severe interventions. Vaccination was ruled out for the commercial reason of seeking to regain FMD-free status quickly (Scudamore 2002). Officials identified over 10,000 premises where animals were to be slaughtered, and over 4 million animals were destroyed. Seventy countries imposed bans on exports of UK animal products during the FMD outbreak, and the net costs to UK farming were estimated to be between £2.5 billion and £8 billion (US$3.6 billion and $11.6 billion) during 2001 (Mathews 2001, USDA 2001d).

The UK rural tourist industry, along with other sectors of the rural economy, was negatively affected by the FMD control program. Disposal of the animal carcasses also created problems. They included concerns that human health might be affected by airborne pollution or contaminated groundwater from carcass-burning pyres in the affected areas.[10] But the intensive control effort had the intended effect. By January 2002 the United Kingdom was again declared to be FMD-free.

FMD status matters to meat-exporting countries because the disease-related SPS trade barriers are applied with country specificity. Meats and other livestock products tend to bring higher prices in the markets of disease-free countries than in other markets. Preferential access to these protected markets is precluded for countries identified as having endemic FMD. Countries that are FMD-free but practice routine vaccination (e.g., Paraguay) must debone, freeze, or heat-treat meat for export.[11] Countries that have sporadic or infrequent outbreaks of FMD can regain FMD-free status, as the United Kingdom did in 2002. Somewhat inconsistent quarantine criteria and durations have been applied by FMD-free importers for different countries experiencing sporadic outbreaks, and this has led to trade frictions.[12]

US import policies toward Uruguay and Argentina illustrate the effects of FMD on trade flows between developed and developing countries. In the 1980s, Uruguay pursued an FMD eradication program. Once the United States recognized Uruguay as FMD-free in October 1995, Uruguay gained access to the US market through a tariff rate quota (TRQ) for a limited quantity of beef exports (Marshall et al. 2002). Later, after Uruguay experienced FMD outbreaks, it chose to vaccinate as part of its control strategy, which led to revocation of its US market access (USDA 2001a).

Argentina has been closely watched as an example of a developing country that is attempting to gain greater access to developed-country markets through higher SPS standards. In 1999 Argentina requested US recognition as FMD-free. In 2000 the USDA appeared ready to lift its ban on importation of fresh and frozen beef from Argentina, until 10 animals were detected with FMD. Like Uruguay, Argentina followed a policy of vaccination to eradicate the disease. As a result, a new US import rule was devised to permit imports from FMD-free regions, and beef imports were allowed into the United States under this rule from

---

10. A monitoring campaign that measured air concentrations of key pollutants from such pyres found little actual risk. The results showed that although the level of pollutants were above normal, the concentrations were unlikely to breach existing air quality standards substantially (Lowles et al. 2001).

11. Such measures increase processing costs and limit export opportunities for their livestock products, and these countries cannot export live animals to FMD-free countries.

12. Similar asymmetry in SPS regulations is found within the world poultry market (Orden, Josling, and Roberts 2002). For example, the United States does not recognize Brazil as free of sporadic outbreaks of highly pathogenic avian influenza, and thus Brazil is not able to ship poultry meat to the US market. But Brazilian poultry is granted access by the European Union and Japan. Such differences in SPS regulations among countries create trade conflicts, but market arbitrage opportunities also mitigate the effects of specific bilateral trade barriers when countries differ in their imposition of regulations.

December 2000 to February 2001. At that point, the USDA prohibited importation of fresh beef from Argentina because additional cases of FMD were detected. In March 2001 Argentina self-suspended exports of fresh beef to its other trading partners (USDA 2001a, 2001c).

In view of the high costs of an FMD outbreak, are stringent sanitary measures of suspending meat imports from a country with FMD optimal for an FMD-free country on a benefit-cost basis? A study of the likely effects of an outbreak of FMD in California illustrates the potential costs of the disease to the United States (Ekboir 1999). The analysis takes into account the direct cost of an aggressive stamping out control strategy, the cost of indirect and induced losses to the California economy, and the cost of losses incurred from trade restrictions. Eight scenarios are presented—from the worst case when the disease spreads throughout two valleys (San Joaquin and Chino) to the somewhat more optimistic scenarios of earlier discovery and an effective control strategy resulting in lower dissemination rates. The estimated costs to the United States of an FMD outbreak range from $6 billion to $13.5 billion. In all scenarios a substantial proportion of the costs (over $5 billion) arise from trade sanctions imposed on California and the rest of the United States by Japan, South Korea, and other FMD-free countries. In the United States, the available domestic meat supply would increase and prices would fall as a result of lower exports. The duration of these effects would depend not only on the effectiveness of the eradication program but also on how long Japan, South Korea, and other countries continue their embargoes after the disease is eliminated.

Philip Paarlberg and John Lee (1998, 2001) extend J.M. Ekboir's analysis to treat the likelihood of an FMD outbreak as endogenous. They relate the risk of an FMD outbreak in the United States to levels of beef imports from countries in four different risk categories. Like that of Orden and Romano (1996), their analysis compares trade benefits with the risk-related costs associated with trade. Utilizing differential tariffs as a policy instrument to determine quantities of beef imports, Paarlberg and Lee find that to achieve maximum national welfare in beef markets, the United States would have to draw almost all of its imports from countries with negligible risk, as under existing quarantine policies. This would be true even if the United States were willing to use proactive control measures: routine vaccinations to avoid outbreaks, along with stamping out if the disease occurred.

Paarlberg and Lee's results reveal that the strong quarantine measures used by the United States are well founded in economic terms when FMD-related risks from imports are taken into account. They also demonstrate the economic gains that other countries can achieve by adopting control programs that eliminate FMD in order to acquire access to the US market, but they do not estimate the feasibility or costs of doing so.

Even with the high costs of recent FMD outbreaks (and estimates such as those by Ekboir and by Paarlberg and Lee), the severity of some FMD regulatory measures has been questioned within the WTO SPS Committee. Of the counter-notifications related to animal diseases, 18 have concerned FMD measures (WTO 2002f). These complaints have asserted that such measures have been unnecessarily stringent given levels of risk in the exporting country, have not been based on a risk assessment, have failed to conform to OIE recommendations, have failed to consider regional disease-free areas, and have been imposed to achieve protectionist objectives. Similar disputes will likely continue to arise as sporadic outbreaks occur and as countries seek to control FMD and gain market access in response to their control efforts. But the basic global framework for prevention of the spread of FMD is not subject to international dispute, and it appears to be reasonably well justified by benefit-cost analysis.

BSE—A New Zoonotic Disease

In 1985 a new zoonotic disease, bovine spongiform encephalopathy, dubbed mad cow disease, was detected in cattle in Great Britain and later was linked to the fatal human variant CJD. The outbreak of this disease provides different circumstances in which to examine the effectiveness of global food regulation. BSE, a slowly progressive degenerative disease that affects the central nervous system of adult cattle, is eventually fatal (Wilesmith et al. 1988). The BSE agent has been detected only in certain tissues of infected cattle, particularly in brain tissue, the spinal cord, and the retina, and mostly in those tissues when the cattle are over 32 months of age.

Through 2002, more than 180,000 cases of BSE have been reported worldwide since it was first detected. Over 95 percent of these cases have been reported in the United Kingdom (table 4.2). Why BSE appeared when it did and why the incidence has been so heavily concentrated in the United Kingdom are not fully understood (Donaldson, Kitching, and Barnett 2000; DEFRA 2000). The emergence of BSE has been associated with feeding rendered animal proteins in meat and bonemeal (MBM) to other animals. But MBM has been used worldwide for 30 years. It seems, in hindsight, that BSE outbreaks could have occurred earlier and possibly in more than one country.

Since the BSE outbreaks, researchers have identified several compounding factors that might explain the timing and geographic concentration of the outbreaks. First, changes in the UK rendering processes during the 1970s and early 1980s may have significantly increased the amount of surviving infective BSE agent and thus contributed to the epidemic.[13] Second, a relatively high percentage of UK beef is a by-product of dairy

---

13. The BSE causal agent is highly stable and is resistant to heat, ultraviolet light, ionizing radiation, and common disinfectants, which normally inactivate viruses or bacteria. Therefore, none of the rendering processes in use before the 1970s was completely

Table 4.2 Cases of BSE, 1989–2002

Year	United Kingdom	Elsewhere	Total
1989	7,228	15	7,243
1990	14,407	17	14,424
1991	25,359	31	25,390
1992	37,280	36	37,316
1993	35,090	49	35,139
1994	24,438	104	24,542
1995	14,562	102	14,664
1996	8,149	161	8,310
1997	4,393	160	4,553
1998	3,235	252	3,487
1999	2,301	336	2,637
2000	1,443	513	1,956
2001	1,019	1,013	2,032
2002	755	1,034	1,789

Source: OIE (2003b).

production, and UK feed manufacturers introduced MBM into rations for dairy calves around 1970, increasing their exposure. Third, UK MBM may have contained a relatively high level of TSE infectious material from sheep. In view of all these factors, it seems likely then that an unusual concatenation of events in the United Kingdom resulted in the emergence of BSE—but that no single cause can be determined. With the long incubation period, the number of affected cattle in the United Kingdom grew until 1992, when more than 37,000 cases were confirmed, equivalent to 1 percent of the national herd.

Once BSE was identified, the United Kingdom undertook measures to eradicate the disease in cattle herds, prevent its transmission to other animal species, and protect consumers of bovine products against any risk of disease transmission to humans. MBM was determined to be a likely BSE vector in December 1987. By July 1988, the United Kingdom had banned the use of ruminant proteins in the preparation of animal feed. Parts of cattle that were considered a risk to humans (then known as specified bovine offal and later as specific risk material, or SRM) were

effective in inactivating the agent. The nature of the agent causing BSE was also uncertain. Scientists have now concluded that the causal agent is composed entirely of the disease-specific isoform of a membrane protein (the "prion" hypothesis), which is consistent with the extreme resistance of the BSE agent to conventional inactivation procedures (Hill et al. 1997, Scott et al. 1999). An opposing view was that the transmissible spongiform encephalopathy agents are virus-like and contain nucleic acid. Identification of multiple strains of scrapie, also a TSE, with characteristic incubation periods and patterns of neuropathological change when transmitted to mice, appeared to support this hypothesis (Narang 1996).

banned in the United Kingdom in 1989, and the list of SRMs was revised and expanded in November 1994, April 1995, and August 1995.

The initial economic costs of BSE were incurred from the changes in production practices to reduce the spread of the disease and from the losses stemming from the disposal of SRM and infected carcasses. By 1995 the BSE incidence in cattle had fallen by half, and its economic cost was expected to continue to decline (Atkinson 1999).

Trade impacts were also limited initially. Because BSE is not highly contagious, it is on the OIE's List B despite its fatal consequences. Some non-European countries banned or restricted imports of live animals or beef meat from the United Kingdom in the 1980s and early 1990s, but intra-EU trade was not sharply affected (Bernstein, Buzby, and Mathews 2003). UK exports of beef dropped off from 1988 to 1992, but then nearly doubled from 1992 to 1995. During those years, nearly 400,000 head of live cattle were exported annually, up slightly from previous years. Still, tensions mounted over the foreboding possibility that BSE in cattle represented a human health threat. This was perplexing because, until 1996, epidemiological studies had found no connection between the exposure of humans to agents causing other animal spongiform encephalopathies and the occurrence of known human TSEs.

On March 20, 1996, the BSE situation was transformed from a livestock disease management problem into a human health management crisis when the UK secretary of state for health announced a probable linkage between BSE and new vCJD. In contrast to the traditional forms of CJD, vCJD affected younger patients than those with CJD, who suffered relatively longer from the illness. The classic form of CJD occurs spontaneously worldwide at an annual rate of about one to two cases per million people, whereas vCJD was detected only in countries in which BSE was known to exist.

From 1990 surveillance had began to identify cases of CJD that could be linked with BSE. The announcement by the government regarding the possible link between BSE and CJD followed consideration of cases of the human disease among people associated with farming and in young people. The secretary concluded, based on the available evidence, that the most likely explanation for cases of vCJD was exposure to the BSE agent (see DEFRA 2000 for a full chronology). Subsequently published studies of the vCJD causal agent provided strong evidence that the same strain of agent derived from BSE is also found in vCJD (Hill et al. 1997, Scott et al. 1999). One early study estimated that the total number of deaths from vCJD could range from 100 to as many as 136,000 (USDA/FSIS 2002).

Substantial adverse consequences and economic losses followed the announcement of a possible zoonotic link between BSE and vCJD (Henson and Mazzocchi 2002). Domestic UK sales of beef products dropped immediately—in April 1996 household consumption was 26 percent below the level of the previous year. Export trade in live cattle and beef was completely disrupted when an EU ban was imposed on UK exports of cattle, meat, and bovine products (such as pharmaceuticals, gelatin, and beef stocks, extracts, and flavorings). The price of beef cattle fell by over 25 percent as domestic and export demand dropped in 1996.

Disease control and eradication measures were intensified in the United Kingdom. Officials imposed a complete ban after 1996 on the use of cattle over 30 months of age for food and ordered the disposal of bull calves that had been exported. Compensation schemes and price support intervention purchases under the European Union's Common Agricultural Policy (CAP) offset as much as 90 percent of the losses to farmers. Other measures taken to control the spread of BSE included new animal identification and traceability requirements, and controls and regulations at slaughter facilities. UK legislation governing the removal and safe disposal of SRMs from the carcasses of domestic animals, and further SRM import controls, became effective in January 1998. The net costs resulting from these measures were estimated to be between £400 million and £600 million (Atkinson 1999).

In the United Kingdom, in retrospect, the initial regulatory responses to detection of BSE in cattle were too modest. Although intentional negligence was not involved, the UK government initially pursued a campaign of reassurance that turned out to be mistaken, undermining consumer confidence in the regulatory authorities (DEFRA 2000). Indeed, the UK regulatory system underestimated the significance of the novelty of BSE, not recognizing its linkage to the fatal zoonotic disease vCJD until 10 years after BSE was first detected among cattle. Fortunately, early estimates that the total number of human deaths from vCJD could reach 100,000 or more have proven unwarranted. The likely eventual number of deaths now appears to be below 1,000 worldwide.[14] In part, this more limited impact arises from limited early cautionary measures, taken while risks were still unknown, and the subsequent vigorous responses of the regulatory system in containing the disease threat once the BSE-vCJD link was recognized.

Control of BSE also intensified elsewhere after the likely BSE-vCJD linkage was acknowledged. The European Union banned the use as human food of materials known to contain the BSE agent in infected cattle, the use of bovine vertebral column in the production of mechanically recovered meat, and the use of stunning techniques that could introduce large pieces of brain into the circulatory systems of slaughtered cattle. The European Union also prohibited the use of cattle over 30 months of age as human food, unless such slaughtered cattle had been tested for BSE.

---

14. From October 1996 to early November 2001, 111 cases of vCJD were reported in the UK, 4 in France, and single cases in the Republic of Ireland and Hong Kong (USDA/FSIS 2002).

Measures undertaken by the United States were typical of those taken by countries distant geographically from the initial BSE outbreaks and apparently free of the disease, including Australia, Canada, and Brazil. Initially, in 1989, the USDA had issued restrictions prohibiting the importation of live ruminants from countries where BSE was known to exist in native cattle. In the early 1990s, and again in 1996 and 2000, the FDA issued recommendations for manufacturers of regulated products intended for human use to avoid bovine-derived materials from countries where BSE was known to exist or might exist. In 1997 the FDA prohibited the use of most mammalian protein in the manufacture of animal feeds given to ruminants. The USDA took further steps in 1997, prohibiting the importation of live ruminants and most ruminant products from all of Europe. In 1999 the FDA issued guide-lines to reduce the theoretical risk of transmission of vCJD to recipients of blood transfusions by excluding potential donors with substantial exposure to food products in countries with BSE.

In December 2000, the USDA prohibited all imports of rendered animal protein products, regardless of species, from countries with BSE because of concern that cattle feed that contained these products may have been cross-contaminated with the BSE agent. Meanwhile, the USDA continues to operate a comprehensive surveillance system for BSE in the United States and has drafted an emergency response plan in case BSE is detected.

In short, the United States and other countries where BSE has not been detected have taken significant steps to avoid introduction of the disease domestically. A study by the Harvard School of Public Health concluded that the actions taken by the USDA and FDA made the United States "highly resistant" to any introduction of BSE and that in the unlikely event BSE did enter the United States only a small amount of potentially dangerous tissues would be likely to reach the human food supply (Cohen et al. 2001). When a single case of BSE was detected in western Canada in May 2003, the United States and other countries quickly embargoed Canadian meat and cattle imports. The very strong responses to this single BSE detection had sharply negative immediate effects on the Canadian beef industry, which usually exports nearly 70 percent of its output to the United States.

Because of its novelty and severity, BSE/vCJD thus sparked the birth of extensive new trade-related health regulations. But as countries began to put regulations in place to minimize BSE risks, some disputes arose among trading partners over implementation of specific measures. Regulatory responses had to be informed by scientific risk assessment, and countries differed in their initial assessments and responses. In the months and years that followed, OIE procedures and WTO notification and dispute resolution processes for coordinating global regulation were put to the test. The OIE became a forum for determining numerous guidelines and standards. As described in chapter 3, from 1995 to 2002 some 50 counter-notifications were raised about TSEs (mostly BSE) within the SPS Committee as countries began to notify numerous new BSE-related regulations to the WTO (see table 3.1).

The BSE counter-notifications fell primarily into two groups (WTO 2002f). First, most countries in Europe were slower than the United States and others to impose restrictions on UK livestock and meat products during 1985 to 1996. As some of these countries began to experience small numbers of BSE detections, other countries imposed restrictions on export products from those countries to ensure their own BSE-free status.[15] Disputes arose about appropriate regulation in high-incidence versus low-incidence countries and about equivalence of alternative control strategies. Thus this first group of counter-notifications arose from European countries with limited BSE detections objecting to the conservative measures adopted by countries in which BSE had not been detected. Likewise, in bilateral negotiations in 2003, Canada complained about the severity of the initial complete US embargo on importation of its meat and cattle, leading in September to some easing of the restrictions under new import licensing rules, in part as a result of close Canadian adherence to OIE disease management recommendations.

The second group of counter-notifications arose from countries that had not detected BSE and that were objecting to restrictions by the European Union. The United States, Brazil, Chile, and others argued that the European Union failed to recognize their BSE-free status, and had placed unnecessary restrictions on a variety of products, including some high-value pharmaceuticals and cosmetics. The European Union responded early in the crisis that no country could be ascertained BSE-free. As the OIE guidelines became more fully established, these disputes receded, but even in 2001 counter-notifications were made over bans on certain products and the criteria by which some countries identified the level of BSE risk associated with imports from specific exporters.

The record of BSE notifications and counter-notifications within the SPS Committee suggests that transparency and risk assessment requirements can play a useful role as national regulatory agencies respond to unfolding events. As nations responded to the unanticipated, significant new BSE disease threat, control measures were imposed in an atmosphere of uncertainty. It therefore took some time for scientific opinions to converge to widely accepted guidelines as specified by the OIE. As with

---

15. BSE was first detected outside of the United Kingdom in 1989, and about 3,800 non-UK cases were reported through 2002 (see table 4.2), primarily in European countries. Substantial numbers of cases (100 or more) have been reported in six countries—France, Germany, Ireland, Portugal, Spain, and Switzerland. Small numbers of cases also have been reported in 11 other European countries, and Israel and Japan reported isolated cases in 2002, probably resulting from the importation of contaminated British feed exports in the early 1990s.

FMD, the WTO disciplines have not fundamentally altered the regulations various countries have adopted to protect their animal herds and public health from BSE/vCJD. It has become clear over time that some of the BSE control measures adopted were overly restrictive. The WTO has provided a forum in which some excessive health regulations could be disciplined and related trade disruptions could be minimized. Still, these issues had to be engaged again, and with significant disruption of trade, when a single BSE case was detected in Canada in May 2003.

Managing Agricultural Trade in the Presence of Risks

Animals and plants are susceptible to threats from pests and diseases that are pervasive and ever evolving. Countries differ significantly in their incidence of various sanitary and phytosanitary risks and in their regulatory strategies and capabilities. When pests are endemic, public efforts to affect their incidence often are minimal, and control measures for individual properties are left primarily to private agents and their farm management practices. When pests are less pervasive or not present, or when effective control of infectious diseases requires collective action, public agencies usually rely on active containment policies, and private-public coordination is involved in pest management strategies. It is in the latter situation that regulatory decisions can affect trade and lead to disputes among countries over whether particular measures are warranted. Responsibility ultimately rests with national authorities, but the WTO, OIE, and IPPC oversee national regulatory decisions, and they and other organizations have sought to achieve international coordination of the management by countries of threats to animal and plant health.

The extent to which animal and plant SPS regulatory measures result in trade conflicts is reflected in ongoing efforts to open specific markets for commercial gain, in unilateral governmental accounts of trade disputes, in bilateral negotiations at technical and political levels, in deliberations in regional bodies, in discussions and decisions at the international standards organizations, and in disputes addressed within the WTO. In the WTO, only a few conflicts among trading partners have gone through the formal dispute settlement process, and even the number of counter-notifications raised in the SPS Committee is relatively small compared with the large number of animal and plant health measures already in place and the new measures being notified to which objections can be raised. These developments suggest a degree of consensus in national assessments of legitimate animal and plant health measures and general conformity to those measures for well-understood pests and diseases. Still, the impact of disputed measures on trade can be substantial when evaluated in terms of access to a specific market by a specific exporting country or in the aggregate. For this reason, efforts to resolve disputes over SPS measures will continue. The WTO record shows some evidence of achieving this objective.

The three examples of SPS regulation and management discussed in this chapter are illustrative of the challenges that must be faced in seeking enhanced integration of the global food system while minimizing proliferation of agricultural pests and diseases to protect animal, plant, and human health. The lengthy negotiations that resulted in partial access for Mexican avocados to the US market are typical of bilateral disputes over specific plant pests. This example demonstrates that borders can gradually be opened by replacing severe quarantine restrictions with a process standard systems approach to pest control. Progress requires clear opportunities for economic gains, persistent attempts to seek market access, sound scientific assessments of the risk associated with the proposed trade, and governments that are committed to opening markets if a good technical case can be made for doing so.

Endemic infestations of FMD pose different problems. FMD demonstrates the importance of vigilance in monitoring livestock diseases and the costs of a breakdown in sanitary control systems, even for a well-known disease risk. The recent outbreaks of FMD in Taiwan and the United Kingdom highlight the threat this disease still poses within world agriculture. The basic quarantine and control measures applied internationally are not under dispute, though applications of these measures in certain situations have been questioned. Eradicating FMD on a worldwide level is impracticable, and the disease continues to affect international trade patterns for live animals and livestock products. Trade essentially differentiates into international flows within the FMD-free region and flows within the infected region. A few countries that are primarily exporters, such as Australia and Canada, are FMD-free. This status gives them access to high-priced markets in high-income countries such as Japan, Korea, the European Union, and the United States, which also trade meat products among themselves and with other countries that strictly prohibit importation of livestock and meats from countries where FMD is present. Other potential exporters, including Taiwan, Argentina, and Uruguay, have found it difficult to establish or retain FMD-free status.

The emergence of BSE and its likely cause—feeding rendered animal proteins to ruminants—also pose a significant global challenge to commercial agriculture and food regulators. Critics of modern agricultural technology might argue that this crisis could have been avoided altogether had a more conservative approach been taken to technology adoption. But such precaution, broadly applied, would incur a high cost in lost productivity and higher food costs. Conversely, had detection efforts been less systematic in the United Kingdom in the mid-1980s, this disease could have become much more endemic before control measures were initiated.

The role of the WTO in resolving disputes that have arisen in the BSE case may be indicative of the larger regulatory oversight role it will play over time. Other new animal, plant, and human health threats will surely materialize and will have to be addressed in the global food system, even if sensible measures are adopted beforehand to avoid any such future crisis.[16] Undertaking measured responses that ensure a reasonable level of animal and human health protection without unduly restricting technology development or global food trade will remain a challenge. The BSE experience demonstrates the importance of strong scientific analysis, national regulatory institutions, and global regulatory disciplines to minimizing the risks inherent in the development of modern agricultural technologies, and the damages incurred—directly and through disruption of trade—when these systems fail.

---

16. The emergence in 2003 of severe acute respiratory syndrome (SARS) drives home the importance of vigilance against new disease outbreaks in human as well as animal health. As the book goes to press, the first case of BSE was discovered in the United States, leading to new control measures and an embargo on US exports by two dozen countries.

5

Food Safety and Control of Human Health Hazards

Consumers increasingly want their governments to assure them that their food supply is safe and reliable, as well as affordable. In recent years, many of the changes in the design of food regulations have been in response to these pressures and to the concern that safety issues are being compromised by commercial or other considerations. But regulatory decisions have costs and face resource constraints. And food regulations are a particular challenge because individual countries differ greatly in both their demand for national regulation and their ability and willingness to cooperate in the design and implementation of coordinated international strategies. In fact, the benefits of coordination need to be weighed against the costs involved, including any related weakening of consumers' confidence in their national regulatory institutions. This chapter explores the options for regulatory actions to provide healthier food within an open global delivery system, and the scope for their misuse, which creates trade conflicts.

Human health can be affected by a variety of organisms, contaminants, and chemicals that enter the food supply chain at various stages, from the feeding of animals and the control of plant pests on the farm to the processing and packing of products for sale in commercial facilities. It is useful to separate these health hazards into two kinds: those that are essentially pathogenic agents in the environment and those that stem from the use of productivity-enhancing inputs and technologies in the food production process. "Natural" food safety risks include the agents that can pose significant health problems for humans, such as *Salmonella*, *E. coli*, and other prevalent disease-causing organisms, and the contaminants that enter during the food-processing and marketing chain. "Man-made" food safety risks linked with the use of yield-increasing technology are posed by the additives used by the food industry, the pesticide residues emanating from agrochemicals, and the hormones and antibiotics used mostly in the production of beef, pigs, poultry, and eggs. The implication of this distinction is that the incidence of natural hazards is not a matter of choice, whereas those linked to inputs and technology can be avoided. However, in practice the distinction is difficult to maintain, because the links between technology and the incidence of natural pathogens are numerous, and control of pathogens is easier under some technologies than others.

The food safety regulations discussed in this chapter are different in several respects from those explored in chapter 4. First, contamination of food products by pathogens is normally not directly related to animal and plant health, though some of the pathogens mentioned in this chapter could be described as zoonotic in that they also cause disease in animals, and this category of problems may be on the increase. Second, it is those in the medical profession and related disciplines, rather than veterinary and plant scientists, that tend to advise on food safety issues. Third, the domestic agencies involved in food safety regulation are often not the same ones involved in animal and plant protection. The capture of food safety agencies by agricultural interests can at times become an issue, but consumer interests tend to be at least as deeply engaged in food regulations with a human health dimension as producer organizations. The persistence of the controversy over the European Union's ban on the use of hormones in beef production has shown the difficulty in resolving trade problems in these areas when producer interests in one country conflict with strongly expressed consumer interests in another.

Food Safety Regulation

Over the last decade, many countries have overhauled their food safety agencies, seeking to achieve a level of consumer confidence that makes the regulatory activity almost invisible and rarely newsworthy. In doing so, reformers also have sought to be comprehensive in coverage, from "farm to fork," at different stages of the food supply chain.[1] A secondary objective has been to coordinate the application of regulations across agencies to avoid duplication and confusion. And a third objective has been to distance the regulation of food safety from the management of the market for agricultural products. As a result of this, food safety regulators have recently become more autonomous, and their traditional connection with agricultural ministries has become weaker.

---

1. Other phrases that popularize this food chain approach are "stable to table" and "plough to plate."

According to Donna Roberts and Laurien Unnevehr (2002), the underlying forces driving new food safety regulation are greater scientific understanding of the sources of food-borne illnesses, growing international trade in food products, and changes in how consumers obtain and prepare food. This combination of changes in science, markets, and consumer awareness has led to a new paradigm for food safety regulation in developed countries. The paradigm that emerged during the 1990s

- identifies public health as the primary goal of food safety regulation,

- bases food regulation firmly on risk analysis and scientific evidence,

- recognizes that a farm-to-fork approach is often desirable for addressing food safety hazards,

- often features the Hazard Analysis and Critical Control Point (HACCP)[2] system as a basis for regulation of microbial pathogens in food,

- increases the stringency of many food safety standards,

- adds more extensive regulation to handle newly identified hazards, and

- improves market performance in food safety by providing consumers with information.

In spite of, or in some cases because of, the introduction of this new paradigm, the range of food regulations among countries within the trade system is wider than ever. Health and safety measures differ by country in the standards set by regulation, the instruments utilized, and the allocation of responsibility for conformity assessment. Countries that already had relatively highly regulated food systems have moved further in that direction.[3] But the capacity of many developing countries to implement

---

2. The HACCP approach is based on identifying those stages in the food chain where contamination can take place and focusing remedial controls on those points.

3. The history of US meat inspection is illustrative of the evolution of relatively highly regulated systems. Meat inspections began in 1891, when Congress enacted legislation to place inspectors in export facilities selling salted pork to Europe. This legislation was prompted by the long-running trade conflict of the nineteenth century mentioned in chapter 2. For many years, Chancellor Otto Bismarck's Germany banned US pork, citing its contamination by a parasite that caused trichinosis in humans eating or handling the pork. Although the United States maintained that its exports were not contaminated, it had no choice but to modify the regulations to satisfy importers' complaints. Inspection was conducted either at the request of the importing country or the exporting firm (Crutchfield et al. 1997). In 1906 inspection was extended to all facilities slaughtering meat for human consumption. Federal inspection of poultry began as a voluntary program, but was made mandatory in the 1946 Agricultural Marketing Act and extended in the 1957 Poultry Products Inspection Act to include the inspection of every carcass that crossed state lines. By the mid-1990s the Food Safety and Inspection Service (FSIS) of the USDA had more

such food safety programs even if they choose to do so is often limited (Henson, Loader, et al. 2000). Similarly, a range of approaches to risk assessment and management is also evident in food safety regulations. In general, countries are increasingly adopting science-based regulations, but they can still differ widely on the role of science and scientists in regulatory decisions. Most countries following the new paradigm have adopted a strong preventative approach toward food safety, along with rapid reaction to food scares. But the shift toward process standards and away from product standards can create trade problems. The new food regulations are often horizontal in nature, covering many products and sectors.

Trade Issues and Food Safety

Most people would agree that the major threat to food systems is underprotection, where welfare losses occur through inadequate or uncoordinated food safety regulations. But overprotection through regulations that are too costly for the degree of safety that they confer, or that confuse rather than protect the consumer, can be a danger as well. On the face of it, one would expect little disagreement on the need for or the means of protecting consumers from food-related illnesses, at least among countries with similar levels of income. But even among such countries, trade conflicts do arise. Some of the clashes among domestic and foreign interests involved in food safety regulation relate to the different interpretations of scientific evidence on the prevalence of microorganisms; others arise from pressures on the regulatory authorities to apply the regulations in a way that gives advantages to domestic interests. Although the need to establish tolerance levels based on scientific knowledge of the effects of pesticide residues and other toxins on health is not in doubt, differences among standards can have a major economic impact on particular firms and countries.

Banning imports is not always the most efficient (or even effective) remedy for achieving food safety. Import bans have costs, not least the higher prices that domestic consumers must bear. Overprotection could arise if medical and biological scientists, who work in a culture of exclusion and eradication of disease, were to exert an undue influence on food safety policy. That culture may clash with the notion of making the best use of resources—a notion that characterizes economic approaches. As for politicians, they often find it easier to adopt the rhetoric of extreme risk aversion, even if they know that, in practice, there are few absolute

---

than 7,400 inspectors in the nation's slaughter and meat-processing facilities (USDA/FSIS 1996)—an extensive and costly regulatory response both to higher infection rates and to elevated consumer concerns. The Pathogen Reduction Regu-lation of 1996 modified the standards for pathogen reductions, although it has not solved all the problems of measurement in this area.

guarantees that pathogens will not be imported and that any attempt to achieve such perfect protection will imply considerable, and unacceptable, economic costs.

The two sets of issues discussed in this chapter—protection against natural hazards and protection against the side effects of technology—exemplify this dilemma. When facing the risks arising from imports of food, and the inadvertent import of natural disease organisms, regulatory authorities take into account the public health consequences of such diseases. Most food-borne illnesses pose a cost only for the consumer who gets sick. Rarely does the disease spread and become an epidemic.[4] The economic cost of human illness can be estimated by calculating lost work time and extra medical care costs.

Consumer reactions to food-related health risks are far greater, however, than such pecuniary losses might imply. They tend to avoid consuming foods that they think might carry health risks, even when such risks are minimal, and regulators are pressured to provide more food safety than a benefit-cost calculation would suggest. Related to this is the dramatic fall in consumption that often follows a food safety "scare"; such a reaction may be out of all proportion to the actual (actuarial) risk involved. Thus regulators have to pay particular care to avoid collapses in market confidence, and can easily slip into overprotection out of a fear of the unexpected.

The fear of illness from eating certain foods is understandable in view of natural pathogens that might pose a risk. But when this fear extends to methods of food production, it is often unsupported by the scientific evidence. Thus mistaken concerns about the safety of the production process can also lead to overprotection.

Some of these concerns stem from the common but not necessarily reliable assumption that the way in which a crop is grown or an animal is raised determines the suitability of the final product for human consumption. The use of chemical pesticides and fertilizers and of growth promotants such as hormones and antibiotics has brought this issue front and center in the public consciousness, thereby considerably enhancing the chances of regulatory overprotection. As regulators focus on the food production process, this can lead to excessive protection from risks that are, on a scientific basis, relatively small. It is no accident that one of the most contentious trade disputes in sanitary and phytosanitary regulation is over the European Union's ban on importation of hormone-treated beef. The approach taken by the European Union in the hormones ban shows evidence of overprotection, but the difficulty in resolving this problem by reference only to science is also apparent. This conundrum

---

4. Control would then become more akin to that applied to animal and plant diseases, except that the costs associated with the disease tend to be much higher when human health is at risk.

poses a significant challenge to multilateral rules that are designed on the assumption that risk assessment is not only a necessary component of domestic regulations but also is sufficient.

Controlling Natural Food-Borne Pathogens

Consumers worldwide recognize the need to prevent contamination of foods by microbial pathogens, and most accept the scientific basis for such consumer protection.[5] Consumers in different countries may have somewhat different tolerance levels for such pathogens, but in general they react somewhat alike to the presence of these microbes. The sources of such contamination also differ among countries; they depend on the level of hygiene of the production and processing facilities and the conditions at the point of sale.[6]

Lower-income countries with generally substandard hygiene levels, when compared with those of their higher-income trading partners, can still enter world markets by developing export-oriented enclaves with higher standards. But there are also "global good" aspects to combating food safety problems that are important. As long as some countries lack clean water, a functioning sanitation system, refrigeration, and hygienic food preparation facilities, efforts to control food-borne pathogens to facilitate an open global food system are unlikely to be fully satisfactory. For the smaller number of infectious diseases spread by the food chain, the global good dimension and the need for collective action become even more compelling.

In large part, the trade system comes under strain because developing and developed countries differ in their ability to administer safe food regulations, in much the same way as they differ in controlling animal diseases. But trade issues arising from the inadvertent transportation of food-borne pathogens are generally confined to the local response to particular hazards and therefore are easier to control than are animal and plant diseases.

---

5. Food-borne pathogens include bacteria, viruses, parasites, and fungi, along with the toxins that some of these parasites secrete. Pathogens can either cause infections, through invasion of the host or through the production of toxins while in the host, or intoxications, where the organism produces toxin in the food that is ingested (CAST 1994). Mycotoxins such as aflatoxin are common intoxicants, and are treated separately from the pathogens that cause infections because control systems tend to differ.

6. Many health hazards can and do enter the food system after the point of sale to consumers; inappropriate storage conditions or improper product handling and cooking may be the culprits. The regulations directed toward minimizing such hazards normally take the form of consumer information, and so are unlikely to be a source of trade conflicts. Allergenicity problems that affect only certain individuals are also appropriately handled as a consumer information issue.

Box 5.1 Common bacteria that can cause food-borne illnesses

Salmonella enteriditis is one of about 2,000 strains of the *Salmonella* bacterium. It is often associated with poultry and eggs, but it is also found widely in the intestinal tracts of warm-blooded animals. *S. enteriditis* causes mild to severe illness, with occasional complications. Other strains of *Salmonella* (*S. pullorum* and *S. gallinarum*) are confined to poultry and do not pose a human health hazard.

Staphlococcus aureus is associated with unhygienic food handling and preparation of meat and other high-protein foods. Illness is rarely severe.

Campylobacter jejuni and *Campylobacter coli* are common bacteria associated with consumption of raw milk, poultry, beef, pork, and shellfish. They produce mild to moderate illness, but occasionally are associated with serious complications. These bacteria are controlled by correct food preparation.

Listeria monocytogenes is a relative newcomer to the list of food-borne organisms that cause human illness. It is also associated with poor food handling and inadequate cooking temperatures. Its effects are most severe in children.

Escherichia coli O157:H7 is one of a number of *E. coli* types that cause illness. Although not common, *E. coli* O157:H7 is associated with insufficiently cooked ground beef and occasionally with milk. Illness can be severe.

Vibrio cholera and *Vibrio parahaemolyticus* are associated with seafood, mainly shell-fish. Illness is usually moderate.

Source: CAST (1994).

Eradication of these food-borne diseases is inherently unlikely. The principal microbial hazards include a small number of common bacterial pathogens with nearly global incidence. The main food-borne pathogens are described briefly in box 5.1. The severity of food-borne illness is usually mild to moderate, and many instances go unreported. The very young and the elderly and those with compromised immune systems, among others, are more at risk than the general population. Thus the public health component of food safety regulations must take into account the vulnerability of particular segments of the population.

Fortunately, the main problems of contamination by microbial pathogens are usually found in only a limited range of foodstuffs, primarily uncooked meat, fresh dairy products, raw eggs, and shellfish, as well as occasionally in fruits, vegetables, and grains. Thus food safety inspectors worldwide devote much of their time to the control of pathogens such as *Salmonella, E. coli, Campylobacter,* and *Listeria* in poultry meat, eggs, dairy products, beef, and shellfish. The differences in the methods that they use to control this limited set of pathogens and hosts have led in turn to some of the more persistent trade tensions among countries.

Most of the national regulation to control microbial contamination, at the border or at various stages during the production and processing chain, is appropriate and necessary. The problems arise when importing countries succumb to the temptation to shade their regulations in favor of domestic producers. If the misuse of health standards to protect domestic producers is widespread, it would be evident in the markets for meat and shellfish products, and perhaps dairy. As noted earlier, many regulations in the poultry market appear to be discriminatory, and protectionist use of regulations is not unknown in the market for fresh dairy products. But, in general, health standards related to pathogenic contamination are less a cause of trade tensions than the animal growth stimulants discussed later in this chapter. The science is less controversial, and the interests of domestic producers are not so obviously benefited by too-high standards. Some overprotection is found in the area of microbial hazards, but to a lesser extent than in several other areas of food regulations.[7]

Import Standards for Food-Borne Pathogens

The common bacterium *Salmonella* is responsible for many cases of illness from food consumption. *Salmonella* is found in a range of raw food products, but it is easily controlled by cooking these products to an adequate temperature. A high proportion of food poisoning caused by eating raw eggs is caused by *Salmonella enteritidis*. *Salmonella typhimurium* accounts for many other cases of food poisoning worldwide, although it is less common in the United States. A virulent form of *S. typhimurium*, known as DT 104 and thought to have developed resistance to common antibiotics, may pose a new threat.

One common complaint among exporters has been that importers discriminate when imposing standards for *Salmonella*. In a case typical of such disputes, the United States complained in October 1996 that some WTO members were discriminating between standards for control of *Salmonella* in domestic and imported poultry products (WTO 2002f). According to the United States, a group of countries (Chile, the Czech Republic, El Salvador, Slovakia, and Honduras) were each applying what they referred to as "zero-tolerance" standards for *Salmonella*. The United States considered these standards to be in effect a trade barrier, because none of these countries appeared to have eradicated *Salmonella* from the domestic poultry flock or to have surveillance systems in place to establish nonexistence of *Salmonella* in domestic products. As a result, imported

---

7. Increased use of preentry inspection has contributed to a reduction in trade conflicts arising from rejection of shipments. By choosing to bring particular processing facilities up to the standards of the importer, an exporting country avoids some of the "randomness" of postentry checks.

poultry was being held to higher standards, in violation of the fundamental WTO principle of national treatment.

The response of the importers varied from denials that such zero-tolerance standards existed to clarifications of the requirements for imports and domestic poultry. The Czech Republic, for example, insisted that its regulations required negative results on *Salmonella* tests in poultry holdings and slaughterhouses, but the United States sent no assurances that these requirements would be met. The Czech Republic then suggested bilateral consultations between veterinary experts, which seems to have resolved the issue.

The dispute with Chile has a longer history. Chile observed that bilateral consultations on *Salmonella* regulations had started in 1992, but that the United States had misunderstood Chile's sanitary requirements, which required tests to determine the level of *Salmonella* in domestic poultry. The result was then compared with the level of prevalence in the exporting country as a part of Chile's risk assessment procedure. Chile claimed that the United States had difficulty complying with this requirement because of the high prevalence of the pathogen domestically. The Chilean government indicated, perhaps tongue in cheek, that it was prepared to show a certain flexibility and would consider imports of irradiated poultry from the United States as a possible alternative. Irradiation of poultry, though now legal in the United States, is not generally thought to be acceptable to consumers in the major importing countries.[8]

Another source of trade contention over *Salmonella* risks has involved sales of fishmeal, for use as animal feed, from Latin America to the European Union. Chile and Peru sought clarification from the WTO SPS Committee of an EU directive that apparently applied to imports of fishmeal but was not applied to substitutes for fishmeal. The exporters maintained that these substitutes could also be contaminated with *Salmonella*, and referred to research carried out in the United Kingdom. The European Union countered that the directive was justified on the basis of the available scientific information, although it was considering whether similar criteria should be applied to feedstuffs of vegetable origin. The European Union admitted that member states themselves were not in agreement on the need for such standards. Some EU member states had

---

8. One indication of the strength of resistance to irradiation in Europe is that EU authorities have been considering irradiation regulations for more than 10 years. Despite the repeated recommendations of the European Union's Scientific Committee on Food to allow the irradiation of products such as fish, fresh meats, poultry, produce, and raw milk cheeses, irradiation opponents note European consumer concerns about this technology, and question the "technological need" for this form of pathogen control (European Commission 2002). Current European Commission proposals for a list of products that may be irradiated have drawn criticism from the United States because the list includes only a few minor products such as frog legs, peeled shrimp, herbs, spices, and seasonings (WTO 1998b, Roberts and Unnevehr 2002).

introduced heat treatment requirements, but others had found that the grounds for introducing such requirements were insufficient.

Although governments feel they are on firm ground when they announce strict health standards on imported foods such as poultry,[9] they must avoid discriminatory application of these standards, either among countries or among related products. The motivations for such standards may on occasion include protection of domestic producers, but as long as standards are consistent and based on scientific evidence, they are allowed under the SPS agreement. Such trade conflicts can persist for some years; exporting firms have incentives to maintain pressure on their governments to try to change the policies of importing countries. But of these cases, the only ones that have moved to informal dispute settlement have been those in which the scientific evidence is clearly absent or being misused, and those in which the main driver of the regulation in question is not the regulation of human health but the management of imports for domestic reasons.

As noted, exporters do from time to time accuse importers of discriminating against imports through the operation of food safety SPS standards. Additional instances further illustrate the issues involved. For example, in June 1998 Switzerland reported that New Zealand and Australia had, without advance notice, halted imports of hard cheeses made from unpasteurized milk on the grounds that the imports did not meet the sanitary requirements. Australia and New Zealand responded that the import standard was intended to ensure the inactivation of pathogenic organisms, particularly E. coli. They explained that the measure had been in place before January 1, 1995, and therefore not been "notified" to the SPS Committee. Compliance was now being reinforced. The Australia New Zealand Food Authority (ANZFA) had apparently conducted a risk assessment and briefed Swiss officials on the result. In November 2000 Switzerland reported that a mutually satisfactory solution had been found. Swiss hard cheese would be allowed into Australia because the treatment of the cheese in Switzerland before export was deemed to be equivalent to the pasteurization process required by the ANZFA rules.

In a parallel incident, the European Union and Australia did not find such a convenient solution. In 1994 Australia had changed its regulations in a way that effectively banned imports of Roquefort cheese. In November 1998 the European Union asked Australia to identify the inter-

9. A high-profile dispute arose in the mid-1990s between the United States and Russia (which was not a WTO member, and therefore was not subject to the disciplines of the SPS agreement) over the Russian ban on imports of US poultry. The dispute involved not only Salmonella levels but also the antibiotics used in feeding. This dispute erupted again in 2002. Suspicion that this ban was in some way connected to the US increase in the tariff on Russian steel is a reminder of the benefits of eventual Russian WTO membership, as that should discourage the retaliatory use of SPS barriers.

national standard on which its import ban on Roquefort cheese was based, or to provide scientific justification and a risk assessment. Australia pointed out that its food standards required all cheese to be made from pasteurized milk or "milk that had undergone an equivalent process." Australia's risk assessment on Roquefort cheese had identified potential problems with pathogenic microorganisms, in particular enterohemorrhagic *E. coli*. In addition to food safety assessments, Roquefort cheese was being evaluated for its risk to animal health.

It is tempting to see in these two cases some reflection of the trade relations between the parties involved. After all, agricultural trade between the European Union (and France in particular) and both Australia and New Zealand is contentious, especially in the dairy market. The European Union is widely blamed in Australia and New Zealand for depressing world dairy prices by means of export subsidies. Thus, there must be little enthusiasm in Canberra or Wellington for easing the way for French cheeses to enter the domestic markets. Moreover, because specific cheeses have a high profile, and their trade is profitable for particular regions of the exporting country, they often singled out for retaliatory duties: exports of Roquefort were targeted by the United States in its retaliation against the European Union's refusal to remove the ban on hormone-treated beef. Nonetheless, the sovereignty rights under the WTO confer a "presumption of innocence" and make it difficult to show that any such considerations are at work if there is adequate scientific evidence to substantiate a risk.

Mycotoxin Standards as a Trade Barrier

Mycotoxins are naturally occurring toxic substances produced by fungi that infest certain food crops. Allowing such infested plant material into the food chain poses a risk to the health of the consumer. The most prevalent of the mycotoxins is aflatoxin, found in cereals, nuts, vegetables, and fruits. The aflatoxins most harmful to humans (B1, B2, G1, and G2) are found in corn and corn products, peanuts (groundnuts) and peanut products, cottonseed, milk, and tree nuts (including Brazil nuts, pecans, pistachio nuts, and walnuts).[10]

The toxic properties of aflatoxins were discovered only in the 1960s, mainly through their effects on animal and plant health. In 1997 the Joint FAO/WHO Expert Committee on Food Additives (JECFA) concluded that "aflatoxins should be treated as carcinogenic food contaminants, the intake of which should be reduced to levels as low as reasonably achievable" (Otsuki, Wilson, and Sewadeh 2001, 267). But the JECFA also illustrated the dilemma in determining what level was "reasonably achievable"

---

10. A detailed account is given in Otsuki, Wilson, and Sewadeh (2001). The information presented here on aflatoxin is from UNDP-FAO (1998) and USFDA (2000).

when it concluded that the difference between two hypothetical standards, 10 parts per billion (ppb) and 20 ppb, could translate into saving annually two persons out of a billion from death by cancer caused by exposure to aflatoxins. Thus the stricter standard could be achieved, but it might not be reasonable if the cost of achieving it was excessive.

The main trade-related aflatoxin controversy has centered on the strict health standards imposed by the European Union. These standards have posed challenges for many countries that supply the EU market. The EU regulations replaced a variety of standards that were in use in the individual member states.[11] For aflatoxin B1 in groundnuts, the tolerances ranged from 1 ppb in France and Denmark to 25 ppb in Portugal (Otsuki, Wilson, and Sewadeh 2001). The initial EU regulation in 1997 set the total aflatoxin standard at 10 ppb for groundnuts destined for further processing and 4 ppb for groundnuts destined for direct consumption. This regulation was amended in 1998 to include a somewhat less restrictive standard of 15 ppb for processing groundnuts and a specific standard for aflatoxin B1 of 8 ppb for processing groundnuts and 2 ppb for those destined for direct consumption.

In March 1998, while the regulation was in draft form, some WTO members argued that the EU proposal would impose severe restrictions on trade while not significantly reducing the health risk to consumers.[12] These countries claimed that the EU proposal did not seem to be based on a proper risk assessment. An international standard on the subject did not exist at that time. The Codex Committee on Food Additives and Contaminants (CCFAC) was considering the matter, but the European Union had made it clear that it did not support the norm that the Codex Alimentarius Commission was considering. According to the European Union, the proposed measure for aflatoxins reflected its desired level of protection, as allowed by the SPS agreement. It was enacted with minor modifications, and came into force on January 1, 1999.[13]

---

11. This example of the EU standards raises two significant points. First, many of the EU standards challenged are those that resulted from the harmonization of such standards in the European Union's single market. In many cases, the EU standards were stricter than those previously in use in some member state markets. It was inevitable that some exporters would face stricter standards as a result of harmonization. Second, the European Commission in effect has faced the same dilemma as the multilateral trade system: how to maintain support for standards without distorting trade patterns by overprotection. The Commission is generally more favorable to risk-based regulatory systems with scientific credibility than to the systems that are favored by member states that wish to maintain some (political) control.

12. These countries were Argentina, Australia, Bolivia, Brazil, The Gambia, India, Indonesia, Malaysia, Philippines, Senegal, and Thailand, and they were supported by Canada, Colombia, Mexico, Pakistan, Paraguay, Peru, the Philippines, South Africa, Turkey, the United States, and Uruguay.

13. An additional problem surrounded the proposed sampling procedure for aflatoxin, which exporting countries regarded as "unduly costly, burdensome and unjust." The

Two particular trade problems illustrate the range of issues involved in the EU measure. In September 1998 Bolivia informed the SPS Committee that the proposed EU measure severely affect its exports of Brazil nuts. Bolivia then entered into bilateral discussions with the European Union to find a mutually agreeable solution. In November 1998 the SPS Committee chairman reported that because of the discussions, Bolivia now better understood the rationale behind the EU measures and subsequent procedures and the European Union understood the effect that some of its measures could have on the Bolivian industry. In March 1999 Bolivia suggested that the European Union apply to Bolivia the WTO principle of special and differential treatment in favor of a low-income country. In doing so, Bolivia outlined the socioeconomic and ecological implications of the European Union's measure for Bolivia's Brazil nut production and on the national economy. The European Union countered that the problems in Bolivia stemmed from production chain and equipment problems—improvements were needed.[14]

A recent World Bank study has estimated the effect of the EU aflatoxin regulations on exports of nuts (groundnuts and groundnut products) and cereals (corn and corn products) from African countries (Otsuki, Wilson, and Sewadeh 2001). The authors found that because of the stricter aflatoxin regulations in the European Union (relative to the proposed Codex standards), the African countries would lose $380 million in exports, or 76 percent of the value, of cereals and cereal products and $287 million in exports, or 53 percent of potential trade, of edible nuts. Thus the total export effect was estimated at $670 million a year. Although Europe would be at a slightly higher risk from increased exposure to aflatoxins, the additional export earnings from a less strict aflatoxin standard would likely generate enough income in Africa to support health improvement with a greater reduction in mortality.

The controversy over aflatoxins illustrates an important aspect of food safety standards. Developed countries' tendency to tighten up health requirements clearly is a problem for developing countries that have actual or potential export interests in agricultural and food goods. Such problems can be aired in the SPS Committee, but developed countries are unlikely to relax the regulation in question, because regulators and politicians in those countries have little room to maneuver in doing so. Where regulations contravene WTO rules, such as by discriminating among

---

European Union argued that because contamination appeared in a small percentage of kernels, a simple sample was not sufficient to minimize risk to consumers. The directive on sampling went into effect on April 5, 2002.

14. Subsequently a project to improve production and storage processes and the livelihood of nut collectors was included in the EU aid program slated for execution in 2002; the European Union also proposed a certification procedure for Bolivian exports.

suppliers or artificially restricting imports in favor of domestic production, the dispute settlement process is at hand to provide remedy. But such action is costly and not always successful. In cases such as the presence of aflatoxins in nuts and cereals, the main hope is to secure assistance from the European Union and others in meeting the high standards set by the importing countries.

The Health Effects of Yield-Enhancing Inputs

More controversial than the prevalence of food-borne bacterial agents or mycotoxins in food are concerns about modern agricultural technologies and their possible detrimental side effects on human health. One prominent example of these health issues is the widespread use of hormones to increase growth rates in cattle or yields in milking cows. The European Union's ban since 1988 on imports of beef raised with the aid of hormones (to match the domestic ban on the use of such hormones) has already posed a major challenge for the multilateral trade system. Hormones are used widely in the production of beef in the United States and Canada, and these countries therefore challenged the legitimacy of the ban under the WTO.

Waiting in the wings is probably another major trade dispute in this area, over the use of antibiotics as growth promoters in poultry rations. Some countries worry that bacterial resistance to such antibiotics could eventually lead to resistance to medical treatments of human bacterial infection. The issue in both the hormones and the antibiotic cases is essentially the same. Countries disagree about which growth promoters should be administered to animals and what impact the consumption of products from those animals has on human health. All these growth promoters are used legally in some producing countries, and the authorities in those countries are convinced of their safety. When they see markets closed to them, exporters in these countries pressure their governments to make the importing countries toe the line.

Sometimes trade conflicts revolve around pesticide residues, though these tend to be less intractable. In 1998 Côte d'Ivoire expressed concern in the WTO SPS Committee about new EU maximum residue levels (MRLs) for pesticides in fruits and vegetables, which would affect Côte d'Ivoire's exports of pineapples, mangoes, papayas, cashew nuts, passion fruits, and green beans, and in turn its small farmers. Côte d'Ivoire found the MRLs (e.g., for ethephon) inconsistent, or lacking basis in a pertinent risk assessment. The European Union had offered technical assistance for pineapple production, but the changes had not been put into effect before the entry into force of the EU directive. Accordingly, Côte d'Ivoire requested a waiver from the EU directive pending the outcome of the planned technical assistance.

The potential significance of such regulations is examined in a 2002 World Bank study that relied on a model similar to that used to estimate the trade impact of tighter aflatoxin standards in the European Union. In the study, John Wilson and Tsunehiro Otsuki (2002) look closely at the impact of tighter-than-existing standards governing the use of the pesticide chlorpyrifos, an organophosphate used widely in banana production throughout the developing world. The European Union, by adopting stricter standards, could cause developing countries to lose an estimated $1.8 billion in banana exports.

The Hormones Dispute

Dwarfing all these other trade disputes in drawing attention has been the beef hormones case. The amount of trade originally involved was only about $100 million, a small fraction of the billions of dollars of trade that flow across the Atlantic in each direction. Nonetheless, the conflict over hormone-treated beef has had a major impact on trade relations far beyond the confines of the beef sector (Josling, Roberts, and Hassan 1999). Along with the more recent conflict over genetically modified food described in chapter 7, it has taken on a symbolic role that has greatly complicated the search for a solution.

Hormones have been used in livestock production worldwide for five decades. Naturally occurring hormones in both cattle and humans can be added to feed or otherwise applied to increase the rate of animal growth (growth promotion purposes), to synchronize the estrus cycles of dairy cattle to lower production costs (zootechnical purposes), or to correct certain endocrine dysfunctions (therapeutic purposes). "Synthetic" hormones, which mimic the action of natural hormones, are used only to promote growth.

The events leading up to the 1988 EU ban on the domestic use of hormones in cattle raising and on imports of hormone-treated beef are important in explaining the political longevity of this US-EU dispute.[15] Trade concerns were not dominant in the early years, and the disciplines applied by trade rules were, in any event, weak. European livestock producers were searching for ways to stimulate growth in cattle, and so took eagerly to the use of hormones. Sometimes, however, they did not know enough about the consequences of misusing such chemicals. At times, regulatory control slipped between the cracks as coordination and harmonization of national regulations progressed haltingly in the European Union.

---

15. Unless otherwise noted, the material in this section is drawn from WTO (1997b) and Josling, Roberts, and Hussan (1999).

European authorities first proposed a hormones ban in response to the public anxieties that emerged after highly publicized reports of "hormone scandals" in the late 1970s. In the first incident, reported in 1977, some schoolchildren in northern Italy exhibited signs of premature hormonal development that investigators initially suspected was linked to illegal growth hormones in veal or poultry served in school lunches. Although an exhaustive examination of possible causes of the abnormalities produced no concrete conclusions, a public furor arose over the use of hormones in livestock production (Kramer 1989). The second incident occurred three years later, again in Italy, when numerous samples of veal-based baby food were found to contain residues of the illegal hormonal drug diethylstilbestrol (DES), further alarming European consumers.[16] Consumer organizations called for a boycott of veal, which had a significant adverse effect on the market—and, incidentally, on the administration of the European Union's Common Agricultural Policy (CAP), which at that time was supporting veal as well as beef prices.

Before the school lunch and baby food incidents in Italy, the use of natural and synthetic hormones had been regulated in Europe by a patchwork of national animal drug regulations and practices. Belgium, Denmark, Germany, Italy, and the Netherlands either banned or severely restricted the use of hormones, and the United Kingdom, France, Ireland, and Luxembourg authorized different hormones under different regulatory protocols. The events in Italy and the ensuing veal boycott created a climate in which European consumers became increasingly wary of modern animal production technology in general, and suspicious of the use of hormones in particular. The immediate legacy of these events was a European Community (EC) ban on the use of hormones for growth promotion in cattle.

The EC Council of (Agriculture) Ministers gave a boost to supranational efforts to craft a new, European-wide regulatory regime for hormones by adopting a declaration in September 1980 that favored a ban on the use of one of the more widely used hormones and supported harmonized legislation on veterinary medicines and animal rearing. The next month, the European Commission advocated a more stringent regime, proposing a ban on the use of *all* hormones in livestock production unless administered for therapeutic purposes. Three months later, the commission revised its initial proposal to allow the use of three natural hormones for zootechnical as well as therapeutic purposes under advised conditions. The European Parliament approved the commission's

---

16. DES is a synthetic estrogen that had been used widely since the late 1930s for both human and animal health purposes until epidemiological evidence linked the use of DES by pregnant women to the development of cervical cancer in their daughters. Medical and livestock uses of DES were eventually banned both in the United States (in 1979) and in Europe (in 1981).

proposals, following adoption of the "Nielson Report" in February 1981, and the EC Economic and Social Committee endorsed the proposals shortly thereafter.[17] However, three of the member states (Belgium, Ireland, and the United Kingdom) advocated retaining use of both natural and synthetic hormones as growth-promoting agents in livestock production. This position was supported by the major non-European beef producers, including Argentina, Australia, Canada, New Zealand, South Africa, and the United States, which feared exclusion from the European market.

To review the safety of hormones, the commission set up a Working Group on Anabolic Agents in Animal Production, made up of 22 European scientists. In 1982 the group released the interim "Lamming Report," which concluded that the three natural hormones (estradiol-17β, testosterone, and progesterone) would not present any harmful health effects when used under appropriate conditions to fatten animals, but that additional data on the two synthetic hormones (trenbolone acetate and zeranol) were needed before an opinion could be given. Three European Commission regulatory committees reviewed the Lamming Report and concurred with its findings.[18] As a result, in 1984 the commission proposed amending the 1981 directive to reflect the Lamming Committee's recommendations.

Before the commission acted, the Lamming Committee report was preempted by the actions of the European Parliament. Following the lead of the EC Economic and Social Committee, it adopted a resolution on October 11, 1985, calling for a complete ban on hormones for growth promotion.[19] The resolution stated that scientific information about hormones was "far from complete and that considerable doubt therefore exists about the desirability of their use and of their effect on human health." However, food safety was not the only justification offered for the proposed ban: the potential impacts of hormone technology on the cost of the European Communities' CAP were also noted. Specifically, the resolution cited "overproduction of meat and meat products in the European Communities which adds considerably to the cost of the CAP" as a rationale for the proposed ban. In deference to this opposition, the commission amended its draft regulation to reflect the European Parliament's sentiments and submitted it to the EC Council on December 19, 1985. The

---

17. At that time it was necessary only to seek an opinion from the Parliament and the EC Economic and Social Committee. Neither had a significant role in decision making. The Commission proposed legislation and the Council (of Ministers) took action. Directives are agreed-on frameworks that must be implemented by national law, whereas regulations have the force of law in all member states.

18. The three bodies were the Scientific Veterinary Committee, the Scientific Committee for Animal Nutrition, and the Scientific Committee for Food.

19. In June 1984 the EC Economic and Social Committee had given a negative opinion of COM(84) 295.

Council adopted it as Directive 85/649/EEC, which banned the use of all hormones as growth promotants in cattle, established a more detailed regulatory regime for the authorized use of the three natural hormones for therapeutic and zootechnical purposes, and banned the use of synthetic hormones altogether.[20] The measures, which came into force on January 1, 1989, applied to both imported and domestic products, to the dismay of the United States and other exporters.

The GATT and WTO Challenges

The United States first took the issue of the EC hormones ban to the GATT in March 1987, alleging that there was no legitimate basis for the ban under the Tokyo Round Standards Code. When bilateral consultations between the European Communities and the United States failed to resolve the matter, the United States requested that a technical expert group be convened pursuant to Article 14.5 of the Standards Code to examine the issue of scientific support for the EC's measure. Under the GATT rules, the European Communities blocked formation of the group, arguing that its ban was related to a process and production method (PPM) that was not covered. As noted in chapter 3, the European Communities argued that its sole obligation under the Standards Code was to abstain from the *intentional* circumvention of the disciplines by formulating its measures as PPMs rather than product standards.

Later in 1987 the Codex JECFA returned an opinion on the use of natural and synthetic hormones, concluding that it could establish maximum residue levels for the two synthetic hormones it was assigned to review. This committee also judged that MRLs were not needed for the three natural hormones if they were used as directed, including for growth-stimulating purposes. This opinion, which was adopted by a very close vote, has been considered highly controversial in the Codex.

As the dispute escalated, both sides publicly considered trade restrictions against the other.[21] When the ban went into effect, the United States retaliated with 100 percent ad valorem duties on a range of products

20. Directive 85/649/EEC was subsequently challenged in the European Court of Justice, and in 1988 it was annulled by the court on procedural grounds. The measures originally proposed in 1985 were reintroduced by the European Commission and re-adopted by the EC Council in March 1988 as Directives 88/146/EEC (the general prohibition on the use of hormones) and 88/299/EEC (which provides for the exceptions to 88/146/EEC, authorizing the use of the three natural hormones and their derivatives for therapeutic and zootechnical purposes). This time, the Court of Justice upheld the directive.

21. For example, in 1988 the US Food Safety and Inspection Service began to request certification from EC authorities that meat produced in EC countries met US safety requirements for hormone residues and that conformity assessment procedures were equivalent to US standards. The EC responded with the announcement of a counterretaliation valued at $360 million (but never implemented) that targeted products such as California walnuts (Kramer 1989).

imported from Europe. The European Communities requested a panel to examine the legitimacy of the retaliation, but this request was blocked by the United States. Later in 1989 a joint US-EC task force agreed to a limited compromise that allowed imports of some US beef products that were certified to be "hormone-free" (the ban had applied to all US beef, because hormones are used widely in the US cattle sector) as well as other beef products destined for pet food.[22] The United States, in response, withdrew some products from its retaliation list.

Further compromise, however, was precluded by the increasing polarization of domestic political forces on both sides of the Atlantic. The US beef industry was convinced that the ban was a protectionist device aimed at restricting trade. The US government worried that in addition to the technical criteria of effectiveness, safety, and reliability, a "fourth criterion"—the economic and social impact of the adoption of a particular technology—was being endorsed by the European Union (as the European Community was known after 1992) in its standard for veterinary and other substances, and would become established as an excuse for protecting other agricultural markets.[23] European producers were determined that US beef would not escape the hormones ban, and the European Parliament appeared desirous of hanging onto a popular cause even at the expense of some embarrassment for the European Commission.

The legal stalemate and ensuing exchange of tit-for-tat measures were widely viewed as one of the more visible failures of the GATT dispute settlement mechanisms. Indeed, the hormones dispute, more than any other case, motivated negotiation of stronger disciplines on technical regulations in the GATT Uruguay Round. Yet even knowing that the hormones

---

22. The United States and other countries that allow the use of hormones also regulate them through product and process standards in the livestock sector. The United States regulates hormone use through controls on the manufacturing of the hormone ear clips (a product standard) and on withdrawal periods before slaughter (a process standard). Conformity assessment can be conducted by testing for the synthetic hormones and by inspection and monitoring for the natural hormones. Testing, inspection, and monitoring requirements are limited by the fact that there is little incentive for cheating (the additional weight gain from using additional clips does not offset the clip and feed costs). Today, the incentives for cheating are greater for producing "hormone-free" beef for export to the European Union. The USDA has been required to step up its conformity assessment program so that the United States can retain access to the European Union for hormone-free beef.

23. While the beef hormone case was winding its way through the GATT dispute settlement process, another growth promotion agent was coming on the market. Recombinant bovine somatotropin (rbST), introduced for use in dairy cattle, promised considerable increases in milk yields. Objections to the use of rbST centered on its structural and economic aspects, although some safety issues were also raised. Because of such controversies, the Codex did not adopt an international rbST standard (see chapter 3). The major supplier of the hormone, Monsanto, later became embroiled in the controversy over genetically modified foods (see chapter 7). Products from rbST-treated cattle are allowed into both the European Union and Canada, even though domestic use is prohibited. In each case, imports are kept to a low level by other trade restrictions, limiting any public concern about such imports.

issue was going to reemerge under these stronger rules, the European Union did not thwart the adoption of the SPS agreement.

After new Uruguay Round rules for SPS measures and dispute settlement procedures were in place, the United States renewed its complaint against the beef import ban. In January 1996 the United States requested formal consultations with the European Union, which were joined by Australia, Canada, and New Zealand. The United States charged that the EU ban violated not only the basic GATT provisions but the TBT and SPS agreements as well. The central claim was that the ban was not based on science. The European Commission responded that the ban was the only feasible option for meeting its very high public health goals. The parties met in March 1996, but were unable to find a mutually satisfactory solution. The next month, the United States asked that the WTO establish a panel to hear the dispute. The European Union countered by requesting a panel to review the legitimacy of the US retaliatory tariffs, whereupon the United States unilaterally rescinded them in July 1996. The first meeting of the panel to hear the complaint by the United States (later joined by Canada) against the EU hormones ban was set for October 1996. As long anticipated, the hormones dispute became a key test of the new disciplines in the SPS agreement.

In its report issued on August 18, 1997, the WTO dispute settlement panel concurred with the complainants that the EU ban on beef treated with hormones for growth promotion purposes was inconsistent with its obligations under the SPS agreement (the outcome of this case was also reviewed briefly in chapter 3). In support of these findings, the panel noted that the scientific evidence cited by the European Commission as informing its regulatory decision fell into two categories. In the first category were those studies that had specifically evaluated the potential toxic effects of hormones used to promote growth in cattle. Those studies had concurred that, at present, there was no indication that these substances posed public health risks when used properly. Into the second category fell other research that, the European Union argued, raised serious questions about the methodology or conclusions of the first group of studies. This research examined the carcinogenic or genotoxic potential of entire *categories* of hormones or the hormones at issue *in general.* As such, the panel stated, these latter studies did not qualify as a risk assessment—in this case, an evaluation of the consequences of consuming beef from cattle treated with growth hormones—as defined in the SPS agreement.[24]

It was anticipated that whatever the outcome, the Appellate Body would be asked to review the panel's decision. And, indeed, all three

---

24. Moreover, the panel noted, the scientific experts whom it had consulted during its proceedings (under the terms of Article 13 of the Dispute Settlement Understanding, or DSU) had concurred that this evidence did not invalidate or contradict the scientific conclusions of the first group of studies.

parties to the dispute requested a review of both the procedural and substantive findings in the panel's report. The Appellate Body released its report in January 1998, ruling on 14 issues. It overruled the panel on several points, but concurred with the panel that the European Commission measure was not in conformity with all of the SPS agreement disciplines (see table 3.3).[25]

After the appeal, the commission said it needed four more years to conduct additional risk assessments before policy changes could be considered. The United States and Canada countered that such action did not constitute compliance, so the matter went to arbitration in Geneva. The arbitrator concluded that 15 months was a reasonable time to comply.[26] The arbitrator also noted that requests for additional time to conduct new studies or consult experts to demonstrate consistency of a measure were not consistent with the requirement for prompt compliance.

The European Commission then announced that it would proceed with scientific studies regardless of the arbitrator's decision. In the interim, the United States and Canada discussed potential compensation schemes or trade concessions that the European Union could offer beef producers to compensate for loss of market access due to the hormones ban. Labeling was discussed as well. The United States agreed that it could label hormone-treated beef as "a product of the USA." It could not agree to a label that would indicate that the level of hormones in the beef was higher than that in a comparable product from the European Union. US negotiators argued that it was unclear that the level would be higher and such a label would be potentially misleading to consumers.[27]

---

25. The Appellate Body held that the statement in the SPS agreement declaring that a measure shall be *based on* an international standard where one exists (except as otherwise provided for in the agreement) does not imply that measures need to *conform to* international standards. If this were so, contended the judges, the SPS agreement would vest international standards (that is, recommendations under the terms of the Codex) with *obligatory* force and effect. To sustain such an assumption, the Appellate Body argued, language far more specific and compelling than that found in Article 3 of the SPS agreement would be needed.

26. The arbitrator who established a May 1999 deadline for compliance had noted, "It would not be in keeping with the requirement of *prompt* compliance to include in the reasonable period of time, time to conduct studies or to consult experts to demonstrate the *consistency* of a measure already judged to be inconsistent." See WTO (1998a).

27. A range of alternative policy instruments, of different degrees of trade restrictiveness, is potentially available to facilitate compliance with the hormone ruling. These include imposing product standards (e.g., residue levels), process standards (e.g., administration of growth hormones by veterinarians), or information remedies (e.g., labeling). Whatever the option chosen, there must be (in the words of the Appellate Body) a "rational relationship" between the measure and the risks it mitigates, and scientific evidence must support this claim. At the conclusion of their report, the original panelists had suggested that a voluntary labeling regime might constitute an acceptable resolution to the hormone dispute. It would provide consumers with information on hormone use that would allow free choice in the marketplace.

Because no compensation scheme was in place, the WTO offered the United States and Canada retaliation in the form of increased tariffs on EU exports totaling about $128 million. In the meantime, the European Commission proceeded with its scientific evaluation of the six hormones through the Scientific Committee on Veterinary Measures for Public Health. The committee opined that it could establish no acceptable daily intake for the hormones. On the basis of this opinion, the European Commission proposed a permanent ban on estradiol and a provisional ban on the other five hormones until another committee could review the evidence again to determine if these five hormones might be used safely for therapeutic and technical purposes. The matter was then put before the European Council, but the Council has taken no action to date.

The effect that the legal resolution of this landmark dispute will have on regulation of hormone use and other food safety cases remains uncertain. But it has defined the scope of the SPS agreement and made more public the dilemma that regulators face in balancing consumer safety based on science with consumer sentiment based on perception. The beef hormones case has dramatically demonstrated the limits of the Dispute Settlement Understanding in imposing politically unacceptable solutions on powerful countries. It has also shown that not all legally sanctioned results of SPS dispute settlement cases yield desirable trade outcomes.

This landmark case has then, for the moment at least, resulted in less rather than more international trade. Trade sanctions are by far the least preferable of the possible outcomes of the WTO dispute settlement process. But the granting of authorized retaliation under the rule of law may still be superior to undisciplined, unilateral tit-for-tat measures, such as those between the United States and European Communities in the 1980s, which can be described as the equivalent of "vigilante justice" in trade. Sanctions are tolerated by the European Union because they are small in cost and diffuse in impact. Short of a change of heart by the US beef industry, which might eventually accept compensating market access for additional hormone-free beef into the European Union, it is not easy to see a resolution to this conflict.

Drug Residues and Antibiotics in Livestock Products

The use of veterinary medicines in food animals was regulated only sporadically until 1990, when the pace of regulatory activity picked up and several countries passed new regulations on drug residue tolerances. Regulation of veterinary antibiotics still varies widely from country to country. Sweden is the only country that has completely banned the use of antibiotics for growth promotion, presumably imposing additional costs on their livestock producers but possibly gaining in domestic market acceptance of meat products. Argentina, Brazil, and the United States do not have national legislation dedicated solely to regulation of the use of antibiotics in food production, although the issue is addressed in general food safety legislation.

Since the entry into force of the SPS and TBT agreements, domestic regulation has been strongly influenced by conformity with international standards such as the Codex MRLs for Residues of Pesticides and Veterinary Drugs in Foods.[28] The Codex Alimentarius Commission has established MRLs for 54 drugs that have been categorized as "acceptable" for use in food animals. It also has established limits for 289 veterinary drugs in the context of "acceptable Good Veterinary Practices in animal husbandry." Adherence can take two forms: "Full Acceptance" and "Free Distribution." Full Acceptance requires compliance in both imports and domestic production; noncomplying products are prohibited. Free Distribution requires Codex compliance for all imported foods, but in contrast to Full Acceptance, domestic production of the food is governed by (different) domestic standards. Though this leads to potentially different treatment of domestic and imported products, in practice it amounts to a kind of "mutual recognition" of the Codex standard even when not fully adopted in the domestic regulations.

The European Union has developed perhaps the most extensive regulations to govern antibiotic use, and four such products were recently banned altogether in animal feed. Council Directive 70/524/EEC, passed in 1970, required that the use of veterinary drugs in animal feed be limited to levels that do not have a negative effect on human health. The European Union passed three additional regulations in the 1990s. Council Directive 96/23/EC regulates the monitoring of residues in animals and animal products. Commission Directive 97/6/EC requires resistance monitoring for feed additive antibiotics and related substances in animal bacteria. And Council Regulation 2821/98 bans the use of the antibiotics bacitracin zinc, virginiamycin, tylosin phosphate, and spiramycin. This regulation continued the trend that began with the banning of avoparcin

---

28. The limits on acceptable amounts of veterinary drugs in animals for food can be defined in two ways. The first is the level of residues of veterinary drugs that have been used in accordance with good veterinary practices allowed by the Codex standards, known as the Acceptable Daily Intake (ADI). These are currently based on toxicological evaluations of veterinary drugs. However, future criteria for ADIs may include antimicrobial activity for veterinary drugs that have a potential impact on human health (FAO 2001). The second way of specifying allowable amounts of drugs in foodstuffs is MRLs. These identify the levels of veterinary drugs that may be found in tissues and are usually achievable within a reasonable period after application of the drug. Evaluation of MRLs also requires estimation of the potential intake of residues based on standard assumptions about individual consumption of meat and dairy products. Both standards are based on the recommendations of JECFA. The JECFA recommendations are also available as a basis for national and regional regulation of animal antibiotics. Final definitions of ADIs and MRLs are made by the Codex Committee on Residues of Veterinary Drugs in Foods (CCRVDF).

in 1997 and ardacin in 1998. At present, no types of veterinary medicine are allowed to be used as growth-promoting agents in the European Union.

In the United States, only one hormone has been approved for poultry use (on roasting chickens), but no hormones are presently being used. Antibiotics, however, are widely used both to prevent poultry disease and to increase feed efficiency (FSIS 1995). A recent report by the US General Accounting Office (GAO) examined the implications for human health of the use of antibiotics in agriculture (GAO 1999). It found that resistant strains of three diseases, *Salmonella, E. coli,* and *Campylobacter,* are linked to the use of antibiotics in animals. The resistance develops while the microorganism is in the animal, and the resistant strain of the pathogen is then transmitted to humans through food or by contact. In addition, the effectiveness of the antibiotics when used in humans may be reduced by continual ingestion of low levels over a period of time. It is likely that the US agencies that regulate antibiotics will come under pressure to limit the use of those drugs that are also used for human treatments.[29] Indeed, one public policy group, the Center for Science in the Public Interest, has already called on the Food and Drug Administration's Center for Veterinary Medicine to institute such a ban, and this body responded by setting up a program to monitor the diminished susceptibility of enteric bacteria to antimicrobial drugs.

Since 1990, there also has been rapid growth in the regulation of animal antibiotics in other industrial countries.[30] Canada passed the Health of Animals Act in 1990, and Australia enacted the Agricultural and Veterinary Chemicals Act (Agvet Code) in 1994. Since 1994, New Zealand has passed 10 regulations for antibiotics, 3 of which were adopted in 2001.

So far, few trade conflicts have arisen over the regulations on antibiotic use. One that did come before the SPS Committee involved not so much the use of antibiotics but the difference between regulations on imports entering under different market access regimes. The case illustrates rather explicitly the substitutability between technical regulations and other trade barriers. In September 1998 the United States, supported by Australia, Brazil, Canada, Chile, Hungary, India, Israel, and New Zealand, expressed concern that Swiss regulations on meat from animals treated

---

29. The US FDA approves antibiotics for use in animals and allowable residues in food. Testing for antibiotic levels in food is the responsibility of the FSIS for meat, including poultry, and of the FDA for eggs. Monitoring resistance to antibiotics in humans is the joint task of USDA, FDA, and the Department of Health and Human Services.

30. Australia, Canada, Japan, and New Zealand had passed relevant laws even before 1990. In 1967 New Zealand passed the New Zealand Animal Remedies Act. Japan restricted the use of antibiotics as growth promoters in animals in 1976. In 1981 Australia adopted standard requirements for veterinary product registration, and Canada passed the Feeds Act in 1985.

with hormones, antibiotics, and similar products and imported under the low-duty Swiss tariff rate quota (TRQ) established under the Uruguay Round Agreement on Agriculture were not based on science or risk assessment. Different requirements were applied to meat imported outside the TRQ, calling into question the validity of the alleged public health objective behind the regulation. The United States maintained that the measure would prohibit imports under the TRQ of eggs and egg products from birds raised in battery cages. Such imports would be more easily permitted outside the TRQ under labeling and additional certification requirements, but would be subject to prohibitively high duties. The United States claimed that discrimination between products imported under the TRQ and outside the TRQ was unjustified.

It is not clear under what conditions domestic regulations on antibiotic use are notifiable under the SPS agreement. The United States has pointed to the failure of the European Union to "notify" the ban adopted in December 1998 on four antibiotics used in animal feed to enhance production. Canada and Australia shared the US concern, and Canada asked to be informed when the European Union reviewed its measure, which it understood to be provisional. The European Union replied that the measure had not been notified because it did not contain any provision applicable to imports and therefore had no effect on trade.

Managing Trade-Related Food Safety Issues

Food safety and health hazards arise from natural pathogens and, at times, from the adoption of modern agricultural technologies. For natural pathogens, attempts to harmonize regulations in the food safety area will always be hindered by the differences among countries in the degree of risk associated with the threat of food contaminants and the differences in willingness to absorb that risk. Individual regulatory authorities have established national standards based on the conditions in their countries and the advice from their scientists. There are therefore significant variations among such regulations and their levels of enforcement. When trade conflicts arise from the discriminatory application of standards to imported and domestic goods, would-be exporters often believe that domestic producers have unduly influenced regulatory enforcement policies.

Trade conflicts also arise from the differences in the standards even when enforced uniformly by authorities in the importing country. Such problems are likely to be magnified by the relative lack of capacity in developing countries to meet testing and certification standards for export markets, a problem that is exacerbated when regulators rely increasingly on process standards to ensure food safety. A public good element in the control of food-borne pathogens—at a minimum, avoidance of unwarranted market collapses from food safety scares—suggests the scope for multilateral coordination and technical assistance in this area. It is also important to weigh the costs imposed abroad as well as domestically against the gains anticipated from regulatory decisions, as the aflatoxin case vividly illustrates. Even when these costs are taken into account, standards, and the ability to enforce them, generally will remain different among countries. This finding suggests that development of specific export-oriented subsectors will be an efficient strategy within some countries. Exporters will have to bear the additional costs of revising production methods and testing for pathogens in foods to retain or gain access to foreign markets, but there can be economic incentives to do so.

The issues arising from the possible health impacts of growth- or yield-enhancing inputs are more complex. The technology is unevenly distributed among countries, and it is not universally accepted. There is always the danger that restrictions on the use of productivity-enhancing inputs (or at least the importation of the resulting products) is inspired by domestic producers anxious to avoid competition. Nonetheless, the political economy becomes more convoluted when differences in consumer preferences among countries are also involved in regulatory decisions. This involvement complicates the resolution of these trade disputes, and trade conflicts such as the beef hormones dispute tend to persist, despite the existence of multilateral rules and the efforts of trade diplomats to resolve them.

6

Regulating Quality Through Labeling and Standards

A market's ability to satisfy diverse consumer preferences regarding quality is an important virtue since not all consumers are willing to pay the same price for particular product attributes. Although consumers generally cite sensory (organoleptic) characteristics and price as the most important factors in their food-purchasing decisions, other nutritional, hedonistic, and process attributes have been growing in importance. Firms in wealthy countries have been especially eager to market the health and nutritional features of their products, including claims that products are "high-fiber," "lite," or "heart smart." Market niches for hedonistic attributes (e.g., "pure" for spring water) and process attributes (e.g., "shade-grown" for coffee) have also emerged. Determining which attributes consumers are willing to pay for is not a trivial task; if it were, "big Madison Avenue advertising firms would be neither be big nor located on Madison Avenue" (Golan, Koehler, et al. 2000, 7).

Historically, the role of governments in regulating quality has been primarily limited to policing voluntary claims to prevent consumer deception and to ensure fair trading practices. Governments also have defined and administered standards, in cooperation with the food industry, to transmit quality information from sellers to distant buyers in the agricultural supply chain (Dimitri 2003). Over the past two decades, the role of the public sector in labeling, particularly for industrial products, has increased through the growing number of regulations that require disclosure of risk information (Noah 1994). More recently, governments have intervened in labeling to align individual consumption choices with social objectives (Magat and Viscusi 1992). The first explicit reference to a link between food labeling and a social goal was found in recommendations that led to the 1990 Nutrition Labeling and Education Act, which established mandatory nutritional labeling in the United States (Jessup 2000).

Consumer organizations continue to campaign vigorously for more labeling, making the political claim that consumers have a "right to know" everything their food contains and how it was produced. In some instances, producers also advocate more labeling regulation. Although more labeling is not always good public policy, governments have responded to the increased demand for regulation. The number of recently proposed labeling regulations for food and other agricultural products that have been notified to the WTO under the requirements of the SPS and TBT agreements is disproportionately large compared with the share of these products in domestic output or international trade. Some government initiatives are aimed at helping producers to differentiate their products in the global market; others are in response to a range of concerns raised by consumer and environmental advocates.

Informational remedies, including labeling, can often enhance welfare by addressing a market failure directly and allowing market forces to determine the attributes to be supplied. However, labeling policies and related standards may at times be more a means of excluding foreign competition than of attaining marketing efficiencies. This is true even for some government regulation of voluntary claims. In the absence of such protectionist motives, the costs of labeling to industry, consumers, and taxpayers may still exceed the benefits if relatively few consumers are willing to pay a sufficient premium for the regulated attribute.

Regardless of whether labeling policies improve national welfare, they might be expected to alleviate rather than exacerbate trade frictions because they can serve as a substitute for more trade-restrictive forms of government regulation. Instead, since the end of the Uruguay Round labeling requirements have emerged at the center of a large number of international disagreements.

This chapter examines the rationale for informational remedies in agricultural markets and analyzes the different roles for the market and the state in the provision of information about the definition, content, and location of production under different labeling regimes. It then looks at four labeling policies to ascertain if and how they improve the functioning of global food markets. The analysis indicates that different regulatory approaches to labeling have markedly different effects on trade. These different effects have implications for ongoing WTO attempts to resolve disagreements over labeling policies in various venues.

Private and Public Provision of Information

Firms must solve two information problems when selling to consumers: firms must decide *what* product information to convey and *how* to make the information credible. The private benefits of labeling are determined by the premium that consumers are willing to pay for a product attribute and the number of consumers willing to do so. Possible industry expenditures associated with labeling attributes include the one-off costs for label redesign, inventory disposal, and administrative expenses; production or marketing costs for product reformulation or product reidentification; and conformity assessment costs for testing, inspection, or other means of verifying attributes.

Firms will voluntarily supply information if the revenues likely to result will exceed the costs.[1] But disclosure of an attribute that could reduce consumer purchases, such as the high fat content of a branded food product, is unlikely to be supplied voluntarily by firms.[2] And in the absence of effective reputation mechanisms, which characterizes a large number of unbranded food products, including fresh fish, seafood, meats, and produce, the market may not supply optimal quality. In particular, the market may not supply an optimal amount of products with the experience and credence characteristics that consumers want. Experience characteristics are those that consumers can evaluate only after purchasing the product; credence characteristics are those that consumers cannot ascertain even after use. Consumers' willingness to pay will not adjust to improvements in quality if they do not know, and cannot cheaply ascertain, the experience or credence characteristics of what they buy. Because quality is generally costly to produce, poor-quality products can outcompete high-quality products, and the market equilibrium may entail the production of a suboptimal share of low-quality output—the "lemon" problem, as described by George Akerlof (1970).

When market failures stem from information failures, labeling regulations may be preferred over other fiat measures to redress the inefficiencies that arise. Labeling can transform the experience or credence characteristic of a food product into a search characteristic, which consumers can ascertain before purchasing a product. The purchasing patterns of well-informed consumers would then be sufficient incentive for producers to provide the range of quality that consumers are willing to pay for without further government intervention.[3]

---

1. Thus a supermarket chain might choose to voluntarily label the country of origin for muscle cuts of meat, but not for ground meat, because of the additional costs possibly involved in tracking multiple sources of supply.

2. However, according to the "unfolding theory" of Ippolito and Mathios (1990), reticence on the part of individual firms to disclose information may not result in information failures. They note that competitors with, for example, a low-fat version of the same product would have an incentive to advertise this attribute, thereby allowing consumers to draw the appropriate inferences about foods without this claim.

3. One example of the benefit of an information approach to regulation is the mandatory labeling of unpasteurized fresh juice. Through such labeling, risk-averse consumers can avoid its consumption and the marketplace avoids imposition of a marketwide standard (e.g., required pasteurization) that would restrict choice for those consumers who prefer fresh apple cider over other alternatives.

In recent years, regulatory authorities have given more consideration to adopting information remedies as a means of influencing economic behavior (Caswell and Mojduszka 1996). Besides regulations that require firms to disclose information, governments may wish to provide various labeling services, if lowering the private costs of providing and verifying information corrects information asymmetries or yields wider social benefits such as a lower incidence of diet-related heart disease. Government information services might include establishing public standards which regulate the use of nouns (e.g., *ice cream*) and adjectives (e.g., *fresh*). The public sector might also provide certification, testing, or inspection services. Ex ante provision of such services may later limit the resources needed to detect and prosecute deceptive claims (Caswell and Padberg 1992).

Countries can choose from several alternative labeling regimes that allocate information tasks to different private- and public-sector actors. These alternatives are illustrated in table 6.1 for the regulatory examples discussed in this chapter.

The first column of the table sets out an example of a labeling regime for geographical indications (GIs) for food and beverage products. In this example, the industry develops and adopts standards that make certain products eligible for designation as being from a specific region. The industry is also responsible for private third-party verification services, which includes accreditation and certification in this example. The private sector is primarily responsible as well for enforcing protection of GIs, through the civil courts if necessary, although, as for every voluntary claim, the government is responsible for preventing consumer deception through the criminal justice system. Other examples of information regimes that are similar to the one described for GIs include "seals of approval" from industry, consumer, environmental, or religious groups, such as the designation *kosher*.

The second column represents a regime in which the government plays a larger role in the regulation of voluntary claims. This column might illustrate the public and private sector's roles in product identification (e.g., "sardines" or "juice"). Governments may establish standards of identity to reduce consumer confusion and, in some cases, deception. In doing so, the government is likely to assume more responsibility for conformity assessment and enforcement. However, standardizing the definition of an attribute can reduce the costs of policing the truthfulness of affirmative claims.

The third and fourth columns of table 6.1 describe two types of regimes that require mandatory disclosure of information. The third column illustrates the costs involved in labeling a process attribute that requires traceability of the attribute through the supply chain. This column could represent labeling the country of origin of a product. The fourth column shows the possible public and private roles in labeling a content attribute, such as the nutritional profile of a product.

Table 6.1 Private and public roles in four quality labeling regimes

Role	Regime 1	Regime 2	Regime 3	Regime 4
Legal status	Voluntary	Voluntary	Mandatory	Mandatory
Standard set by	Private sector	Government	Government	Government
Attribute	Process	Content	Process	Content
Implementation	Adoption of stipulated production practices	Product reformulation or re-identification	Segregation and identity preservation	Product reformulation
Conformity assessment				
Accreditation	Private sector			
Certification	Private sector			
Testing		Private sector		Private sector
Documentation			Private sector	
Inspection/audit		Government	Government	Government
Legal enforcement	Private sector and government	Government	Government	Government
Example	Geographical indications	Standards of identity	Country-of-origin labels	Nutritional labels in the United States

Table 6.1 illustrates three points. First, all labeling regimes require standards, verification, and enforcement so that consumers can confidently use labels to guide their purchases. Second, industry will always bear the initial costs of implementing a standard, whether it requires product reformulation, a change in production or harvesting practices, or segregation and identity preservation. If firms do not believe that consumers will pay a premium to compensate them for these additional costs, they will not participate in voluntary schemes. Third, government can provide some informational services, such as creating public standards or providing verification services to induce firms to participate in voluntary schemes, or to lower costs to producers and consumers (at the expense of taxpayers) for mandatory regimes. The public sector therefore has several tools at its disposal to remedy market failures stemming from imperfect information.

Food Quality Regulations in Practice

The examples shown in table 6.1 highlight different issues that arise in the regulation of food quality. Geographical indications for products such as wine, cheese, and rice are intended to help producers from a specific area to reap reputational rents. One of the principal challenges facing the WTO in food labeling is determining how the use of GIs should be governed at the multilateral level. Strengthening and extending the protection of these property rights is favored by a coalition of European and developing countries that seek exclusive access to names for cheeses, specialty meats, teas, rice, and silk and other textile products. Major commodity exporters in the New World, including Australia, Argentina, and the United States, vigorously oppose proposals that link increased legal protection for GIs to a multilateral notification system in the ongoing TRIPS negotiations, or to market access offers in the Doha Round agricultural negotiations.

Governments and the Codex Alimentarius Commission have long been in the business of establishing standards of identity to protect consumer interests by preventing deceptive claims. But problems have arisen as governments have used these measures to, in effect, differentiate domestic from foreign products. Even though definitional standards are used only to regulate voluntary claims, they can restrict trade by raising costs for foreign suppliers. The role that international standards can play in counterbalancing the pressures to use such measures to thwart foreign competition was recently highlighted in the WTO dispute case brought by Peru against the European Union's definitional standard for sardines. Other examples of definitional standards that have raised objections from trading partners include the European Union's standard for scallops (DS 7, DS 12, and DS 14 in table 3.2) and the US standards for catfish and ginseng that were recently established by the US Congress in the context of 2002 farm subsidy legislation.

Country-of-origin labeling is of interest because the United States and Japan currently have different options under consideration. This type of regulation also raises broader systemic issues related to the labeling of process attributes—issues that currently are under scrutiny at the WTO and are discussed in chapter 7. Although requiring disclosure of a product's country or countries of origin is primarily rationalized by the claim that it is the consumers' right to know where their food was produced, some advocates also intend consumers to use these disclosures as risk information.

Finally, nutritional labeling has been relatively uncontroversial because the verification and enforcement costs are generally minimal and nondiscriminatory. Estimates of the benefits of nutritional labeling requirements easily exceed their estimated costs. Even so, regulation of nutrition labeling is one area in which coordination among governments could increase the net benefits of such regimes without apparent sacrifice of national objectives. The lack of coordination, together with the limited impact of an international standard, points up the limits of harmonization in this area of policy.

Geographical Indications

GIs can be thought of as a type of collective trademark that helps producers to sell their products to consumers as differentiated goods and so avoid the need to compete solely on the basis of price in global food markets. GIs can be used for industrial products, but the vast majority are used for agricultural products. Some governments, particularly those in Europe, have recognized the growing potential for GIs in international markets and have actively promoted them to support rural development (Zago and Pick 2002). Although most governments afforded GIs some protection prior to the Uruguay Round, the TRIPS identification of GIs as a form of intellectual property rights has increased the legal standing of these indications and has redefined this area of the global food system.

One reason for increasing interest in GIs is that governments, under pressure to reduce subsidies and phase out trade policies that benefit domestic producers, want to encourage the private sector to adopt market-oriented mechanisms to increase producer income. The key question is how far such initiatives should proceed. In most countries, the private sector itself has historically enforced the protection of this form of intellectual property, using the legal infrastructure provided by the public sector. Judgment about expanding multilateral protection for GIs, whether through TRIPS Article 23 protection for products other than wines and spirits or through a centralized registry that requires countries to protect the GIs of others, hinges on understanding how public-sector enforcement costs in importing countries will change. It also is important to gauge the effects these initiatives will have on consumers of these products in importing countries, as well as on producers and consumers of close substitutes. Aside from efficiency considerations, the governance of GIs also raises distributional issues. At least in the short term, producers in developed countries will probably register far more GIs than their counterparts in developing countries.

The TRIPs agreement is built on earlier multilateral conventions such as the 1951 International Convention for the Use of *Appellations d'Origine* and Denominations of Cheeses (Stresa Convention), the 1958 Lisbon agreement for the Protection of Appellations of Origins and their International Registration (Lisbon agreement), and the 1986 International Agreement on Olive Oil and Table Olives (table 6.2). Before the Uruguay Round, the Lisbon agreement was the most important convention for the protection of GIs. Most of the 18 countries that joined the Lisbon Union established by the 1958 agreement did so in the 20 years after its adoption.[4]

Together, the parties to the Lisbon agreement have registered 738 GIs (or *appellations d'origine*) for a large range of products, including wines and spirits, other beverages, fruits and vegetables, dairy products, meat products, fish, honey, various other agricultural products, handicraft products, and extractive products such as salt and silica (WTO 1997b). France alone accounts for more than half of the registered GIs. Other European countries, including Bulgaria, the Czech Republic, Hungary, Italy, and

---

4. Only one country, Costa Rica, has joined in the past 20 years.

Table 6.2 Multilateral conventions for the protection of geographical indications (GIs)

Convention	Members	Number of protected GIs
Lisbon Agreement for the Protection of Appellations of Origins and Their International Registration (Lisbon agreement)	Algeria, Bulgaria, Burkina Faso, Congo, Costa Rica, Cuba, Czech Republic, France, Gabon, Haiti, Hungary, Israel, Italy, Mexico, Portugal, Slovak Republic, Togo, Tunisia	738
International Convention for the Use of *Appellations d'Origine* and Denominations of Cheeses (Stresa Convention)	Australia, Denmark, France, Italy, Netherlands, Norway, Switzerland	34
International Agreement on Olive Oil and Table Olives	Algeria, Croatia, Cyprus, European Union and member states, Egypt, Israel, Lebanon, Morocco, Syrian Arab Republic, Tunisia, Yugoslavia	Unknown

Sources: WTO (1997b, 1999c).

the Slovak Republic, have each registered between 30 and 70 GIs. Algeria, Cuba, Israel, Mexico, Portugal, and Tunisia each registered fewer than 30 GIs, and six countries did not register any. Lisbon Union members are obliged to protect each other's GIs, provided that they are protected as such in the country of origin and registered at the World Intellectual Property Organization (WIPO).

More recently, the European Union has negotiated new bilateral agreements for reciprocal protection of wines and spirits with Australia, Chile, and South Africa. Interest in GI protection is evident in North America as well. The North American Free Trade Agreement (NAFTA) affords protection to GIs for products such as "tequila," "Tennessee Whiskey," and "Canadian Whiskey" (WTO 1997b). Although the European Union and Switzerland are the strongest proponents of strengthening and extending GI property rights, some developing countries have also signaled a strong interest in additional GI protection in both the TRIPS Council and the WTO agriculture negotiations. Examples include additional protection for basmati rice and Darjeeling tea (India), Ceylon tea (Sri Lanka), jasmine rice and Thai silk (Thailand), yogurt (Bulgaria), salami (Hungary), and carpets (Turkey).

The renewed interest in GIs, together with the Doha negotiations over their governance, highlights some unresolved questions (WTO 2003b). Most fundamental is the uncertainty over the definition of *geographical indication*, which has not yet been interpreted or tested in dispute settlement proceedings. In practice, a variety of definitions are used by WTO members. Some countries, particularly the European Union, accept country names as GIs only in exceptional cases, on the understanding that a GI, by definition, must be smaller than the entire territory of a country. The European Union has also questioned the use of geographical identifiers that no longer reference a geopolitical entity, such as Ceylon. The use of GIs for different plant varieties such as basmati or jasmine rice that can be grown in other countries, and for blended products such as Darjeeling tea that use products from different regions, is also unresolved. Questions have also arisen about the use of traditional expressions (TEs) in conjunction with GIs. The new EU regulation for labeling wine accords protection to TEs such as "ruby," "tawny," and "vintage" for port, with the justification that some TEs are so closely linked to a GI that they themselves meet the TRIPS definition of a GI.[5]

Some ambiguity also surrounds the status of existing product trademarks that could be interpreted as a claim of origin. Under the TRIPS agreement, a country can cancel the trademark of a domestic or foreign company if officials believe that it misleads consumers about the origin of the product. This issue lies at the heart of the only formal WTO dispute over GIs to emerge over the first seven years of the TRIPS agreement (DS 174 in table 3.2). The Czech Republic has successfully canceled the Anheuser-Busch company's trademarks Budweiser™ and Bud™ in four European countries by claiming that these trademarks are GIs for beer from the Czech town of České Budějovice. Some WTO members, including the European Union, generally view GIs as superior in right to a trademark, while others, such as the United States, adhere to the "first-in-time, first-in-right" principle for GI and trademark protection (OECD 2000, Meltzer 2001).[6]

These unresolved questions about GIs seriously complicate calculations of national interest in the Doha negotiations. Developing countries, in

---

5. The difficulty in interpreting the scope of legal protection for GIs, even within the European Union, has been illustrated in the recent case brought by the Consorzio del Prosciutto di Parma against a British supermarket chain that was slicing and packaging Parma ham for sale in its stores. In an unusual move, the European Court of Justice overturned an earlier opinion issued by the Advocate General, which would have allowed the supermarket chain to slice, package, and sell Parma ham. However, the court ruled in May 2003 that the product must be sliced and packed in Parma, Italy, itself in order to be marketed with its name of origin. The ruling does allow the slicing of Parma ham by retailers and restaurants outside the region as long as it is done in front of the consumer or at least so that the consumer can verify that the ham used bears the name of the market of origin (European Court of Justice 2003).

6. EU legislation addressing geographical indications excludes mineral waters, thereby protecting the trademarks of companies that often include geographical names. For example, Eviana mineral water bears the name of the French Alpine village in which the spring is located.

particular, face choices that are difficult in view of the current uncertainties. They must judge first whether the indications that are of most interest to their producers actually rise to the level of a GI. If so, they must provide legal protection for these GIs in their domestic market before they are eligible for protection in foreign markets. Protection of GIs in foreign markets is then secured in different ways, as no one mechanism is specified in the TRIPS agreement. For example, in the United States GIs can be registered as certification marks or collective marks under trademark laws. Protection for GIs in the European Union can only be secured via a bilateral treaty, unless EU authorities determine that the petitioners are from a country with an equivalent regime for protecting GIs.[7] And countries must keep in mind that the return on such investments may be diminished in some key markets by the generic and grandfather exemptions, unless these too are revised in upcoming negotiations. For example, under current rules US courts could rule that *yogurt* is a generic term in the United States, thereby eroding the value of that GI for Bulgarian producers.

Standards of Identity

Standards of identity, which establish the generic names under which products can be marketed, are especially important in agricultural markets. The demands of the marketplace for increased convenience and lower costs have led to unprecedented innovations in food technology in recent years, and, in turn, a stream of new food products.

As a result, food regulators are faced with determining which products can lay claim to generic identifiers such as *fruit juice, ice cream*, or even *cappuccino* (*World Food Chemical News* 1998). One difficulty for regulators is ascertaining when the benefits of providing information through standards outweigh the costs of establishing and policing them. Another is that some subjectivity might be involved in determining the essential characteristics for a product identifier. Science can aid in policing selected content attributes, but may be less useful in determining which organoleptic characteristics—such as texture, taste, and smell—or other attributes are relevant to consumers.

For manufacturers of multiple-ingredient products, definitional standards create bounds within which a manufacturer can produce a differentiated

---

7. The difference between these two systems is highlighted by the status of European and US GIs in each other's markets. The United States does not have a bilateral agreement with the European Union, nor is its level of protection recognized as equivalent by EU regulators. As a consequence, no US GI is protected in the European market. By contrast, several European GIs are registered in the United States as certification marks (e.g., Parma ham, Roquefort cheese) because producer groups registered them under US trademark law.

good to attract consumer purchases. The controversy sometimes engendered in setting or moving these bounds attests to the economic significance of these regulations for industry stakeholders. For example, the European Union (and the Codex) struggled for 25 years to establish a definition for *chocolate*. If a standard for a multiple-ingredient product is upgraded, manufacturers must determine which option is more profitable: reformulating the product and incurring higher production costs, or reidentifying the product and incurring higher marketing costs. The choices are the same for producers of single-ingredient foods, except that product reformulation may not be possible if they cannot grow, catch, or raise the required varieties, species, or breeds.

The WTO dispute over the EU definitional standard for labeling preserved sardines (DS 231 in table 3.2) illuminates several public policy issues related to identity standards in global food markets.[8] EU Council Regulation 2136/89 first established common marketing standards for preserved sardines in 1989. The standard specified, among other things, that preserved sardines must be prepared exclusively from the fish of the species *Sardina pilchardus* Walbaum, a species found off the coast of Western Europe and Morocco. The EU standard harmonized the differing standards for preserved sardines in Europe through adoption of the standard prevailing in Spain, Portugal, and France, and was notified under the Tokyo Round TBT agreement.

The European Union's standard was substantially more restrictive than the Codex standard for preserved sardines, which initially was adopted for canned sardines and sardine-type products in 1978 and revised in 1995 (Codex Stan 94-1981, Rev.1-1995). Article 2.1 of the Codex standard establishes that canned sardines or sardine-type products must be prepared from fresh or frozen fish from a list of 21 species, among them *Sardina pilchardus* and *Sardinops sagax*. A new species of fish may be added to the list, but only after reports from at least three independent laboratories state that the organoleptic properties of the species after processing conform to those of the species already included in the standard.

Article 6 of the Codex standard states that in addition to the provision of the General Standard for the Labeling of Prepackaged Foods (Codex Stan 1-1985, Rev. 3-1999), the following specific provisions are to apply: The name of the products shall be:

1) "Sardines" (to be reserved exclusively for *Sardina pilchardus* (Walbaum)); or

2) "X sardines" of a specific country, a geographic area, the species, or the common name of the species in accordance with the law and custom of the country in which the product is sold, and in a manner not to mislead the consumer.

---

8. The discussion of the sardines case in this section is drawn from WTO (2002a, 2002b).

In 2001 Peru formally requested a WTO panel to rule on its complaint against the EU labeling standard. Canada, Chile, Colombia, Ecuador, the United States, and Venezuela reserved their rights to comment as third parties in the case. The complainants acknowledged the legitimacy of the European Union's stated objectives of market transparency, consumer protection, and fair competition, but claimed that other measures could accomplish the same goal in this instance. In particular, Peru argued that the same objectives could be achieved if *Sardinops sagax* could be marketed under the name "Pacific sardines" in the European Union, as provided for in the international standard.

The case centered primarily on whether the European Union's standard violated the TBT agreement's conditional requirement to use international standards, although the complainants also claimed that the standard violated other provisions of the TBT agreement and the GATT. The complainants argued that the European Union had not used the Codex standard "as a basis" for its labeling regulation. They also asserted that the Codex standard was not "ineffective or inappropriate" to fulfill the European Union's legitimate objectives, and as a consequence, the EU regulation was in violation of Article 2.4 of the TBT agreement, which requires WTO members to base their measures on international standards in these circumstances. The complainants also claimed that the EU measure violated Article 2.2 of the TBT agreement because it was "more trade-restrictive than necessary," and that, because *Sardina pilchardus* and *Sardinops sagax* are like products, Articles 2.1 of the TBT agreement and Article III.4 of the GATT had been violated as well.

The European Union countered that it did in fact use the Codex labeling standard as a basis for its regulation. The European Union claimed that the international standard offered options, including choosing between "X sardines" and the common name of the species (in this case *Sardinops sagax*), and that it had chosen the latter option. The European Union also recalled that the Appellate Body had already ruled in the hormones case that "based on" cannot be interpreted as meaning "conform to," and therefore it had reversed a panel ruling that reflected this interpretation. On this basis, the European Union expressed the concern that the obligation to amend a technical regulation when a new international standard is adopted would turn standardization bodies into "world legislators."

The European Union also criticized the process by which the Codex standard had been created, as well as the standard itself. First, the European Union asserted that adoption of the standard did not really reflect an international consensus, claiming that dissenters had been deterred from voicing objections during Codex deliberations because they believed they would have lost a vote on the measure anyway. Second, the European Union maintained that the Codex had violated its own rules of procedures by changing the wording of the standard at its meeting, resulting in a substantive rather than an editorial change that should have been referred back to the Committee on Food Labeling. Third, the European Union argued that questions about the suitability of the standard for the global food system were raised by the fact that only 18 countries had adopted the standard—a list that did not include the European Union or Peru.

The European Union also submitted that regardless of the circumstances in other markets, European consumers did not consider different species to be so "like" that they should bear the same name. Canada challenged this assertion, claiming that there was no evidence that European consumers expected sardines to be *Sardina pilchardus*; to the contrary, Canada pointed out, until the adoption of the EU regulation Canadian exporters had successfully marketed their preserved sardines (*Clupea harengus harengus*) in the United Kingdom and the Netherlands for over 50 years. Canada further argued that consumers' expectations were related to the culinary and nutritional characteristics of the processed products, and that these characteristics were not necessarily aligned with biological taxonomies. Venezuela agreed, stating that the European sardine case was probably the only one in which attempts had been made to match the trade description with the scientific name. Venezuela noted, for example, that "mussel" and "tuna" are common trade descriptions for multiple species. The complainants concluded that the EU measure actively undermined market transparency and fair competition through the creation of a monopoly under the name "sardines" for its own domestic species and that of a few other countries, such as Morocco, where the European Union was investing heavily in sardine production.

The panel concurred with the complainants, but limited its findings to issues related to the international standard. The panel first examined whether the European Union had used the Codex standard "as a basis" for its regulation. After determining that the European Union had not, the panel further examined whether the standard was "ineffective or inappropriate" for achieving the European Union's stated objectives of market transparency, consumer protection, and fair competition. The panel noted that the European Union's regulation was based on the factual premise that consumers in the European Union associate "sardines" exclusively with *Sardina pilchardus*, but observed that this premise was called into question by the evidence presented by the European Union itself. The European Union had asserted that in most member states the term *sardines* had corresponded to the particular consumer expectations that underpinned its regulation, but had also acknowledged that in some member states, it was the regulation that "created" those "uniform" consumer expectations. The panel stated:

> If we were to accept that a WTO Member can "create" consumer expectations and thereafter find justification for the trade-restrictive measure which created those consumer expectations, we would be endorsing the permissibility of "self-justifying" regulatory trade barriers. Indeed, the danger is that Members, by

shaping consumer expectations through regulatory intervention in the market, would be able to justify thereafter the legitimacy of that very same regulatory intervention on the basis of the governmentally created consumer expectations. (Para. 7.127)

The panel therefore found that the EU regulation was inconsistent with Article 2.4 of the TBT agreement, but it declined to rule on other matters related to Article 2 of the TBT agreement or Article III.4 of the GATT. When the decision was appealed, the Appellate Body also determined that the EU regulation violated the obligations set out in Article 2.4, and concurred with the panel that it was therefore unnecessary to examine the measure's consistency with other WTO disciplines. The two parties to the dispute subsequently agreed that the sardine labeling regulation should be brought into compliance with the TBT agreement by April 2003, bringing the case to a successful conclusion for the complainant.

The judicial economy adopted by the panel and the Appellate Body in the sardines case is in accordance with the Dispute Settlement Understanding (DSU), but it leaves open several questions related to other standards recently adopted by countries in instances in which there were no international standards. In particular, the 2002 US farm bill (Food Security and Rural Investment Act) sets out definitions for "catfish" and "ginseng" that correspond to catfish species raised in the southern United States and ginseng grown in Wisconsin. Producers in Vietnam and other Asian countries have objected informally to these definitions. If these issues remain unresolved through informal discussions, they could be raised at the WTO (Elizabeth Becker, "Catfish Are Catfish, Unless They're Caught in a Trade War," *The New York Times*, January 16, 2002, 1).

The final outcome of the dispute over the European Union's labeling regulations for preserved sardines, like the earlier settlement of a similar dispute over the European Union's labeling regulations for scallops, illustrates how government regulation of voluntary claims can restrict trade. These disputes also raise questions about the conclusion that labeling regulations always benefit consumers. Standards of definition can improve the functioning of markets, but even standards that are not egregiously protectionist can be tailored to domestic production at the expense of domestic consumers as well as exporters.

Country-of-Origin Labels

Interest in country-of-origin labels for food has increased along with the volume of imports. Domestic producers are in many instances the strongest advocates of country-of-origin labeling. The leading rationale that advocates offer for such requirements is the consumer's right to know. Consumer surveys commissioned by producer groups indicate that a large majority of US consumers would like to purchase domestic products (*World*

Table 6.3 Government country-of-origin labeling requirements, selected countries, 1998

Product	Required at retail	Required only at customs entry	Not required
Fresh fruits and vegetables	Australia	Argentina Canada France	Brazil Japan[a] New Zealand
Frozen vegetables	Australia Brazil	Argentina Canada France	Japan New Zealand
Meat/poultry carcass	—	Argentina Australia Canada France	Brazil Japan New Zealand
Meat/poultry cuts	Brazil France	Argentina Australia Canada	Japan New Zealand
Processed meat/poultry products	Brazil Canada[b] France	Australia France	Japan New Zealand

— = not reported

a. Except for five vegetables: ginger, taro, broccoli, garlic, and fresh mushrooms.
b. If more than 51 percent of the value of the product is from foreign sources.

Source: USDA (1998).

Food Chemical News 1998, FSIS 2000). Consumer groups support country-of-origin labeling as well, citing concerns about the safety of imported products, and producer advocates now also cite consumer concerns as a rationale (*World Food Chemical News* 2002a).[9]

Many countries require country-of-origin labeling, and the trend is increasing. A 1998 US Department of Agriculture survey indicated that many key trading partners required origin labels for products in five categories: fresh fruits and vegetables, frozen vegetables, meat and poultry carcasses, meat and poultry cuts, and processed meat and poultry products. The summary report notes, however, that the legal requirements are not enforced in some instances, and in others are satisfied by normal import documents (USDA 1998). Table 6.3 presents the country-

---

9. For example, Rep. Helen Chenoweth-Hage (R-Idaho) stated, "Without a country-of-origin label for meat, American consumers are at risk of purchasing a low-quality foreign product that could contain food-borne disease under the false assumption that they are buying high-quality American meat" (*World Food Chemical News* 2000, 19).

of-origin requirements for some of the more important countries in international agricultural markets.

US federal law, including Section 304 of the amended US Tariff Act of 1930, the Federal Meat Inspection Act as amended, and other legislation, has long required most imports to bear labels informing the "ultimate purchaser" of the country of origin. An "ultimate purchaser" is defined as the last US person receiving the article in the form in which it was imported. Thus under these laws, shippers, processors, wholesalers, or retailers generally qualified as the ultimate purchaser for most agricultural products, because even final consumer goods such as produce and meats were more often shipped in bulk containers rather than in consumer-ready packaging.

This feature of the marketing system for agricultural products implied that exporters could comply with US federal laws by simply marking containers, boxes, or cartons with the country of origin, and that retailers were generally not required to identify the source of perishable products that they offered for sale.[10] Retailers could therefore display produce from multiple sources in the same bin and commingle meats from different countries in the same refrigerated cases. However, they also could choose to segregate and label products from different countries, provided they could supply documentation to support their voluntary claims.

These rules were changed for some agricultural commodities by the 2002 Food Security and Rural Investment Act, which included sweeping new requirements for point-of-sale labeling for a range of products, including beef, lamb, pork, fish, fresh produce, and peanuts. Congress directed the USDA to develop guidelines for voluntary labeling of these products which would in effect remain until September 30, 2004, when mandatory labeling requirements are scheduled to come into force.

The USDA guidelines set out criteria that must be met to qualify for the designation "United States Country of Origin Labeling" (US COOL). Products of mixed origin must indicate where each stage of production took place, according to the USDA guidelines. If current trade flows are not changed by the US COOL requirements, a sizable percentage of steaks and roasts on display in US retail outlets will bear the label "Born in Canada (or Mexico), raised and processed in the United States." The US COOL requirements also extend to blended products, such as hamburger, with all components to be labeled for origin in descending order of predominance by weight. USDA guidelines also specify what means can be

---

10. Some country-of-origin requirements have been adopted by state legislatures. Several states, including Florida, Idaho, Maine, Wyoming, Kansas, North Dakota, and South Dakota, have laws requiring country-of-origin labeling for a range of goods. Regulations in Florida, for example, require country-of-origin labeling for fresh produce, and Idaho's law requires labeling of imported meat. According to the USDA's Food Safety and Inspection Service (FSIS), federal meat and poultry inspection laws prohibit states from passing labeling requirements that differ from those imposed by the US Congress.

used to inform consumers at the point of sale, such as individual stickers, stamps, or marks, or, alternatively, placards or signs for holding units or bins. They also set out guidelines for a traceability system throughout the supply chain, so that retailers and upstream suppliers know what documentation and record-keeping system will be sufficient to verify the source of the product.

Article IX of the GATT explicitly allows countries to require marks of country origin, subject to some conditions. Requirements must apply to all like products of third countries and are to be no more onerous than necessary to protect consumers from fraudulent or misleading indications. Furthermore, country-of-origin measures must not seriously damage the product, materially reduce its value, or unreasonably increase its cost.

To date, no formal WTO dispute has emerged over country-of-origin regulations, and so the multilateral rules await interpretation by a panel or the Appellate Body. Nonetheless, complaints related to such measures have repeatedly surfaced in the TBT Committee since 2000, shortly after Japan notified the WTO that it had revised its Law Concerning Standardization and Proper Labeling of Agricultural and Forestry Products (1950 Law No. 175), which required phasing in new country-of-origin requirements for foods and beverages. The Japanese requirements apply to processed foods, fresh foods, brown and milled rice, and marine products (WTO 1999b). Both developed and developing countries have registered objections to the Japanese country-of-origin regulations in the TBT Committee, and Canada, a leading exporter of meat to the United States, has raised questions about the US COOL regime (WTO 2002g).

Even if point-of-sale, country-of-origin requirements are legal under the WTO, they are not necessarily good public policy. The costs of this labeling regime, including the private and public costs of implementation, verification, and enforcement throughout the agricultural supply chain, may outweigh the benefits. Compliance with such requirements could result in additional costs for exporters, such as individual stickers for fruit. However, many of the operational and administrative costs associated with country-of-origin are more likely to be borne initially by domestic agents in the food system, including shippers, handlers, and processors. These costs include segregation costs (i.e., processing meats from cattle with different places of birth on different days of the week) and industry's fixed and variable costs of record keeping to maintain verifiable audit trails (Hammonds 2003). Eventually, these costs would likely be passed back to foreign and domestic producers or forward to consumers, depending on the relative price responsiveness of supply and demand. Taxpayers in the importing country would generally bear the costs of policing and otherwise enforcing country-of-origin regulations.

The market effects of mandatory country-of-origin labeling could be larger for foreign suppliers if the regime increases demand for domestic products, as intended by at least some of its advocates. However, if mar-kets have failed to create incentives for voluntarily labeling of what is asserted to be a positive attribute, the resulting shift in demand could be slight. The consumer, producer, and government costs of mandatory labeling could well exceed the benefits in such circumstances.

Given the reality of the marketplace—including limited space in retail outlets and the expectation that consumers will choose products based on attributes other than their national origin—many wholesalers and re-tailers may choose to avoid the transactions costs of segregation and simply sell domestic products, which normally account for a large percentage of total supply. As a result, consumers may end up paying an even higher price for labeled foods, regardless of whether they are indifferent to whether a product is foreign or domestic. Country-of-origin labeling also runs the risk of misinforming consumers if they conclude erroneously that domestic products are safer than imported ones, when both are required to meet the same safety standards. Consumers may believe that a higher price for a domestic product reflects a safety premium rather than higher production costs unrelated to safety.

Nutritional Labels

Many firms now market the nutritional attributes of their products, and governments have, as a consequence, adopted policies to regulate these voluntary claims. Some governments have gone further, requiring all nutritional information to be labeled, especially for packaged products. For some products, producers do not have an incentive to disclose the nutritional profile, although consumers would like such information to inform their food purchases. Thus an a priori case exists for some form of regulation, although whether the benefits of any particular regime exceed its costs is an empirical question.

The US Nutrition Labeling and Education Act of 1990 (NLEA) regu-lates nutritional labeling in the United States. This act mandates the types of nutritional information required on almost all packaged foods and beverages, standardizes the presentation of this information on labels, and bans certain types of claims.[11] It also requires scientific proof for all voluntary claims that an ingredient or food is beneficial to health, or is a "functional" food. The NLEA now has 15 mandatory components and 10 optional components.[12] Optional components become mandatory if claims are made about them or if they are added to enrich or fortify the food.

At present, most other countries do not have mandatory nutritional labeling. One exception is Canada, which notified its mandatory nutritional

---

11. Nutritional labeling in the United States is voluntary for raw fruits, vegetables, and fish.

12. The first significant amendment to the NLEA, the requirement to label trans-fatty acids, was adopted by FDA in July 2003. The rule will come into effect in 2006.

Box 6.1 Nutritional labeling components in the United States and Canada

Canada	United States	
Mandatory	Mandatory	Voluntary
Calories	Total calories	Calories from saturated fat
Fat	Calories from fat	Polyunsaturated fat
Saturated fat	Total fat	Monounsaturated fat
Trans fat	Saturated fat	Potassium
	Trans fat	
Cholesterol	Cholesterol	Soluble fiber
Sodium	Sodium	Insoluble fiber
Carbohydrate	Total carbohydrate	Sugar alcohol
Fiber	Dietary fiber	Other carbohydrate
Sugars	Sugars	Percent of vitamin A as beta carotene
Protein	Protein	Other essential vitamins and minerals
Vitamin A	Vitamin A	
Vitamin C	Vitamin C	
Calcium	Calcium	
Iron	Iron	

Note: Canada requires the listing of omega-3 and omega-6 fatty acids when polyunsaturated fats are listed.

Source: Federal Register (1991) and Health Canada (2003).

labeling regime to the WTO in 2001 and published its final regulation on January 1, 2003, making nutrition labeling mandatory for most packaged foods and beverages after a transition period. Although US and Canadian nutrition labeling regulations are similar in many ways, there are some important differences (box 6.1). Most important, each country uses its own reference values to calculate the "percent daily value" (%DV) for each nutrient, based on a daily diet of 2,000 calories. Canada also requires that omega-3 and omega-6 fatty acids accompany a listing of polyunsaturated fats. Finally, the two countries have different requirements for labeling cholesterol: the United States requires a declaration of the %DV for cholesterol; Canada does not allow it.

Nutritional labeling gives consumers not only the information they need to improve their general health but also the means for reducing the incidence of chronic, rather than acute, health hazards such as heart disease and diabetes. Mandatory labeling also can significantly influence product formulation by creating incentives for producers to use healthier ingredients (Caswell and Padberg 1992). The industry costs of nutritional labeling (aside from reformulation) include administrative, product analysis, labeling redesign, and inventory costs. The latter two costs are significantly defrayed by a suitable phase-in time for the regulation. Government enforcement costs are minor, because the nutritional information can be verified by periodic testing of products rather than continuous monitoring or on-site inspection of production facilities or retail outlets.

Economic evaluations of mandatory nutritional labeling have indicated that the benefits of this policy, although not dramatic, outweigh its costs even if changes in dietary habits are modest (*Federal Register* 1991). The US Food and Drug Administration estimated in 1991 that the benefits of mandatory labeling included $0.6 billion in reduced medical costs over 20 years. The FDA study also estimated that consumers were willing to pay $3.6 billion for reductions in deaths attributable to cancer and coronary heart disease associated with fat and cholesterol consumption. This $4.2 billion in total social benefits exceeded the estimated industry costs of $2.6 billion over 20 years, even though consumers' willingness to pay to avoid other diet-related illnesses, such as diabetes, was not included in the benefit estimates (Jessup 2000).

A study commissioned by the Canadian government found that the benefits of mandatory nutritional labeling exceeded its costs by a larger amount. The estimated benefits of mandatory nutritional labeling in Canada totaled C$5 billion in overall savings to the health care system over 20 years, while industry costs for the regime were estimated to range from C$263 million to C$476 million, depending on the length of the phase-in period (Health Canada 2003).

One earlier study that examined nutritional labeling regulations in global food markets concluded that although the Codex initially established guidelines for nutritional labeling in 1985 and revised them in 1993, there had been little coordination of national policies across countries (Caswell 1997). The subsequent differences that emerged between the US and Canadian regimes support this conclusion. This lack of coordination increases the transactions costs of trade between the two countries, according to industry sources, requiring food manufacturers to run two separate packaging lines for US and Canadian markets. Both the Grocery Manufacturers of America and the National Food Processors Association have urged the harmonization, or at least mutual recognition, of US and Canadian labeling requirements in order to facilitate trade between these two trading partners, each the most important export market for the agricultural products of the other (*World Food Chemical News* 2001).

Impacts of Labeling and Standards on Trade

When firms are able to make positive claims about product attributes—that is, when they can advertise that their products contain desirable properties or are free of those that are not—the appropriate role for governments in information provision will usually be limited to policing the truthfulness of the voluntary claims. This limited government role may not be the case if negative attributes are integral to the product, such as the high fat content of butter, or if a government seeks to *modify* as well as *inform* consumer choice in order to achieve social welfare objectives. Labeling regulations are demand-led instruments that can improve quality signaling when private market incentives are insufficient. Although they can be attractive alternatives to other fiat measures, they should, nonetheless, be subject to benefit-cost tests. They are more likely to pass such tests if they are designed so that they do not create obstacles to trade.

The roles for the public and private sector in GI labeling regimes have been relatively uncontroversial prior to recent initiatives to change the prevailing balance. Governments generally provide only the legal infrastructure for private-sector enforcement of GI property rights (although that in itself creates the value of the property rights). The private sector is usually responsible for all other costs associated with the creation, adoption, and ongoing verification of products bearing the GI. The value of such investments is determined by consumer preferences in domestic and foreign markets. Producers will abandon GIs if their additional production and marketing costs are not matched by additional revenues.

The TRIPS negotiations, however, raise the prospect of increased use of public-sector resources for the promotion of GI products. In view of the current legal uncertainties over the definition of a GI, the status of GIs versus trademarks, and the required mechanisms for fulfilling TRIPS obligations, evaluation of such initiatives is difficult. It is clear that at present developed countries have far more GIs than developing counties, and that producers in developed countries are likely to have an advantage in the development of these marketing tools over their developing-country counterparts for some time. However, the fact that the reputational rents generated through the application of GIs will primarily accrue to developed-country producers for some time does not imply that increased protection for GIs will not also benefit consumers in developing countries, reducing search costs and curbing misleading claims. Globally, it is important to assess whether the benefits that accrue to producers and consumers of differentiated products outweigh the higher enforcement costs that are intrinsic to strengthened GI protection. For many countries, it may be that investments in other components of their legal infrastructure will yield higher payoffs.

The importance of standards of identity in food trade has generally been overlooked. But the evidence is growing that policymakers are interested in this tool to help domestic producers differentiate their products from foreign products. However, definitional standards determined by domestic production circumstances may not benefit consumers if such standards increase the costs or reduce the availability of close substitutes. These measures can raise exporters' marketing costs, at a minimum, or exclude competition altogether. Thus, although mandatory disclosure requirements are generally more controversial, government regulation of voluntary claims, such as product identifiers, can also disrupt trade.

In the sardines case, an international standard counterbalanced the attempt to transform a generic product identifier into a GI for the domestic market by restricting use of the term *sardine* to a local species of fish. The outcome of the case appears to bring additional pressures to bear on the international standards organizations, particularly the Codex. The Codex's higher legal standing in the multilateral system has already disrupted its decision-making process when health and safety issues are at stake. The increased scrutiny of the Codex could similarly slow the development of international standards for quality attributes that are often advocated as a mechanism for helping developing countries to export to developed country markets.

Labeling of process attributes—country-of-origin (just discussed) and genetically modified, organic, free-range, or other attributes discussed in chapter 7—requires credible traceability regimes. The uncertainty about cross-border conformity assessment arrangements has increased opposition to initiatives to modify WTO rules to explicitly recognize the legitimacy of labeling process attributes. The potential role of private certification in international transactions, which might facilitate trade as labeling becomes used more widely, remains largely unexplored for agriculture and food, but is the prevalent practice in markets for industrial goods.

Nutritional labeling is an example of a mandatory regime with a positive net effect. Nutritional labels provide product information that firms may not supply voluntarily but that has the potential to reduce health care costs and provide other health benefits. It requires industry to absorb minimal, onetime compliance costs (unless a firm chooses to reformulate its product), involves modest enforcement costs, and is nondiscriminatory. The objective nature of the information and the verification process leaves little scope for firms to use nutritional labeling to discriminate against imported products. Other regimes sharing this profile are also likely to be welfare-enhancing.

However, it should be noted that the different nutritional labeling regulations in Canada and the United States could fragment markets that are already highly integrated for processed food products, thereby offsetting some of the benefits of such policies to consumers. Different regimes have emerged, despite numerous factors that should have led to harmonized requirements: the shared objective and approach of improving consumers' health through informed choice; the participation of the two countries' regulators in the Codex Committee on Food Labeling and the NAFTA Technical Working Group on Food Labeling, Packaging, and Standards; the lengthy deliberations over the regulations prior to their adoption in each country; and the amount of commerce between the two neighbors. The lack of harmonization also apparent with other developed countries suggests an indifference to the potential benefits of trade to consumers and a limited interest in harmonization in international food markets even under the most propitious of circumstances.

The confluence of heightened interest in labeling together with some ambiguity in the multilateral rules that govern its use represents a significant challenge for the global food system. Specifically, it is unclear whether consumers' "right-to-know" imperative will qualify as a legitimate objective under the TBT agreement, or whether a more specific objective will have to be identified. It also is uncertain whether arguments that a voluntary labeling regime is an effective and less trade-restrictive alternative to mandatory labeling could be successful. And it is unknown how government enforcement costs will change if governance of geographical indications becomes more centralized. Current legal uncertainties are exacerbating trade tensions, because developed countries' intensified interest in labeling seems, in some cases, to be directed at foreclosing opportunities otherwise created by trade liberalization. Such cases undermine trust among trading partners, invite skepticism about the fine print of other labeling initiatives, and harden opposition to any issue related to nontrade concerns raised in the Doha Round agricultural negotiations.

7

Emerging Food Regulation Issues

Of the food regulatory issues that are emerging in the area of trade, the most contentious revolve around the regulation of process attributes to achieve quality goals.[1] In meeting the new challenges posed by process attributes, countries face additional choices in deciding how to regulate, what information producers should provide, and whether to make such information mandatory. Because these emerging challenges address the credence characteristics of foods, the regulations adopted will often require extensive traceability for conformity assessment and enforcement.

The new challenges also broaden the debate on labeling, specifically by raising the issue as to whether to include information that may imply facts about safety and environmental impacts that are not agreed-on among countries. Any regulation on food labeling can spark lively trade disputes. An even greater challenge to the trade system, however, is the more general trend toward identifying foods by process as well as content attributes, where the uniqueness or relevance of the process is contentious.

The multilateral framework of rules governing process attributes is less well developed than that for most other areas of food regulation. Eventually, these rules will have to be revised through negotiations or reviewed when they are the subject of the WTO dispute settlement process, although such review could lead to further trade tensions. Indeed,

---

1. Some of these process attributes were introduced in the discussion in chapter 6 of the labeling of foods by country of origin and the protection of intellectual property held by groups of producers.

trade rules in this area are more likely to be driven by particular conflicts than by abstract regulatory principles. Still, analysis of the broad issues involved can be useful in reaching consensus on an agreed-on regulatory framework.

This chapter elaborates on three emerging issues that will test the interpretation and usefulness of international regulatory disciplines and define their scope. These issues are

- the regulation of trade in genetically modified (GM) crops and food products, and the requirements that such goods be labeled;

- the rapid growth in the market for organic foods and the problems that this growth raises for the compatibility of national regulations; and

- new concerns in some countries over the welfare of farm animals, particularly in the context of intensive livestock production.

Each of these issues raises fundamental questions about the balance between public- and private-sector decisions on labeling and providing consumers with information, and about the nature of national and international regulation. In addition, each of these issues has raised the problem of distinguishing between risk and quality goals. By claiming that each issue involves risk factors, those who advocate further regulation seek to bolster their case by enlisting the regulatory apparatus of the state to provide information to consumers and influence choice. Those who oppose such further regulation argue that the role of the state in providing information should be strictly limited to acknowledged health and safety issues.

Scope for Trade Conflicts

The issues that arise in connection with the regulation of process attributes such as biotechnology, organic methods, and animal welfare standards differ in important ways from the topics discussed in the last three chapters. For process attributes, where universally recognized health and safety reasons do not exist for the regulation, and the attribute does not represent an identifiable and testable feature of the product itself, the scope for trade distortions increases.

The problem is systemic. The global trade system is largely predicated on the exchange of goods with inherent characteristics that can be revealed in final content. Whether inspection is done "at the border," at a "pre-border" site in the exporting country, or "post-border" at a wholesaling point in the importing country, the control has traditionally been on the product and its content attributes. Even when a process attribute is identified, such as geographical indication (GI) or country of origin at the point of sale, this step generally is taken in order to describe implicitly some aspect of the product. Likewise, the application of rules of origin in trade agreements requires identification of a source country, and that often requires in turn some form of traceability to earlier stages of production. But this is to categorize the good for customs purposes rather than as information for the consumer.

The requirement of process identification other than a geographical source for a good calls into question the whole concept of "like products" on which essential elements of the trade system, such as the transparency of customs classification and the principle of nondiscrimination, are based. When the process itself is regarded as an integral part of the product, the potential for regulatory confusion and for protectionist capture is considerable. If the process defines the product, countries may need to rethink many of the conventions of trade policy. The question arises whether it is possible through careful design of process attribute regulations to alleviate the conditions that are most likely to lead to conflicts.

By far, the most controversial of the emerging process attribute issues has been that precipitated by the rapid development, adoption, and incorporation into the food supply of transgenic (GM) crops. Transgenic crops are produced by shifting genetic material—derived from another plant, a bacterium, or other living organism—into the plant to be modified. The result is similar to regular breeding practices, although the selection of genetic material is much greater because the limits of normal reproductive activity can be exceeded. To date, the most important traits embedded in plants by this process are pest resistance (by incorporating the natural Bt pesticide) and resistance to the herbicide glyphosate (sold as Roundup™) which can then be used on crops for weed control. Genetically modified organisms (GMOs) commonly found on the market include Roundup-ready soybeans and Bt corn and cotton.

The introduction of these biotech products into the food supply has been one of the most rapid adoptions of technology in history, although the science behind the technology has been under development for many years. The reaction against the technology also has been swift and dramatic. First in Europe and then increasingly in other countries, environmental and consumer groups have launched vigorous campaigns against the spread of genetically modified foods. Scientists, however, have generally considered the health impacts of consuming foods made from transgenic crops to be minimal and manageable. The one health concern that has surfaced is the allergenicity of some introduced proteins from crops such as nuts, but this problem is generally covered by existing national regulations that provide adequate consumer information, usually through labeling. Environmental concerns have more scientific credibility, and the interaction of genetically modified crops with other varieties and species is still under intensive investigation.

There is a fundamental disagreement among countries (and often within countries) on the need for tight controls on this new technology and its products. Conflicts have emerged between those countries that wish to see the technology constrained by new regulations that reflect concerns, regardless of the current evidence, that transgenic crops and animals could pose either health or environmental threats and those that argue that current regulations are adequate to guard against such negative side effects.[2] The countries that have adopted the technology in their export agriculture believe its use is not a reason to regulate otherwise safe food-stuffs, while importers tend to take the view that in this case "process matters." Those countries wishing to constrain the technology argue that the process itself is relevant to the definition of the product and should therefore be subject to restraints. The group content with current safe-guards argues that regulation should not hinge on the technology un-derlying a new product, and that this technology, a logical application of advances in the life sciences, should not be singled out for special treatment.

While key governments are lining up on each side of this issue, private-sector traders are struggling with the prospect of a bifurcated world market where genetically modified products have to be segregated from those that are not, and import regulators in other countries have to decide whether to allow genetically modified products into their food supply.[3] No issue poses a more immediate challenge to the harmonious develop-ment of the global food system.

Compared to biotech-assisted crop production, "organic" food is often considered its antithesis. Organic food is usually grown without the range of fertilizers and pesticides that characterize modern agriculture.[4] In the developed world, the availability of organic foods has increased sharply in recent years. Although still only a small share of total food and agri-cultural products, the organic market is important in certain countries and for certain products, usually fruits and vegetables but increasingly meats and dairy goods.

Organic foods are entering the mainstream of the food system because they have increasingly been adopted by supermarkets, initially suspicious

---

2. The impacts of intellectual property rights and investment flows on the development and adoption of transgenic technologies in world agriculture are clearly summarized in Victor and Runge (2002) and are not considered here.

3. Robert Paarlberg (2002) argues that under these conditions, exporters themselves will reject the technology so they can retain access to the major import markets, and that this stance will essentially block adoption of a technology that offers great potential for developing-country farmers.

4. As discussed later in this chapter, the link between GM and organic regulations is reinforced in many countries by the exclusion of genetically modified foods from the category of "organic" products, even though the GM technology is often designed to reduce the use of chemical pesticides.

of the "niche" nature of the demand, and because large farming enterprises are finding them increasingly attractive. Governments have been somewhat reluctant to enter this arena where the justification for public intervention is hard to pin down. As a result, most governments limit their intervention to establishing voluntary standards and supervising certification and verification procedures. Problems only surface at the multilateral level when the national, voluntary certification schemes conflict and governments feel obliged to assist in reconciling them.[5]

The third emerging issue in the food system examined in this chapter is animal welfare, which, in many ways, most clearly illustrates the new demands for regulation of process attributes.[6] Animal welfare legislation is at present the province of only a handful of developed countries. But the potential for trade disputes is considerable as consumers ask for more information about how animals were raised, transported, and slaughtered. Producers have begun to demand some compensation for the extra costs associated with adhering to consumer-inspired legislation on animal welfare, and retailers are looking for ways to assure their customers that they are buying only from responsible, humane producers. In this environment, and in the absence of an international consensus on acceptable standards for the treatment of animals, government responses to domestic pressures could easily lead to trade conflicts.

Labeling Process Attributes

Table 7.1 illustrates three different types of labeling regime for process attributes. The first column characterizes the European Union's GM labeling regime, which is discussed later in this chapter. Under this regime, any genetically modified product must, under defined conditions, carry a label. The chain of accreditation, conformity assessment, and enforcement is all in the public sector. By contrast, the United States has issued guidelines for the private sector on the use of voluntary claims for GM-free products.

The second column of table 7.1 shows the label regime typical for

5. At least some members of the European Union are eager, however, to encourage organic farming as part of agricultural policy. But once a government gives incentives through agricultural policy, it must develop a consistent and rigorous oversight capacity.

6. A distinction can be drawn between animal welfare and animal rights. Animal welfare refers to the humane treatment of animals that many would regard as an integral aspect of civilized society. The concept of animal rights is somewhat less generally accepted because it implies significant restrictions of the ways in which animals are put to use in the service of humans. The practical basis of animal rights seems controversial, because these rights must be conferred on animals in the absence of their ability to claim them. Although many of the more active animal welfare groups support the concept of animal rights, this concept is not integral to the support of animal welfare legislation.

Table 7.1 Private and public roles in three process-attribute labeling regimes

Role	Regime 1	Regime 2	Regime 3
Legal status	Mandatory	Voluntary	Voluntary
Standard set by	Government	Government	Government
Attribute	Process	Process	Process
Implementation by firms	Segregation of crop supplies	Change in input use	Change in harvest techniques
Conformity assessment			
Accreditation	Government	Government	
Certification	Government	Private sector	Government
Testing	Government		
Documentation	Government		
Inspection/audit	Government		Government
Legal enforcement	Government	Government	Government
Example	Genetically modified organisms in European Union	Organics in United States	Dolphin-safe labels in United States

organic foods, and the third column applies a regime to one animal welfare issue that has been the subject of international dispute: the protection of dolphins during tuna fishing. The government lowers the private sector's cost of making information available on these voluntary regimes by establishing the standard, providing the verification services (accreditation in the first case, certification and inspection in the second), and prosecuting false claims.

Like the label regimes described in chapter 6, all credible process-labeling regimes require standards, verification, and enforcement. Industry initially bears the cost of a change in production and harvesting practices, segregation, and identity preservation. Firms will participate in voluntary schemes only if they believe consumers will pay a premium that covers the additional costs of such regimes over the long run.

Aside from mandatory disclosure requirements, the public sector has several tools at its disposal to substantially affect the provision of information. For example, it can itself provide some informational services, such as creating and certifying public standards that may induce firms to participate in voluntary labeling regimes. Much of the debate is over the effectiveness of those alternatives.

International Regulation of Process Attributes

The disciplines on the regulation of process attributes in the existing multilateral framework of rules and institutions are neither specific nor extensive. As described in chapter 3, the most significant international treatment of labeling process attributes is found in the TBT agreement, which explicitly covers the matter of protecting consumers from misleading labels and other forms of deception. The growing demands for governments in developed countries to provide consumers with even more information on quality-related process attributes is placing an additional burden on the interpretation of the TBT agreement and other international rules.

Although the Uruguay Round made it clear that the new TBT agreement covered production processes, it is still not clear whether process attributes that do not materially affect the final product are subject to the disciplines of the agreement. The TBT agreement is therefore ambiguous in terms of carrying the burden of providing global disciplines for the process attribute regulations examined in this chapter. There is neither an agreed-on interpretation as to whether such process standards are covered or very well defined guidelines for addressing the extended set of consumer information issues.

Lack of clear interpretation of the TBT agreement has not prevented counter-notifications from being raised in the TBT Committee, the predominant ones related to the labeling systems introduced by developed countries. Among the 38 food-labeling regulations challenged by WTO members between 1997 and 2001, 9 dealt specifically with the process attributes discussed in this chapter. A summary of these nine cases is presented in table 7.2.

Although the discussion of process labeling here and later in this chapter focuses largely on the European Union's policy for labeling GM foods, the GM labeling regimes of Australia/New Zealand, Brazil, and Chile also have attracted attention. In addition, Japan's organic food–labeling regime was challenged by several food exporters as being inconsistent with the provisions of the TBT agreement, and the United States was questioned about its regulations on the use of "dolphin-safe" labels on tuna—Brazil, Egypt, Mexico, and Thailand raised doubts about whether the labeling requirement was really "voluntary."[7] Process labeling issues have also arisen in the Committee on Sanitary and Phytosanitary Measures, in particular over the European Union's labeling proposals for GM foods. This matter also has been the focus of several committees within

---

7. Although the GATT panel had ruled against the United States on mandatory measures to enforce its dolphin regulations (see chapter 3), the tuna/dolphin case also was an important test of the role of labeling as part of the trade system. Voluntary labeling was approved by a GATT panel in both the first (1991) and second (1994) reports on this case. The panel upheld the US legislation providing for voluntary "dolphin-safe" labels on the grounds that it conformed to the requirements of the SPS panels, because it had an identified legitimate objective, involved a quantification of the objective, and established a direct relationship between the measure and the objective (Phillips and Josling 2002).

Table 7.2 TBT Committee discussions on process-attribute regulations, 1997–2001

Regulating country	Country(ies) questioning regulation	Notification leading to the complaint
1997		
European Union	Canada, United States	Compulsory indication on the labeling of foodstuffs produced from genetically modified organisms (GMOs)
1998		
European Union	Argentina, Brazil, Canada, New Zealand, United States	Compulsory indication on the labeling of foodstuffs produced from GMOs
1999		
Japan	Australia, Canada, New Zealand, United States	Standards for labeling of organic agricultural products
New Zealand, Australia	Canada	Labeling of food produced using gene technology
2000		
European Union	Canada, India, United States	Marketing standards for eggs
United States	Brazil, Egypt, Mexico, Thailand	Dolphin-safe labels for tuna
2001		
Brazil	United States	Labeling requirements for packed food products containing or produced by GMOs
Chile	Canada	Labeling system for transgenic (GM) foodstuffs
European Union	Argentina, Australia, Brazil, Canada, United States	Traceability and labeling of food and feed products produced from GMOs

Source: Authors' tabulation based on WTO (2002g).

the Codex Alimentarius Commission, as discussed in more detail later in this chapter. Yet governments have been reluctant to push the GM labeling dispute beyond the stage of various committee discussions. This reluctance reflects in part the lack of precision of the TBT agreement and in part the fact that many labeling regulations are only just being put into place.

For biotechnology, another set of multilateral discussions, under the auspices of the 1992 Convention on Biodiversity—known as the Rio Declaration—and emphasizing the risks GM crops pose for the environment, has paralleled those of the WTO. The Rio Declaration confirmed the right of all countries to control the importation of genetic material, including that modified by biotechnology. After much debate, this provision found its expression in the Biosafety (Cartagena) Protocol of 2000, which, following ratification, approval, or acceptance by 50 signatories, came into effect in September 2003. The Biosafety Protocol sidesteps the GM food issue by dealing primarily with "living modified organisms" (LMOs), such as seeds, rather than those incorporated into foods and feeds. The Biosafety Protocol contains a labeling obligation ("may contain living modified organisms") for transboundary movements of materials intended for processing, but does not force segregation of the supply chains themselves. To this extent, the Biosafety Protocol seems to acknowledge the right of domestic regimes to require mandatory labeling. The Biosafety Protocol tries to avoid any negative signaling effect of labels and does not address the question of who has to pay for any subsequently implied segregation of distribution channels.

The Biosafety Protocol, by permitting mandatory labeling even in the absence of evidence of environmental risk, applies the precautionary principle to trade in LMOs. Whether the precautionary principle as expressed within the protocol includes measures on nonliving genetically modified material is not entirely clear. The Biosafety Protocol acknowledges a country's right to make a "final decision regarding domestic use, including placing on the market," of GM products (Article 11.1). Furthermore, it establishes in Articles 15 and 16 basic rules for risk assessment and risk management and addresses questions of handling, transport, packaging, and identification in Article 18. These regulations are clearly related to international trade.

The relationship between the Biosafety Protocol and the WTO is at best uncertain. The preamble of the protocol states that it "shall not be interpreted as implying a change in the rights and obligations of a Party under any existing international agreements," and clarifies that the WTO agreements provide the relevant disciplines when judging domestic measures for living GM products (such as bulk corn or soybeans) related to international trade. But the protocol itself allows trade regulations, including import bans and labeling requirements, as described, and declares itself not to be subservient to other agreements. Further negotiations, or WTO panel and Appellate Body reports, may be needed to resolve this ambiguity.

One example of this tension is the use of labels for provably GM foods in accordance with the Biosafety Protocol for the purposes of avoiding environmental spillovers. Would this be defensible under Article 2.2 of the TBT agreement because it is aimed at protecting the environment?

Dirk Heumueller and Tim Josling (2001) argue that a dispute settlement panel would probably recognize the multinational approach expressed in the protocol and hence take it into account. But how a panel would judge a labeling requirement for altered foods such as soybean oil in which the GM attribute is not detectable and the environmental effect negligible is much more open to question.

Recent Regulatory Developments: Genetically Modified Foods, Organics, and Animal Welfare

For each of the three emerging food regulatory issues discussed in this chapter, the past few years have brought substantial policy developments. Recent regulatory decisions by countries reflect evolving consumer perceptions and domestic political pressures, and each has substantial implications for the global food system.

Genetically Modified Foods

Three interrelated concerns have emerged about the regulation of GM foods. The first is approval of varieties for use by domestic producers. So far, only a few countries allow GM plants to be grown domestically, and several have halted or delayed the field trials needed to test new varieties. Although it is not clear that trade rules impose any constraints on the speed of a national approval process for introducing new varieties, the pace of adoption may be the most significant factor determining the use of genetically modified foods.[8] A domestic regulatory issue translates into a trade issue if the pace of adoption is substantially different in different countries.

The second issue is the approval of varieties for sale on the domestic market (as opposed to their use in production). This approval can cause larger problems for trade because exporters wishing to sell into those markets view delays as disguised protection. The current US-EU controversy over GM foods stems in large part from the slow pace of adoption of varieties acceptable for sale in the EU domestic market rather than the acceptability of new varieties for production in the European Union. It approved several varieties of corn and soybeans for domestic sale in 1996, but has had an informal embargo on new approvals since 1998. The United States argues that the embargo is equivalent to an import ban without scientific justification, and is therefore subject to the SPS agreement. In

---

8. Robert Paarlberg (2002) describes the tortuous and politicized path toward approval for trials and commercial adoption in several developing countries and argues that this comes at a high cost for those countries.

May 2003 the United States initiated formal consultations with the European Union under the WTO dispute resolution process, and later requested the formation of a panel as the consultations proved inconclusive.

The third GM regulatory issue is the labeling and traceability of GM foods and the products made from GM ingredients. The questions here revolve around the nature of the labels (what standards are to be met and whether the labels are voluntary or mandatory) and the verification process. Much of the discussion in the WTO has focused on these questions, and the trade rules are coming under scrutiny to determine which particular labeling schemes are allowable. Moreover, the label issue is intertwined with the approval issue. For example, if GM imports are banned, the labeling issue is moot. But if labeled imports are allowed and local use is not approved, domestic farmers may be placed at a cost disadvantage in production, but only foreign producers may have to incur traceability and segregation costs to label their products.

Conflicting Approaches to GM Foods

These three concerns over the regulation of GM foods illustrate the tensions that can arise when countries choose different approaches. Even countries that decide to require labels have a choice of how to proceed. For example, a government decision to regulate the labeling of GMs as a process attribute would require tracking of the regulated product at every stage of the supply chain to verify that products bearing "GM-free" labels have been segregated from conventionally produced commodities. EU regulations for mandatory labeling of GM foods, which require that all ingredients produced from GM commodities be traceable—even processed ingredients such as soy oil from which the novel protein has been removed—incorporate such process attribute standards and enforcement.[9] Alternatively, regulators could choose to require labeling of a content attribute for altered DNA, set a product standard (e.g., a product must contain no more than 0.5 percent or 1.0 percent GM material to make the claim "GM-free"), and specify a product sampling and testing protocol to verify compliance. The Australia New Zealand Food Authority (ANZFA) regime for mandatory labeling of GM food products, which accepts testing for novel protein as a means for verifying the absence of GM ingredients, has adopted this approach. The choices made among these methods of regulation can substantially affect the level and distribution of the costs of the regulation.

The trade impacts of the disagreements over GM foods are potentially very significant, but so far they have been moderated by the substitution

---

9. The new EU labeling regulations will be among the most stringent of any country. Labeling and traceability will be required for all products produced from GM material, even when detection of the modified protein is impossible. The contamination tolerance for GM-free products will be only 0.5 percent.

possibilities in the international markets. Several corn varieties used in the United States have not, because of the moratorium, received approval for importation into the European Union. This situation has hindered sales of US corn to the European Union, although imports are also limited by high levels of protection at the border and an EU exportable surplus of cereals. US-produced Bt corn, used largely for animal feed, can still be sold in most importing markets, as can the livestock fed on this corn. US glyphosate-resistant (GR) soybeans can still be sold in the European Union and go largely into food products, but manufacturers and retailers in Europe have been able to buy increasingly from non-GM sources. GM canola oil from Canada finds a market in other countries, and Bt cotton is used in the textile and clothing industry without segregation. But the trade frictions will grow as new biotechnology crops become available. US producer interests, for example, are keen to see the WTO case proceed against the EU moratorium on new GM approvals as a way of dissuading other countries from following the European Union's example.[10]

Underlying the GM trade issues are the divergent ways in which countries have approached the regulation of products from agricultural biotechnology. Many countries are still in the process of deciding on their regulatory approaches to GM foods, but both the United States and the European Union have established their divergent frameworks, though each in a somewhat roundabout way.

In the United States, a markedly cautious approach to regulation has historically characterized food safety issues, at least until 1984.[11] In case after case, regulatory decisions emphasized precaution and minimal risk to consumers and the environment.[12] Consistent use of scientific risk assessment was not a hallmark of US food regulation, and regulation of biotechnology followed a similar path in its early development. And yet by the mid-1980s, the United States was charting a rather different regulatory approach to biotechnology, as the Food and Drug Administration

---

10. US producers put the loss of corn exports to the European Union at about $300 million in 2002. Introduction of a new GM corn variety in 2003 could increase these stakes if it puts at risk EU purchases of corn gluten (a by-product of use of corn for sweetener production). This situation led midwestern farmers to debate the advisability of adopting the new variety.

11. For a fuller discussion of the regulatory differences between the United States and the European Union in the area of biotech, see Patterson and Josling (2001), Vogel (2001), and Pollack and Shaffer (2001).

12. This approach reached its peak in the Delaney Clause, contained in a 1958 amendment to the Food, Drug and Cosmetic Act of 1954. The clause banned the use of any food additive if tests revealed that it caused cancer in either laboratory animals or humans (Vogel 2001). As a result, air quality standards, pesticide restrictions, drug safety tests, and groundwater contamination rules all focused on the "potential" rather than the "probable" findings of hazards.

worked with the industry to devise a framework that was conducive to investment and not unduly burdensome (Vogel 2001).[13] A biotech product that was "substantially equivalent" to a conventionally produced food product that was, in turn, "generally recognized as safe" needed no label or special testing. The requirements for establishing substantial equivalence were not so onerous that they kept GM foods off the market, and the incorporation of modified corn and soybeans into the food chain followed directly from this decision by the FDA.

The European Union also followed a product-based model in the early 1980s. Before the widespread utilization of recombinant DNA (rDNA) techniques in a variety of industries, most food and agricultural products were evaluated on the safety, quality, and efficacy of the final product—not on the process by which the product was produced. The widespread use of rDNA, however, led some EU policymakers to advocate regulations based on the production process. These ideas found their way into the legislation when the European Union adopted a process-based, horizontal, precautionary approach to biotech regulation. This set the stage for the trade tensions that emerged with the United States at the end of the 1990s.

To complicate trade matters, private-sector food firms began to develop strategies to deal with the problem of low consumer acceptance of GM foods in major (mostly European) markets. By announcing their own policies—ranging from avoiding all GM ingredients in products carrying their own labels (two of the supermarket chains in the United Kingdom) to avoiding the sale of meat from animals fed GM cereals or oilseed products (two other UK chains)—private-sector firms tried to maintain consumer trust even if it compromised their own access to low-cost supply sources (Grant 1999). The private sector therefore engaged in self-regulation as a way of dealing with the problem of standard setting in the global marketplace, but the result was elaborate segregation of supplies, at considerable cost to suppliers and with no demonstrable health and safety benefits for consumers. And the self-regulation appears to have increased rather than decreased the calls for mandatory labeling and traceability in Europe.

The Debate on Labeling

As a proxy for the underlying debate about the acceptability of GM foods, the debate among countries on whether to require labels and on the coverage of those labels has assumed enhanced significance. The European Union has argued that strict labeling regulations are a prerequisite to

---

13. The US biotech industry also received a strong economic incentive from the landmark decision by the US Supreme Court in 1980 (*Diamond v. Chakrabarty*) to allow patents to be awarded for products of biotech, even if such products were in effect "life forms." This decision set off a string of mergers and acquisitions that left the agricultural seed industry heavily concentrated in a few companies.

new GM food approvals.[14] Accordingly, much of the discussion in international institutions has revolved around the issue of GM labeling and traceability rather than the desirability of adopting the technology at the production level, or even the health and safety of consuming genetically modified products.

Labeling GM foods is both popular with consumers and an apparently reasonable way of allowing the market to decide on the premiums for desired attributes. At one level, the differences in consumer perception and sensitivity between countries could be handled by providing information in the form of labels. European consumers could exercise their right to avoid GM foods, and the US consumers, should they choose, could ignore the information on the label as being of no particular relevance to their consumption decision. However, labels are by no means an easy solution, and merely move the debate to how to label and how to enforce the labeling regulation. Moreover, the act of labeling can itself be a signal. The main concern of the food-processing industry and the exporting countries about labels is their impact on consumers' perceptions. A label that stigmatizes a product could cause a drop in market demand. Even a neutral label could be used by opponents of the technology to convince consumers that the product is associated with health or environmental problems.

Because the debate over labels mirrors that over the acceptability of the GM products themselves, exporting countries tend to favor voluntary labels, at least for other countries, as a way of avoiding stigmatization of their products. Importing countries, which have less of a problem with the notion of mandatory labels, are content to take the higher ground of advocating the consumer's right to know and leave it up to the exporter to bear the cost of segregation and of persuading consumers of product safety. In contrast to more traditional protectionism, mandatory labeling schemes are rarely the result of producer pressure but rather of consumer and environmental concerns expressed through a variety of channels. But exporters still see their market as potentially constrained by the fact that the government feels obliged to tell consumers about some characteristic of their product or process. For that reason, labeling is the subject of a continuing dispute among the countries exporting GM foods and those that are reluctant to import these products.

The main venue for disputes over GM labeling within the WTO has

---

14. This emphasis has stemmed in large part from the fact that the European Commission needs to obtain the agreement of certain member states to restart the approval process for GM foods. These countries have insisted that labeling and traceability systems be put into place before they will allow approval of more GM varieties. The commission has indicated that it might take these countries to the European Court of Justice for unduly delaying an obligation to consider the new varieties. The commission in 2003 attempted to persuade the US Congress that as the approval process was expected to start by the end of the year, a formal WTO challenge would be counterproductive.

been the TBT Committee, and the main subject of disputes has been the European Union's evolving regulations. Marketing genetically modified soybeans and genetically modified maize (corn) had been authorized without any special labeling requirements prior to the entry into force of Regulation (EC) No. 258/97 in 1997, known widely as the "Novel Foods Regulation." Regulation (EC) No. 1813/97 first prescribed specific labeling requirements for foods and food ingredients produced from GM soybeans or maize that were judged not equivalent to their conventional counterparts. The latter regulation was replaced by Regulation (EC) No. 1139/98, "Concerning the Compulsory Indication of the Labeling of Certain Foodstuffs Produced from Genetically Modified Organisms," adopted by the Council of Ministers of the European Union in May 1998 and entered into force in September 1998.

The European Union first notified its modified labeling regulation to the TBT Committee in December 1997.[15] The regulation required that a food or food ingredient, produced from GM soybeans or maize containing DNA or protein resulting from such genetic modification, bear the words "produced from genetically modified soybeans" or "produced from genetically modified maize" on the ingredient list or on the food label. The EU regulation stated that, among other objectives, the labeling requirements were

> necessary to ensure that the final consumer is informed of any characteristic or food property, such as composition, nutritional value or nutritional effects of the intended use of the food, which renders a food or food ingredient no longer equivalent to an existing food or food ingredient.

Exporting countries were less than satisfied. The US delegation to the WTO made it clear they did not object to the goal of providing useful information to consumers, but questioned whether the regulation would achieve this objective, and the others set forth in the preamble to the regulation. The United States, supported by Canada, pointed out that problems with the implementation of the regulations would "make compliance difficult, at best" (WTO 1998c).

Canada raised concerns about the trade disruptions that might result from the EU GM labeling requirement, the ability of the EU labeling scheme to provide consumers with meaningful information on GM food ingredients, and the difficulties to be faced in ensuring and enforcing compliance.[16] Moreover, Canada pointed out, similar labels, with their

---

15. Details of the debate over the European Union's labeling regime are drawn primarily from the TBT Committee reports cited.

16. According to the European Union, the label would give consumers information about the composition of a food by indicating that it had modified characteristics. But Canada doubted that the statement "produced from genetically modified soybeans" conveyed information about the composition or characteristics of a food.

implications, could spread to other sectors such as animal welfare; forestry, mining, and fisheries with eco-labeling schemes; and manufacturing with labeling schemes based on labor standards. Canada, on its domestic market, had taken the approach of developing a voluntary scheme for the labeling of products derived from modern biotechnology as a practical means of providing information to consumers while upholding its WTO obligations (WTO 1999d).

The European Union was not alone in being criticized. Canada also raised questions about the TBT notification from New Zealand. It stated that New Zealand and Australia might amend ANZFA Standard A18 to require labeling of products derived from "gene technology" even if they were substantially equivalent to traditionally derived products. Canada was concerned about the labeling of "like products" simply because they were produced by a different production or processing method. Canada also asked why this technical regulation was necessary, how the proposed labeling scheme would be made consistent with international trade obligations that required nondiscrimination among like products, how the scheme would be verified and enforced, what methods of analysis and sampling would be used to ensure the accuracy of the labeling, how and when all the necessary methods of analysis would be developed, and whether all methods of analysis and sampling schemes would be subject to international scrutiny and verification.[17]

The issue of GM labeling has also been raised in the SPS Committee, but the discussion began with an issue not related to labeling. In June 2000 Thailand formally challenged Egypt's decision to restrict food imports containing GMOs and requested consultations through the Dispute Settlement Understanding (DSU) (DS 205 in table 3.2). Thailand, citing its exports of canned tuna affected by the Egyptian decision, argued that tuna exported to Egypt did not contain soybean oil produced from genetically modified plants. Moreover, Thailand claimed it was not possible to identify the origin of soybean oil because the final processing stages destroyed genetic material. Thailand therefore found the restrictions on its canned tuna discriminatory, and asked the Egyptian government to lift them.[18]

This case, although not between major agricultural trading partners, raised a fundamental question that the SPS (and TBT) Committees have eventually to face: Can a label or trade restriction that relates to a process

---

17. But this issue was not entirely new; regulation of process attributes had already been raised within the WTO in another context. Trade ministers had called on the WTO Committee on Trade and the Environment to discuss "labeling for environmental purposes," and this discussion had led to more complex issues such as labeling for the sole purpose of describing a "life-cycle analysis" (LCA) that examines the full environmental impact of a single product, including water and energy use and release of various pollutants. For more information, see IISD and UNEP (2000).

18. No resolution to this conflict was reported to the SPS Committee, nor has the dispute been directed to a panel.

be justified when the product itself is not practically (in this instance, chemically) distinguishable from similar products that did not come from that process?

The series of discussions that have taken place in the SPS Committee have mainly revolved around the European Union's proposed revision of its labeling regulations for GM foods. In October 2001 the United States expressed concerns in the SPS Committee that the European Communities (EC) proposals on traceability and labeling of agricultural biotechnology products had been notified only under the TBT agreement and not the SPS agreement, although the proposals made it clear they were intended to address unforeseen adverse effects to human and animal health.

At the same meeting of the SPS Committee, the United States pointed out that no functioning approval process had been in place in the European Union for agricultural biotechnology products since 1998. It went on to argue that under the SPS agreement the European Union was obligated to have a functioning approval process, and decisions on pending applications should not be delayed.

Canada was concerned that the European Union was fundamentally altering the regulation of agriculture and food products to discriminate on the basis of how a product was produced rather than its characteristics. Canada also considered the proposed EU regulations to be arbitrary because they required labeling for highly refined products, such as oil, that did not contain detectable DNA or protein, while not requiring similar controls on products that could present equal risk but were produced by other methods, such as mutation breeding or mutagenesis. Moreover, the proposed regulations discriminated against goods produced *from* genetically modified products, but not against goods such as cheese and wine produced *with* genetically modified organisms. Canada argued that the proposed regulations were not commensurate with the risks and lacked scientific basis.

Finally, Canada and the United States sought clarification about whether the draft regulations were intended to improve food safety or human health. Argentina also noted that GM food did not affect health, and sought clarification about whether the labeling requirements extended to pharmaceutical products for human or animal use. The European Union stated that discussions should continue in the TBT Committee.

The experience of the TBT and SPS Committees has been one of predictable sparring between the GM-exporting countries and those that have not adopted GM technology in their domestic agriculture. The latter claim adamantly that consumers need labeling to make reasoned choices. The GM-exporting countries argue that such labels would stigmatize GM foods and not add to food safety. When a panel reports in the US dispute with the European Union on the moratorium on GM approvals, it will provide a significant formal test of the extent to which multilateral rules can be used to resolve GM trade conflicts. The outcome could also exacerbate transatlantic tensions and erode some of the political support for the WTO.

Because little consensus has emerged from the debate in the TBT and SPS Committees, the labeling issue has also been taken up by the Codex, through its Committee on Food Labeling (CCFL). In May 2000 the Codex established a drafting group to elaborate a guideline for labeling foods derived through biotechnology. At its May 2000 meeting, the CCFL considered the options of either mandatory labeling based on health and safety considerations or mandatory labeling based on the method of production as well as on health and safety considerations. In general, the committee advocated labeling when food and food ingredients are no longer equivalent to their conventional counterparts, when they are composed of or contain a GM organism or protein or DNA resulting from gene technology, and when they are produced from but do not contain GM organisms, protein, or DNA resulting from gene technology.[19] The purpose of the CCFL draft guidelines for labeling was simply to "set out a number of approaches and related information that could be used for labeling of food and food ingredients obtained through techniques of genetic modification/genetic engineering" (Patterson and Josling 2001, 7).

A CCFL meeting held in Halifax, Nova Scotia, in May 2002 made no progress in reaching an agreement on biotech labeling. The discussion revolved around two different issues: (1) the definition of biotech foods in the general standard for labeling prepackaged foods, and (2) guidelines for national GM food labeling regulations. The definition was a choice between products of "modern biotechnology" and "genetically modified/engineered" foods. The country positions reflected the split between the producers and the potential importers of GM foods. Exporters felt that consumers would not be put off by the notion of foods being produced by modern biotech methods, but that they might object to the concept of genetic engineering. The importers and the observers from nongovernmental organizations (NGOs) supported the more familiar, if more sinister, notion of engineered foods. On the labeling issue, the division reflected the views already expressed in the SPS and TBT Committees. Exporters objected to the notion of mandatory labels for process attributes, and the importers insisted that labels would tell consumers what they wanted to know. Both issues were held at their respective steps in the Codex approval process.[20]

Codex members also looked at safety assessments for GM foods and how to conduct them. The Ad Hoc Intergovernmental Task Force on Foods Derived from Biotechnology held its first meeting in March 2000.

---

19. The full proposed draft recommendation can be found at www.fao.org/codex/alinorm01/al0122ae.pdf.

20. The definition issue is at step 6 of the eight-step process to full approval described in chapter 3; the labeling guidelines are at step 3.

The task force agreed that a list of analytical methods for detecting and identifying foods or food ingredients derived from biotechnology should be compiled. The committee's preliminary report was submitted to the Codex in July 2001.[21]

Resolution of the debate over trade in GM foods is becoming urgent. A transatlantic conflict more ominous than the hormones dispute is brewing, and the stakes are higher this time. Developing countries are caught in the middle of this dispute, facing the uncomfortable choice of whether to line up behind the United States or the European Union on the question of GM foods. The dilemma is critical for a country that might wish to import corn or soybeans from the United States for human consumption, or approve GM products for domestic production, yet still seek to export crop or livestock products to the European Union.[22] The developing country may take advantage of low-price imports or cost-reducing new technology at the risk of losing export markets. Solving this problem alone would have an important, beneficial impact on the operation of the world food system, particularly for some of those people most at risk of food insecurity. The broader outline of a resolution to the GM dispute does not, however, appear to be in sight.

Organic Foods

Organic foods are one of the fastest-growing segments of the food market in many developed countries. The potential for profits appears to be considerable from consumers willing to pay premium prices for organic foods. Governments have stepped in to give credibility to the national certification schemes and help consumers to navigate the sea of competing claims. Because the lure of profits has attracted larger enterprises into the market, this in itself ensures that some trade tensions will emerge as exporters compete with domestic producers and small farmers with large corporations. The divergence in national organic food regulations could quickly become a trade issue if not managed within an appropriate framework. Such trade problems are likely to center on conflicts over the definition and accreditation of organic produce. This section looks first at the growing market for organic foods and then at national approaches to regulation that may affect trade.

---

21. The report is available on the Codex Web site, www.fao.org/codex/alinorm01/al0134ae.pdf.

22. This issue surfaced recently when three African countries declined shipments of US corn as food aid. Though the issue was posed as one of food safety, the underlying problem was that food exports from these countries to the European Union might be compromised in the future if farmers planted some of the corn designated for food aid. The solution was to require that the corn be ground before distribution in the recipient country. A similar dilemma can occur if a country imports soybeans or oil from the United States and exports processed foods, such as in the Thailand-Egypt dispute.

The Growing Market for Organics

The growth of the market for organic food has been widespread in developed countries. Although organic products make up less than 5 percent of total food purchases, Luanne Lohr (2001) reports growth rates of 15 to 30 percent in the size of the market in Europe, the United States, and Japan during the past five years. Market surveys indicate that between 20 and 30 percent of consumers in North America, Europe, and Japan purchase organic food regularly.[23] Not all the growth has been satisfied by increases in domestic production: imports account for a significant portion of organic foods (about 10 percent in the Japanese and French markets, but higher in other European markets), and that share could rise significantly as constraints on domestic organic production become apparent.

Consumers buy organic food for its higher quality and freshness, for its supposed health benefits, out of concern for the environment, and as a "lifestyle" statement about the merits of independent, local producers selling more directly to the public. Each of these presumed qualities is linked to a different aspect of the regulation of food. Indeed, because of this complexity of attributes the regulation of organics differs by country and thus poses a challenge to multilateral rules.

Julie Caswell (1997) points out that governments use process regulations in defining product characteristics of organic foods. The use of process standards to indicate to farmers what they can and cannot do in producing organic products results in content attributes (absence of pesticides) as well as process attributes (earth-friendliness). And consumers may see in such process regulations other product attributes such as health and quality. These latter attributes pose a dilemma for regulators. Public oversight of the food system is desired to ensure that all food sold is healthy and safe, to the limits of resources and administrative skills. Therefore, any recognition of a "healthier" type of food production process is immediately a problem. To sustain the health link, organic as well as conventional foods would have to be tested on the same grounds, a process the supporters of organic food have always rejected. Limits on the types of pesticide used, a major criterion in most organic standards, might be attractive to risk-averse consumers, but other organic practices, such as the reliance on organic fertilizer, may introduce new risks.[24]

---

23. The current value of organics sales in Japan is about $3 billion. The size of the market in Europe is $5.3 billion and that in the United States is estimated at $6.6 billion (Lohr 2001). Within Europe, the German market for organics is by far the largest, at almost $2 billion.

24. Lohr (2001) suggests that conflicting data on the nutritional, environmental, and human safety qualities of organics, along with strict truth-in-advertising laws, have made US retailers wary about claims for organics. Some states explicitly prohibit comparisons with conventional produce that may imply that such conventional goods are inferior.

If the predominant consumer motive for buying organics is quality rather than health, the market should meet consumer demands through appropriate voluntary labeling because organic foods will have desirable experience characteristics. Only light supervision would be needed to avoid deceptive practices. On the other hand, if the consumer believes that organics promote health because no toxic chemicals were used in their production, the authorities would probably be obliged to regulate the market more intensively. Otherwise, the consumer would not be able to ascertain whether the claims are justified (organic food would have credence characteristics, and the temptation to cut corners would be irresistible for some producers). This situation would pose a multiple jurisdictional problem for trade because the certification of production and processing methods would often be in another country. There also would be more direct pressure to compare organic and nonorganic foods for their health benefits because the producers of "conventional" foods are unlikely to quietly cede the notion that they are selling anything less healthy to the public.

If, by contrast, a consumer's primary motive for buying organic food is that it is good for the environment, even more trade problems may arise. A certification about the chemicals used (or not used) in organics would go partway toward describing the "life-cycle" effect of the product on the environment in which the food is produced. But a more substantial environmental impact statements might also be needed, adding to cost and offering another avenue for discrimination against foreign produce. On the other hand, if the demand for organic food is in fact a personal statement about support for local merchants and small farmers in their struggle against multinational corporations and large-scale farming operations, then a fundamental conflict exists between the growing demand for such local produce (sometimes called "food sovereignty") and the concept of an open global market. Although it is not clear what role the government will assume in the organics market besides validating certification and preventing the most egregious false advertising, political pressure will undoubtedly be brought to bear for definitions of organic farming that make it more difficult for foreign producers to compete.[25]

Evidence accumulated by Lohr (2001) suggests that the balance among these various motivations for buying organic foods differs among countries. In the United States and Europe, quality, freshness, and taste are the main reasons given for purchase of organic foods. In Japan, food safety is the driving force, listed as the main concern by 80 percent of consumers in a 1995 survey. Japanese retailers emphasize this perception of organics

---

25. A hands-off policy may be particularly difficult when a green party is in power (particularly at the national level), because the promotion of particular lifestyles may then become government policy. The appointment of a Green Party minister of consumer protection, food, and agriculture in Germany in early 2001 made this question anything but academic.

in their advertisements, although freshness and quality also are thought to be important to consumers. European retailers have emphasized food safety aspects as well, in light of a series of food scares and the lack of acceptance of GM foods. US supermarket chains have been reluctant to use arguments for buying organics that may imply that conventional foods are anything less than safe. Overall, each of the motivations described here will be reflected in certain aspects of the regulations governing the production and marketing of organic foods.

National Approaches to Regulation

Organic foods have been available for many years, but it was not until the early 1990s that regulation of organic production and products began to be more widespread through a series of nonmandatory compliance initiatives and the establishment of nonbinding national standards. The United States and the European Union led the early wave of regulatory activity. The US Organic Foods Production Act (1990) established national standards for production and marketing and regulated domestic interstate commerce. The EU Council Regulation on Organic Foods (EEC No. 2092/91), passed in 1991, specifically addressed international trade issues, and it required third-country government assurances that their standards were equivalent to those used in the European Union. Australia followed suit with the National Standards for Organic and Bio-Dynamic Produce in 1992. Argentina became the first country in the Americas to establish standards equivalent to those of the European Union when both the International Federation of Organic Agriculture Movements (IFOAM) and the European Union recognized Argentine organic certification.

A second round of regulatory activity occurred in the late 1990s. Brazil's first organic regulation, Directive 505 published in 1998, applied to vegetable and animal products and addressed both production and handling issues. In 1999 Canada established the National Standard for Organic Agriculture. These standards, which defined organic products and acceptable production methods, specifically identified genetic modification and ionizing radiation as nonorganic processes. In Japan, a series of eight regulatory instruments were established in 2000, under the umbrella of the Law Concerning Standardization and Proper Labeling of Agricultural and Forestry Products.

During the late 1990s, both the United States and the European Union revised earlier regulations. The EU legislation (Regulation (EEC) No. 1804/99) covered a wide range of issues from crop and livestock production to labeling, processing, inspection, and marketing. It also regulated trade among EU member states and between the European Union and third countries. The United States established the National Standards on Organic Agricultural Production and Handling in 2000 pursuant to the Organic Foods Production Act of 1990. These standards delineated organic products, labeling criteria, methods, practices, substances, and production and handling procedures for crops and livestock—for both processed and fresh products. Like Canadian standards, the US standards prohibit genetic engineering methods and ionizing radiation. These standards became effective in 2003. Meanwhile, Argentina also passed a revised National Law on Organic Production in 1999.

Each of these countries regulates organic foods using a mix of government and industry initiatives. But government involvement can vary considerably from country to country. In Canada, compliance with the National Standard for Organic Agriculture is voluntary, as is true for most Canadian national standards. This standard functions more as a guideline than as a regulation. Federal or provincial regulations are implemented only in cases involving potential risks to public health and safety. Compliance with organic standards is also voluntary in New Zealand, but Argentina, Brazil, and the European Union have laws and regulations that require mandatory compliance for those who claim to sell "organic" produce. The US standards are also mandatory and take precedence over state and private standards. The US standards require a product to have a minimum of 70 percent organic ingredients to be labeled "Made with Organic Ingredients."[26] Australia and Japan have both voluntary and mandatory elements. Although there are no legal restrictions on use of the terms organic and bio-dynamic in Australia, organic exports require certification. The National Standards for Organic and Bio-dynamic Produce function as a minimum basis for such certification. Japan has mandatory labeling regulations for produce sold as organic, but compliance with organic production processes is left up to the manufacturers (Takahashi 1999).

Although each of these regulations appears to have been driven by local considerations, regulators have kept a steady eye on the trade implications. All of the countries just mentioned have been keen to ensure access for their organic products to the large EU market. This access plays a key role in defining the specifics of their organic regulations as well as the impetus for and timing of regulations overall. The EU organic regulations therefore appear to be the driving force in the development of standards on an international level. Countries must either establish equivalent standards to those of the European Union or lose out on a major import market.[27] The rapid responses by national governments are

---

26. This percentage is a change from the 50 percent requirement suggested in an earlier draft of the standards, and it is of particular importance because it establishes a minimum requirement that is consistent with EU standards.

27. This statement is supported by the fact that the organic accreditation bodies of several countries, including Australia, Argentina, Israel, and Switzerland, have been recognized as having standards equivalent to those of the European Union. Talks between the European Union and the United States on mutual recognition of organic standards have so far proved unfruitful, though the European Union also has an interest in maintaining access to the US market for organic produce.

indicative of a race to create and adjust domestic standards in the face of a shift in the EU regulatory framework. This regulatory race reveals, and at the same time solidifies, the increasing interdependence of regulations in the global context.

Trade problems in organic foods are likely to take the form of disputes over the way in which an imported organic food has been produced under different standards. Even where the regulations concerned are public certification of essentially voluntary schemes, differences in definitions are likely to result in complaints that certification schemes are being used to discriminate against imports. Despite emergence of the EU standards influencing global regulation, the significant differences among national organic standards could constitute a minefield for trade policy. The credibility of foreign standards is also likely to be an issue. The concept of equivalence may be germane in this regard, but only if countries are willing to negotiate mutual recognition agreements, like that recently concluded between Japan and the United States.

This being said, organic produce regulations have yet to surface as a major trade irritant. However, the sensitivity of this issue is heightened in part by its connection with the dispute over trade in genetically modified foods and, to a lesser extent, through its link with animal welfare. By specifically excluding GM foods from the definition of "organic," countries have inadvertently boosted the market for organic products. The controversy over GM labeling is not unrelated to the issue of organic certification. If mandatory GM labels are introduced, organic producers will find it easier to distinguish their products in the market and capitalize on consumer distrust of the health and safety impacts of GM foods.[28] As for the link with animal welfare, some of the standards for organic foods include a requirement that animals be treated in a particular way. Thus the organic standards could develop in a way that is complementary to those for animal welfare and GM foods: purchasing organic foods may give the consumer some indication of the animal welfare practices employed and some assurance of the absence of GM ingredients.

Animal Welfare

Government regulation of animal welfare responds to the varying sensitivities of consumers to certain agricultural practices. These sensitivities usually reflect income, cultural, and other factors. Industrialized countries—particularly the United States, European Union, Canada, and Japan—have been the first to enact animal welfare regulations, while even relatively

---

28. Another important link between GM crops and organic producers is that organic farmers often use the naturally occurring Bt bacteria for pest control. To the extent that widespread cultivation of Bt crops spurs pest resistance to the insecticide, organic producers fear that their own production practices may be compromised.

high-income developing countries, such as Argentina and Brazil, do not as yet have such regulations.

Animal Welfare and Trade

The major divergence in the demand for, and existence of, animal welfare regulations is a cause for concern in the trade system. If countries cannot agree on the need for domestic regulations in a particular area, they are unlikely to be able to reach an international consensus on such standards. Animal welfare issues have been raised in the Doha Round agriculture negotiations and have revived fears that they are a cover for protectionism. They have not yet led to important multilateral regulatory conflicts, but this may soon change.

The nature of the animal welfare regulations in those countries that have implemented them governs in large part the extent to which trade conflicts occur. Voluntary animal welfare standards should have a relatively benign effect on the food system, much like voluntary organic marketing standards in one or more countries that may not be inconsistent with open markets. Even so, such regulations, by their nature, require controls on production and processing methods, because the way in which an animal has been treated will presumably not be expressed in any measurable characteristic of the product on the dinner table.[29] And they will tend to involve costs to producers, who will notice an effect on their competitiveness.

Animal welfare may be a desired attribute when attached to a food, but it is also a credence characteristic: no amount of search or experience will allow the consumer of meat to know for certain how the animal was treated when alive. This situation suggests a possible role for the government, at least in establishing credible labeling. If governments instituted such labeling schemes, then suppliers both at home and abroad could sell into the market without further regulation. A certification system would, however, have to be in place to ensure that consumers could be sure of the way in which the product was produced.

Mandatory regulations governing the conditions of production, transportation, and slaughter of animals pose greater problems, because they usually add more to costs. Almost inevitably, then, domestic producers will demand subsidies to offset the additional costs or protection at the border against producers in other countries. Thus the trade impacts could

---

29. The conditions under which an animal is raised can, of course, influence the quality of its meat. Grain-fed and grass-fed beef, for example, have a notably different texture and taste. But the treatment of animals within any particular farm system is unlikely to be reflected in the meat. Moreover, the label could be misleading: "free-range" chickens and "grass-fed" beef may still have been treated in ways that consumers might find degrading. The farming technology is only a proxy for the actual treatment of the animals.

escalate as the spread of mandatory animal welfare regulations leads to more demands for protection.[30]

Trade problems associated with mandatory animal welfare are distinct from the more traditional agricultural regulatory issues because the pressures on politicians and trade diplomats come from a different source. It is unusual to find producer groups actively pushing animal welfare regulation. The pressures come essentially from consumer-oriented animal welfare groups, often linked with like-minded groups in other countries. Counterpressure from producer groups for expanded agricultural subsidies to offset cost differences imputed to domestic regulations represents another minefield for trade, especially because of the controversy over the already high levels of subsidies in developed countries.

Trade conflicts over animal welfare could occur between developed countries when their differing emphases and values clash, or between developed and developing countries when the producers in developing countries are pressured to adjust their production processes for exports to conform to regulations of the wealthier countries. Mandatory, process-based regulations tend to deny consumers some freedom of choice, and they may require producers in other countries to follow suit. Consumers who otherwise would choose to buy lower-priced foods that do not meet such mandatory standards must pay a higher price. Such regulation is likely to be regressive in effect, because food price increases affect poor consumers proportionately more than the affluent. Overall, the trade benefits from harmonization of animal welfare legislation are likely to be considerable, at least from the viewpoint of reducing transactions costs, but harmonization in the face of very different public sensitivities can lead to overprotection. Those consumers who care less about the conditions of production than about the price of the product will in effect be forced to support a higher level of animal welfare than they wish.

Animal Welfare Regulations

The roots of current animal welfare regulations go at least as far back as the US Humane Slaughter Act of 1958 (see table 7.3). In 1973 Japan enacted the Law Concerning the Protection and Control of Animals that prohibited cruelty and abandonment. Several other countries also enacted animal welfare regulations in the 1970s and 1980s, in response to some well-publicized animal welfare abuses and pressure by nongovernmental organizations.[31] The first EC regulation of farm animals

---

30. The political economy asymmetry is apparent. Producers do not offer to be taxed when domestic regulations are less onerous than those of trading partners or argue for subsidies on imports when foreign regulations are more burdensome.

31. Greenpeace, later the leading NGO critic of GM foods, became well known during this period for its campaigns to "save the whales" and to prevent the clubbing of baby seals in the Arctic. Although these issues were not related to food and farming,

Table 7.3   Examples of animal welfare regulations in selected countries

Type of law	Requirement	Law or country
Defines and requires general standards of treatment	Mandates that all animals be allowed adequate food, exercise, and freedom from torture and overwork	California penal code, Maine statutes
	Mandates that animals not be treated cruelly or abandoned	Japan's Law Concerning the Protection and Control of Animals, 1973
Regulates slaughter	Specifies how animals must be treated during the slaughtering process	US Humane Slaughter Act of 1958
	Specifies rules for slaughterhouse conditions and the slaughtering process	European Convention for the Protection of Animals for Slaughter—EU Council Directive 93/119/EC, 1993
Regulates the area and methods for confining animals	Specifies minimum cage sizes for hens of 450–600 cm^2	Australia
	Prohibits hog tethering	Australia
	Outlines general requirements for keeping animals on farms, including provision of food, freedom of movement, inspections, lighting that is altered to resemble night and day, air circulation, and pens that can be cleaned	European Convention for the Protection of Animals Kept for Farming Purposes—EU Council Directive 98/58/EC, 1998
	Mandates, by the year 2003, hen cage sizes that allow laying hens a minimum of 550 cm^2 in which to move around	EU Council Directive 1999/74/EC, 1999
Governs animals during transport	Provides regulations for the treatment of animals during transport, which specify the intervals during which animals are to be fed and the characteristics of the space in which they can be confined	European Convention for the Protection of Animals During International Transport—EC Council Directive 91/628/EEC, 1991

Source: Mitchell (2001).

addressed minimum requirements for battery hen cages (EC Council Directive 86/113/EC). In 1988 the Council of Europe in Strasbourg (unrelated to the European Union and with no enforcement powers) agreed to two conventions to promote the humane treatment and slaughter of livestock.[32] The Canadian Health of Animals Act of 1990 regulates the treatment and transportation of animals and establishes voluntary "Codes of Practice."

In the 1990s the European Union became much more active in this area of legislation, and enacted numerous regulations addressing animal welfare.[33] Several of the regulations address specific animals such as calves, pigs, and hens or specific procedures such as transport or slaughter.[34] Of most importance internationally, EU Council Directive 1999/74/EC established new regulations for laying hens.[35] This directive foresees the phasing out of cage systems in favor of noncage systems over a period of 10 years and the institutionalization of registration of all

---

they generated considerable support for animal welfare legislation. Other controversies included the use of leg-hold traps in controlling wildlife (the European Union banned such traps and attempted to restrict imports from those countries that did not) and the transportation of horses and cattle in arguably inhumane conditions across the English Channel. In many countries, controversies are ongoing about the ethics of using animals for sporting activities or for hunting, but these controversies do not seem to generate much tension in trade relations. One major exception is trade in endangered species and products such as ivory. An international agreement, the Convention on International Trade in Endangered Species (CITES), has been moderately successful in regulating such trade.

32. They are the Council of Europe Convention for the Protection of Animals Kept for Farming Purposes and the Council of Europe Convention for the Protection of Animals for Slaughter.

33. A declaration on animal welfare was annexed to the Treaty of the European Union (Maastricht Treaty) in 1992, and the Amsterdam Treaty of 1997 made animal welfare a formal obligation of the European Union and its policies. But in what may be a backlash to the breadth of EU Council Directive 98/58/EC, the Treaty of Amsterdam Protocol on the Protection and Welfare of Animals limits EU legislative competence and specifies areas that remain under the competence of member state governments.

34. Council Directive 91/629/EEC covered the feeding, tethering, and penning of calves. Council Directive 91/630/EEC addressed the weaning, tethering, castration, tooth clipping, and tail docking of pigs, and it established minimum surface requirements for different categories of pigs. Council Directive 91/628/EEC required registration of live animal transporters, limited traveling time, called for compulsory resting time for feed and water, and specified maximum loading densities. Council Directive 93/119/EC regulated the transportation, restraint, and slaughter of animals. This directive prohibited avoidable excitement, pain, or suffering, and it required that animals be stunned before slaughter or killed instantaneously. It also addressed the skill, ability, and knowledge required of staff involved in slaughtering.

35. Among the most common animal welfare regulations are those that deal with the size of poultry cages. The animal welfare complaints center on the amount of space given to laying hens, the practice of debeaking, and the alleged cruelty of the practice of culling day-old chicks in standard poultry production.

egg production units to ensure that all eggs can be traced back to their source. This directive entered into force on January 1, 2002. Currently, the European Union is developing regulations that address the welfare of ducks and geese. The most comprehensive EU regulation to date (EU Council Directive 98/58/EC) takes a step toward "animal rights," and is based on the Farm Animal Welfare Council's "Five Freedoms." Such freedoms are extended to "all species kept for the production of food, wool, skin or fur or for other farming purposes, including fish, reptiles or amphibians."

The United States and New Zealand also updated their animal welfare regulations in the late 1990s and broadened the scope of coverage. The US Code of Federal Regulations on animal welfare was revised in 1999 to include standards addressing health and husbandry systems as well as transportation. New Zealand enacted the Animal Welfare Act in 1999 with similar provisions. The United States continues to allow industry to self-regulate animal welfare where possible. One significant recent development in the US private sector was the decision by McDonald's restaurants, in response to suggestions from animal welfare and animal rights activists, to require suppliers to adopt a code of good practice in housing and raising laying hens and to meet defined standards for cattle slaughter.

Animal Welfare and Trade Conflicts

The aspect of animal welfare legislation that could serve as tinder for trade conflicts is the growing gap in perceptions between the developed and developing world in this area. A delegate to the WTO from a developing country put it bluntly when confronted with the European Union's negotiating paper on the subject: "We are interested in people welfare, not animal welfare." This statement highlights the fact that many in the developing world believe the enactment of animal welfare legislation could damage their trade interests, in much the same way that they fear labor standards in the industrial countries, seeing them as a disguised way of hindering access to rich-country markets. Like environmental protection measures, animal welfare regulations certainly could increase producers' costs and thus affect trade flows. From there it is a short step to demands by producers for compensating subsidies or trade restrictions on imports from countries with less onerous animal welfare standards.

The concept of animal welfare is not covered explicitly in any WTO texts, and no international body is charged developing rules or guidelines in this area. Yet the WTO is having to grapple in the Doha Round negotiations on agriculture with the possibility that subsidies could be paid to farmers in the European Union on the basis of their animal welfare–related farming practices.

In the recent midterm review of the Common Agricultural Policy, the European Council agreed that animal welfare practices could serve as a condition for receiving support payments. Thus the issue of whether these payments are deemed to be minimally trade distorting—along with those assigned to improve environmental practices, for example or are deemed to directly affect production and trade and thus are subject—to WTO disciplines, will have to be addressed, at least implicitly.[36] The development of cage-size legislation for laying hens in the European Union also could well spark a trade dispute if it places any restrictions on imports from countries that do not have similar regulations in place. Although no such restrictions are planned, a move in this direction could be forthcoming if producer pressures intensify.

In 1995 the GATT was faced with a well-known trade dispute that raised animal welfare issues—the conflict between the United States and Mexico over the effects on dolphins of the tuna-catching methods used in the Eastern Pacific. The tuna/dolphin case is usually labeled an environmental conflict in which the US law protecting marine mammals was being enforced globally through trade sanctions. But the case also dealt fundamentally with the ability of a country to develop animal welfare legislation that has an impact on other countries.

As Mexico saw it, the issue was the extraterritorial scope of the US Marine Mammal Protection Act. No one doubted the right of the United States to enact animal welfare legislation within its borders or to apply that legislation to its own fishing fleet. But the demand that Mexico place the same restrictions on its own fleet or be denied access to US markets for tuna was taking animal welfare legislation into a new dimension.

The GATT panel found that the United States was in breach of its obligations by using unilateral trade restrictions to back up its domestic laws. The panel indicated that to achieve a WTO-compatible solution, the United States and Mexico should agree to a convention to protect dolphins. In other words, the panel suggested that an international agreement on this aspect of animal welfare would be a constructive way to avoid the use of trade sanctions to impose one country's laws on another. However, the Appellate Body report in the more recent WTO shrimp/turtle case, discussed in chapter 3, has modified this interpretation somewhat, giving the United States more leeway within the WTO to impose trade sanctions to achieve environmental goals as long as a "good faith" effort is made to reach accommodation with any complainants.

Trade and regulatory conflicts in animal welfare also have other similarities to those in environmental rules and in labor. Like advocates for environmental and labor causes, some advocates for animal welfare take the view that treating animals well is a universal obligation. If a particular method of livestock rearing offends consumer sensitivities in one country, then moving the production to other countries does not solve the problem.

---

36. Payments to farmers for compliance with environmental programs are in the "green box" of acceptable subsidies under the WTO Agreement on Agriculture.

Monitoring production, transportation, and slaughtering methods in the other countries also is required, along with commonly agreed-on standards. But unlike in environmental protection, where at least a base of common objectives can be agreed-on, and in labor, where a set of core labor standards exists, in animal welfare there is little agreement on the basic principles. Even if some degree of minimal responsibility for animal welfare was to be accepted, the chances of an international agreement on animal-raising practices are remote. Countries differ greatly in sensitivity to certain practices, and these cultural differences are unlikely to be resolved by international negotiations.

The Challenges Ahead

The three emerging issues in the regulation of process attributes—GM foods, organic products, and animal welfare—pose particular challenges to the formulation of a consistent and open food system. Although they may seem very different, these three issues all raise the point that the definition of a good as incorporating process as well as content attributes complicates trade policy in fundamental ways. It is not clear what the definition of *like product*, *national treatment*, or *nondiscrimination* means when each product has its own life-cycle history. Voluntary private-sector information systems that let the consumer know this history seem to be the appropriate way of accommodating taste differences and create the fewest opportunities for imposition of protectionist measures.

Trade issues related to food process attributes are not likely to go away. Of the three issues considered here, the GM foods issue is on the front burner at present. What makes the GM debate particularly problematic is the symbolism that surrounds the issue, primarily in Europe. For consumer and environmental groups, the introduction of GM foods represents a threat to small farmers, developing countries, and a rural way of life; an extension of corporate control through laws on intellectual property; a potential environmental threat through the accidental "release" into the countryside of the modified genetic material and the cross-contamination of other crops; a threat to organic farming through the development of super bugs resistant to organic pesticides; and a further example of technology driving human lifestyles.

Although much of this criticism is of dubious scientific or economic merit, it has provided a convenient rallying cry for public interest groups opposed to GM foods. Thus the regulatory challenge plays out at two levels. On the one hand, governments have to sort out what types of regulations on process attributes are allowed and how they should be disciplined in the interests of an open food system. On the other hand, those same officials and legislators have to respond to the objections of consumer and environmental groups, who may have less regard for the functioning of the food system at a global level. Under such conditions, good policy is hard to devise and still harder to implement.

Even more complex and controversial issues await the regulatory agenda. The next big controversy over biotechnology may be that over the introduction of transgenic wheat, which is perhaps more basic a foodstuff than corn in the minds of consumers. US authorities are still weighing approval of this product, and producers are undecided about whether to adopt this product if it is approved.

In a similar limbo between regulatory approval and commercialization is the first example of a transgenic animal. Public reaction may delay its introduction and prevent its full development, but the technology for implanting genetic material in animals is already producing results with commercial prospects. The first animal biotech product marketed as food is likely to be a transgenic salmon, which grows considerably faster than regular salmon.[37] Scientists and regulators recognize that an escaped genetically modified fish could interbreed with the wild population, and that the dominance of the GM fish could give it an advantage in breeding and feeding and reduce the native salmon population. It remains to be seen whether the product will be approved and whether environmental regulations will be adequate to prevent untoward release into the wild. So far, no one has raised any serious questions about the human health consequences of eating the super-salmon, though that could be anticipated. As with transgenic crops, the beneficiaries of modified salmon will be the early-adopting producer, who would gain from the increase in efficiency of feed conversion, and the owner of the intellectual property, who can share in the cost savings by way of licensing fees. The consumer will also reap a considerable benefit if the price of salmon is reduced.

In addition, the debate on animal biotech is likely to include echoes of the debate over the ethics of cloning. Such ethical arguments are likely to come to the fore even more than those associated with crop agriculture. The animal welfare aspect of transgenic animals is also likely to emerge as a complicating factor. But, at least for the moment, the "multinational corporation" stigma does not seem to be attached to the early transgenic pigs, sheep, and poultry experiments. Their primary use to date has been in medical biotechnology, where public acceptance has not been a major problem.[38]

---

37. Many other animal biotech developments also are under way. One involves raising pigs that have the ability to absorb phosphates, thus alleviating the main run-off contaminant from intensive pig production. Several other biotech projects have aimed at using animals to produce medicines for human use—that is, in essence turning animals into living protein factories that would replace the existing methods of producing such substances (brewing in vats). Somewhat more appealing to the consumer is the prospect of "designer" animals that would have beneficial health characteristics, such as producing meat with a low fat content.

38. The use of crops for the development and manufacture of pharmaceuticals has, however, raised some protests. Rice and wheat plants can be used as "factories" to produce

Organics are the other side of the coin. On the face of it, the issue of different voluntary labeling regimes in different countries seems somewhat trivial. If countries choose for domestic reasons to define "organic" in different ways, it should not cause a large problem. If the various certification schemes are run without any bias toward domestic producers and are transparent and consistently applied, then implementation of those schemes would be merely another frictional cost of meeting divergent market requirements. International trade will be somewhat affected, but at least the distortion of forcing all countries to adopt inappropriate uniform regulations would be avoided.

It is not clear, however, that the trade system is heading in this direction on organics. Uniform labeling regulations can at times be efficient, and the multitude of different regulations could hamper trade. The greater problem is that the temptation to use the definition of organic produce to favor domestic producers will be strong. So long as profits are to be had in this growing market, there will be those who will seek some protection from the regulations. Producer capture of the regulatory process may follow consumer capture of the legislative process, as the real and imagined benefits of organic foods lead to the identification of those benefits with local production at the expense of market access for foreign suppliers.

Animal welfare regulations appear to share some of the features of organic certification schemes: organic milk and meats often incorporate rules about the treatment of animals. But the main difference is that animal welfare regulations are generally mandatory, and thus pose an additional challenge to trade. Mandatory labels could be a way of providing consumers with information, if such information is not provided reliably by producers. Producers, however, typically seek compensation for the extra costs associated with compliance with animal welfare regulations, in the form either of subsidies or border protection. Thus the trade conflicts in this case are likely to be as much about the domestic reaction to perceived loss of competitiveness as about the scientific or other basis for the regulations themselves.

In each of these three emerging trade regulatory areas, developing countries may find it more difficult than developed countries to comply with the increasingly complex and strict import requirements and compliance certificates. The question for developing countries is whether, with the spread of these "rich country" consumer sensitivity issues into the global trade system, the costs of meeting these regulations are compensated by increased premiums. If so, the additional market rents from product differentiation could be valuable. If not, developing countries may find themselves increasingly marginalized in the global food market.

---

certain medicines effective in the treatment of immune deficiency, but the risk of these traits moving to other crops has hampered this development.

8

Toward a Safe and Open Global Food Supply

The objectives of this book have been to assess in broad terms the need for and the state of regulation in the global food system, to highlight ways to achieve more open trade with sustained or enhanced food safety and quality, and to examine the obstacles impeding progress toward this goal. Critical elements of this assessment have included a characterization of national food regulation, an evaluation of the international institutions charged with overseeing national regulatory decisions, and an investigation into how well these institutions have performed in the past, particularly since the launch of the WTO in 1995.

Today, national food markets are highly integrated through global trade and investment, yet nations retain the principal authority over almost all dimensions of their food regulation and standards. Although the private sector undertakes most food production, processing, distribution, and marketing activities, optimal management of national food supplies involves various forms of government intervention. Without exception, governments regulate their food sectors. The economic justifications for a government role in food markets stem from both the public goods aspects of disease and pest control and the opportunities to reduce market transactions costs for firms and consumers. National regulations can be designed to protect animal, plant, and human health and to secure provision of product information so as to increase social welfare net of industry, consumer, and government costs.

The justifications for international oversight of national regulation, and for regulatory coordination among countries, follow similar lines. Global public goods tend to be underprovided by national governments, requiring positive action by bilateral, regional, and multilateral bodies. The transactions costs of international trade can be reduced, to the advantage of producers and consumers in exporting and importing countries, by avoiding duplicative, conflicting, and inconsistent national standards. By striving for more coherent decision making among themselves, countries can influence the conditions under which international trade is conducted and thereby address common risks, improve product information, and foster welfare-enhancing transactions.

These justifications for national food regulation and for effective discipline and coordination internationally do not prevent controversy and conflict in the food system. Regulation is so often the subject of international disputes because national institutions are subject to domestic political pressures. Food regulation can be used to restrict trade flows both by shifting relative costs among importers and exporters and by influencing the market demand for specific products.

Appraisal of the net benefits of trade against any costs that arise from risks or market information failures linked to an open food system is a useful counterweight to interest group pressure for trade-related regulation. Such an appraisal entails an analysis of the expected benefits and costs of measures that includes a gains-from-trade calculation. Underprotection—that is, when too much trade is allowed by the regulations and standards in place or by their inadequate enforcement—is likely to be a problem at times. But overprotection, when relaxation of regulation would yield net welfare gains, is also evident in the food system.

Two broad challenges must be faced to improve existing food regulation. The first is to achieve the appropriate balance within countries between reliance on domestically determined and internationally agreed-on product specifications. Common risk-reducing measures can facilitate trade in low-cost, safe products, and the benefits of trade can be enhanced by lowering transactions costs through international harmonization. But, conversely, adoption of the appropriate risk-reduction measures may depend on countries' specific circumstances, making harmonization inappropriate. Undue harmonization might also impose limits on consumer choice. Finding the right degree of international coordination is essential to resolving this dilemma.

The second broad challenge facing food regulation is to maintain both the confidence of consumers and the cooperation of producers in implementing regulations and standards, while avoiding regulatory capture by either group. The resolution of this dilemma is found in improving national regulatory capacities and developing the competence and authority of international institutions to define and enforce disciplines on national regulators.

The examples of domestic and multilateral regulation examined in the preceding chapters allow some generalizations about the workings of the current global food regulatory framework and the extent to which it meets these challenges. The sections that follow provide a summary assessment of the regulatory issues related to risk and food quality goals, the accomplishments of the WTO in disciplining and encouraging coordination of national food regulations and standards, and those aspects of the food regulation agenda under negotiation in the Doha Round. Some recommendations are made at the national and international levels to help address the two broad challenges that must be faced in enhancing the performance of the food sector. Although these recommendations do not always offer a solution for a particular dispute, they point the way to how best to implement national regulation and international oversight to improve the efficiency of the global food system.

Assessment of the State of Food Regulation

The goals of food regulation can be classified, as is done throughout this book, as either risk-reducing or related to product quality. The measures used can also be categorized by whether they focus on content or process attributes of products and by their breadth, scope, and instrumentation. Knowledge of the requirements for verifying compliance or equivalence with a measure is also important in assessments of food regulations. These classificatory variables allow some generalizations to be made about the appropriateness of regulations in achieving their objectives.

The provision of public goods is at the core of the justification for many risk-related measures. For example, regulation may be required to capture the public good of improved production capacity resulting from reduced hazards to animal and plant health. Risk-related measures can also remedy market failures stemming from imperfect information about the safety of a food product. Public intervention is justified economically when a food safety measure, such as legally mandated limits on naturally occurring toxins, improves social welfare net of industry costs.

The regulation of product quality aims to safeguard the integrity of market transactions through remedies for imperfect information that might otherwise increase the costs of exchange for firms and consumers. These remedies include labeling, grades and standards, and measures that protect product trade names and identifiers. The governance of food quality is more diffuse than that for risk because a greater proportion of food quality measures are both established and enforced by the private sector. Yet, increasingly, food quality is becoming subject to national regulation as advocates demand either specific attributes or disclosure of information about the attributes of foods.

One argument that emerges from the analysis in this book is that regulations are most often the appropriate instrument for risk-related goals. By contrast, measures undertaken voluntarily by the private sector—albeit with varying and sometimes significant degrees of government involvement, including prosecution of deceptive claims—are the preferred approach when food quality goals are at stake. This argument is not to deny that risk-related regulations are sometimes distorted for protectionist purposes, or to reject the claim that market failures occur in the provision of product quality information. The former warrants international disciplines and the latter some degree of government intervention. Yet the global food system is best served when regulations are used predominantly for risk reduction and sparingly to govern food quality. The market, rather than the government, is likely to be the more agile institution for accommodating a wide range of continually evolving consumer preferences.

From this perspective, some of the most serious tests facing the global food system arise from the dynamics affecting the pattern of national regulation. Increased consumer demand for quality-related product differentiation is a positive, income-driven phenomenon, attainable at declining cost as information technology advances. Acting on this demand, interest groups that feel strongly about specific food attributes have an incentive to seek greater government regulation of product quality. In international discussions, some governments have argued that increased regulation reflects a new era in the food sector in which policymakers must be attuned to the demands of consumer as well as producer advocates. But the new focus on quality in regulation can lead to regulatory overprotection, despite whatever good intentions underlie the political pressure. Producer groups also favor stronger regulations on quality in those instances in which they can gain market advantage, such as from receiving exclusive rights to various product names. This situation can also lead to overprotection and thus distort trade.

Risk-Reducing Measures

Regulatory measures that address risk in agricultural production and food consumption underpin the structure of market transactions within countries and influence competitive advantage among trade partners. On the supply side, individual producers can take steps to control damage to their own crops and livestock through their management decisions, but they have little control over the prevalence of pests and diseases within their larger environment. Their private costs can become excessive without collective action to manage risk hazards. Likewise, consumers can mitigate risks by means of their food consumption and handling choices, but they cannot observe food-borne hazards such as pesticide levels or microbial contamination. Regulatory oversight of food safety is therefore essential, particularly for the large number of unbranded food products in the global marketplace.

For animal and plant pests and diseases, the basic standards for disease control are broadly accepted internationally. The costs of new infestations or epidemics can be high, such as when FMD breaks out in a country previously considered FMD-free or when a new disease emerges, such as BSE.

Yet international borders sometimes become a convenient surrogate for risk differentiation, leading to inappropriate regulatory discrimination among products by country of origin. A range of disputes has arisen over specific regulatory measures imposed for plant and animal pest and disease control, and new disputes will arise as pest populations and disease organisms evolve and migrate and as new trade opportunities emerge. WTO rules requiring reform of unnecessary sanitary and phytosanitary barriers to trade, in tandem with the multilateral standards organizations' dissemination of relevant scientific research, are therefore critical to sustain an open global food system.

The adoption after four years of negotiations of a systems approach to risk management to facilitate US importation of Mexican avocados provides one example of reform of phytosanitary regulation. The reform entailed replacement of the long-standing US ban on imports of Mexican avocados with process standards to mitigate pest risks while allowing trade. This case demonstrates the confluence of scientific assessments, economic opportunity, persistence by claimants, and political will required for successful resolution of a bilateral dispute.

International standards can also play an important role in disputes over risk-reducing measures. Although the ability of the international standards organizations—L'Office International des Epizooties (OIE), the International Plant Protection Convention (IPPC), and the Codex Alimentarius Commission—to control the spread of agricultural and food-borne pests and disease or to discipline the regulations of sovereign countries should not be overstated, their assessments can be constructive. This constructive role was illustrated by the OIE's standards for disease vectors after the announcement of a possible BSE link to variant Creutzfeldt-Jakob disease in 1996 disrupted world trade in beef and bovine products. Countries are quick to adopt strong regulations when confronted with new risks in an environment of uncertainty, but slower to remove such measures when they are no longer necessary. The specification of international standards, reinforced by WTO disciplines, can sometimes bring countries to make the needed changes and avoid trade disputes.

The regulation of food safety poses challenges for somewhat different reasons than the regulation of animal and plant pests and diseases. Risk perceptions can affect estimates of the benefits of food regulation, which authorities weigh against the costs to industry of reducing food-borne hazards. It has long been recognized that unnatural and unfamiliar risks such as those that might be associated with new food production technologies are more alarming to consumers than natural and familiar risks. Even when a natural contaminant, such as *Salmonella*, is identified as the source of food-borne illness, broad consumer avoidance of the implicated product can trigger a dramatic fall in consumption out of proportion to the actual risk involved. Thus the global food system has much to gain from well-designed and rigorously enforced food safety regulations that target hazards that threaten consumer health and undermine confidence in the food supply. Under the right conditions, consumers trust their regulatory institutions to ensure the safety of their food and to respond rapidly to any breakdown in risk management. Problems occur when such trust is lacking, and both domestic and foreign suppliers, as well as consumers, suffer from the ensuing loss of confidence.

The governance of food safety regulation from a global perspective is challenging because demands for protection among countries from food-borne hazards depend on income differences and other determinants of consumers' risk aversion. The capacity to regulate effectively also varies with levels of national income and development. Poorer countries will typically have less comprehensive programs in place for the assurance of food safety. The increase in exports of high-value and processed foods from some developing countries suggests that consumers in developed countries are prepared to trust imported food if it meets the standards set in the domestic market. But it follows that the impact on developing-country exports can be severe if those countries are unable to meet these high standards. High standards can have a restrictive impact on trade opportunities, such as when the harmonization of EU aflatoxin tolerances hindered exports of grains and nuts from Africa and Latin America.

The reform of food safety regulation, particularly in the wealthy countries, has also placed greater emphasis on using process standards, including those that might be part of a Hazard Analysis and Critical Control Point (HACCP) program, to achieve desired content attributes. Process standards are more difficult to implement internationally than product standards because they involve complex verification and enforcement procedures by regulatory institutions in two or more countries. Judgments about the capabilities of the testing and certification institutions in the exporting countries figure importantly in these regulatory decisions. Trade problems can arise from lack of trust in the regulatory processes across borders, inadequate public-sector enforcement capacity in some countries, and differences in accountability imposed on domestic and foreign products. Developing countries are likely to have difficulty meeting food regulatory and traceability requirements imposed by the process standards of developed countries. Yet disagreements over process standards also arise between high-income countries with high regulatory standards and enforcement capacity, as illustrated by the long negotiations over a veterinary equivalence agreement between the United States and European Union. It is difficult to avoid the conclusion that in some instances, differences over process standards among developed countries are attributable to regulatory protectionism, bureaucratic intransigence, or both.

More controversial than regulations about natural food pathogens are food safety regulations that address the use of production-enhancing technologies, including pesticides and other agrochemicals, hormones, veterinary drugs, and product-enhancing food additives. For these technologies, the scientific basis for the regulation may itself be unknown or in dispute. Just as often, disputes arise when differences in public perceptions of risk persist among countries despite scientific consensus, or when countries have made different political choices about the desirability of adopting new technologies for reasons unrelated to safety. When strong differences in public perceptions are in play, or when risk-related and other goals become interlocked, international conflicts over regulations are often exacerbated.

The long-unresolved hormones dispute between the United States and European Union shows how difficult it can be to resolve these issues. The hormones dispute remains intractable after 25 years because it has juxtaposed producer and health issues and become politically charged on both sides. Producer interests on the export side of this dispute seek market access for their product: Scientific evidence indicates the absence of risk and their products have long been accepted at home. Consumers in importing countries are equally insistent that they have the right to preclude a product if they choose, either on the grounds that the health effects can never be known with certainty, or simply on the basis of their preferences about the process attributes of foods. The duration and intensity of the hormones dispute seem out of proportion to the relatively small economic stakes, but the highly politicized interests on both sides have allowed little room for the respective governments to find a satisfactory resolution.

Quality-Related Measures

Regulations related to quality cover a wide range of characteristics both of products and, increasingly, of how they are produced and handled. Not unexpectedly, governments play a larger role in regulating the quality of agricultural products than of industrial products, because a higher proportion of goods are unbranded in food markets and suppliers therefore have fewer incentives to maintain quality than those firms that rely on their market reputation.

Governments intervene in this situation by creating public standards for unbranded products, such as identity standards for fish and seafood or quality standards for organic produce. Or a government may take another type of approach by setting disclosure requirements, such as country-of-origin labeling that distinguishes among products based on the location of firms involved in their production. Still other measures support the creation of brand identity through geographical indications (GIs) that may have reputational connotations for consumers and thus are of value to firms in specific localities. Governments can also remedy informational failures related to branded products. Examples include setting identity standards for processed foods to prevent consumer deception, or requiring labeling of nutritional information so that consumers have information that private firms do not have an incentive to disclose.

Of these various regulatory measures that governments might adopt, identity standards and nutritional labeling involve product attributes that can be readily verified through product testing. Geographical indications and country-of-origin identification are, by implication, related to process attributes that are not materially present in the final product. Depending on the breadth, depth, and precision required by particular regimes, verification of process attributes can impose higher regulation costs and can lead to claims of discrimination and exclusion from markets.

The proliferation of demands for government regulators to distinguish among products based on process attributes that are unrelated to detectable product characteristics is a critical new issue in food regulation. Within this issue, regulation of trade in GM products based on their production process is perhaps the paramount controversy. An intense dispute is under way among countries over the acceptance and labeling of biotech products. The trade aspect of the GM controversy hinges on whether GM and non-GM variants of the same crop are substantially equivalent. If they are, trade restrictions or labeling requirements for the GM varieties impose a discriminatory burden. If some but not all consumers value GM-free foods, then markets would likely respond to these differing preferences, with private firms seeking market recognition by making voluntary claims about the absence (or presence) of GM content in their products. Such claims might be backed up by public standards and oversight. But moves to go beyond that—moves that prohibit importation of GM foods or require mandatory labels related to this process technology—threaten a costly bifurcation of global food markets and contentious trade disputes.

International disciplines may or may not prove up to the task of limiting other barriers to trade that rest on process attribute distinctions. To date, as regulations for organic products have become more widespread, countries have generally chosen regulatory approaches that allow markets to stay open. Voluntary labeling claims are less disruptive of trade than import bans, and governments are finding their way toward equivalence recognition as different national standards for the voluntary use of the organic claim emerge. But pressures may grow to tilt organic food regulations to favor domestic producers, and it is unclear how the WTO would mediate a dispute between an exporter and an importer with incompatible but domestically suitable production requirements for organic products.

As for animal welfare issues, international disciplines preclude most attempts to impose one country's domestic production standards on other countries. But the production subsidies sometimes proposed to offset the additional costs of animal welfare regulations, on the grounds that the competitiveness of domestic producers has been reduced, are troubling. Subsidies to offset regulatory costs are largely precluded for nonagricultural products under WTO rules. Whether agriculture will be treated differently from other industries in this particular area of trade disciplines remains to be seen.

Role of the WTO in the Food Regulatory Framework

National governments may have paramount responsibility for food regulation, but the WTO has an important role in both enforcing disciplines on national regulatory decisions and achieving international coordination of regulations and standards. In doing so, WTO members must consider questions such as, If regulation is necessary to attain risk-reducing or quality-related goals, how should multilateral commitments be fulfilled to avoid the tendency for measures to slip into protectionism? If a degree of multilateral harmonization is justified, how much harmonization should be imposed?

The WTO agreements provide rules intended to direct countries to answers to these and related questions. The SPS and TBT agreements, supported by the technical expertise of the international standards organizations, offer the fundamental disciplines, which are backed up by recourse to the WTO's dispute settlement procedures. Other agreements— including the TRIPS agreement, the GATT, and some multilateral environmental agreements—also play a role in defining the latitude and limits to regulation within the food sector.

The SPS agreement contains principles to guide regulation, including transparency, harmonization, science-based risk management, equivalence, and regionalization. The TBT agreement likewise encourages transparency and coordination of national regulations and standards through adoption of international norms. The WTO has had some success in each of the areas covered by these agreements, yet application of the basic principles has not progressed as far as it might have, and improvements can still be made.

The WTO has been successful in promoting symmetry of information about regulations and standards among its members. Countries have provided advance notice of thousands of regulations under the terms of the SPS and TBT agreements. Notification of new or modified measures has given firms a chance to change production methods to meet new import requirements. Notification also has provided WTO members with the opportunity to question, propose modification, or challenge new or existing measures in the committees that implement the two agreements. This increased regulatory transparency has led to far greater scrutiny of measures than occurred under the GATT.

The WTO's promotion of harmonization has been less successful than its attempts to increase transparency. A lack of agreed-on international standards for food products in many cases is not surprising. Because international standards are a global public good, it is expected that national authorities will underinvest in such measures. Not only are there too few international standards in the food area, but too many of the current international standards are outmoded, contributing to the low adoption rate for those standards that do exist.

The obligation under the SPS agreement to base measures on scientific risk assessment has been more successful in reducing the disingenuous use of sanitary and phytosanitary regulations and in promoting some convergence of SPS measures among countries. The impact of the risk management requirements of the SPS agreement has extended beyond WTO complaints and dispute settlement decisions to spur broad-based regulatory reviews by countries to determine whether they and their trading partners are complying with the obligation to base decisions on scientific risk assessments. In many cases, the evidence suggests that regulatory authorities are either unilaterally modifying regulations or voluntarily modifying regulations after technical exchanges, as in the avocado case. However, it is evident that some gaps remain in convergence around the principle of using science as a basis for regulation. In some circumstances, countries' reliance on the precautionary principle to guide risk management decisions has led to high-profile trade disputes, as in the hormones and GM food cases.

Equivalence is an alternative to harmonization. The SPS and TBT agreements require WTO members to allow imports from countries that have measures equivalent to their own. This provision endorses regulatory flexibility which allows countries to allocate scarce resources efficiently rather than identically. Despite the conceptual appeal of equivalence, its use is constrained by various factors, both operational and political. The administrative burden of equivalence determinations is often significant, as the six-year negotiation of the veterinary agreement between the United States and European Union illustrates. Moreover, recognizing the equivalence of an alternative regulatory regime may require national regulators to offer the same alternative to domestic producers, requiring in turn new or revised domestic regulations before foreign producers can gain access to the market. Some progress has been made, but seven years of experience suggests that negotiating equivalence agreements is difficult and their use is not common.

Regionalization under the SPS agreement has also met so far with only limited success, and the successful cases have depended heavily on the efforts of the exporting countries. Argentina's numerous setbacks in its efforts to eradicate FMD underscores the fact that investments in public-sector regulatory infrastructure are needed to act as an incentive to private sector eradication efforts and thus establishment of the preconditions for regionalization. But it is also evident that national regulation will not always work: Transborder pest or disease controls may be required where there are insufficient natural barriers or when animals (including wildlife) move freely across borders. Creating or reinforcing regional sanitary and phytosanitary measures across countries will often be necessary to fully realize the gains from trade.

Other aspects of the WTO agreements also contribute to the global framework of food regulation. Labeling based on GM and other process attributes has been an ongoing topic of discussion within the TBT Committee, and eco-labeling has received similar attention in the Trade and Environment Committee. The TRIPS Council continues to discuss the extent to which protection will be afforded to GIs around the world. Although progress on resolving differences over the interpretation of existing WTO rules (for labeling) or the commitment to negotiate new rules (for GIs) has been slow, these WTO venues have nonetheless provided a useful forum for deliberations over systemic legal issues as well as individual measures between rounds of multilateral trade negotiations.

To sum up, the WTO agreements and committee procedures, together with the reviews that WTO rules have encouraged at national, bilateral, and regional levels, have provided valuable channels through which countries can strengthen the framework for global food regulation. They may also challenge policies of their trade partners through these channels when they have doubts about whether regulations conform to international rules as they apply to food trade. It is clear that WTO members increasingly shape, if not determine, regulation in the global food system because of the institutional innovations that emerged from the Uruguay Round.

Lessons from WTO Dispute Resolution

The compliance of countries with the WTO agreements is reinforced by the organization's formal dispute settlement procedures. Only a few conflicts over food regulations have led to the establishment of dispute panels, but these few cases have played a critical role in defining the scope of WTO rules and obligations.

Of 32 formal requests for consultations about food regulations during 1995 to 2002, only seven complaints (related to six distinct cases) proceeded to panel and Appellate Body rulings. In the four SPS cases— hormones, salmon, varietal testing, and apples—developed countries challenged the regulations of other developed countries, and in each case the panel and Appellate Body concurred that the regulation in question violated the requirement that it be based on a valid risk assessment. These outcomes demonstrate the importance accorded to the principle of science-based risk management in the SPS agreement and show that even the measures of countries with advanced scientific establishments are not immune to challenge. The outcome in the hormones case demonstrates further that the WTO Appellate Body can rule against measures based on popular consumer misconceptions of risks, as well as more overtly discriminatory measures. This result removes a degree of national political sovereignty for regulations in cases in which evidence has not been marshaled to demonstrate any risk from trade.

In the other two cases of food regulation that advanced to rulings by the Appellate Body, developing countries lodged complaints against measures of developed countries. In the sardines case, brought by Peru, the Codex Alimentarius international standard was found to be effective and appropriate to achieve EU objectives of transparency, consumer protection, and fair competition. The importance of this case lies in demonstrating that international standards can take precedence over national regulatory decisions and can set bounds on the use of policies that, in effect, limit imports. In the second case, India, Malaysia, Pakistan, and Thailand challenged US restrictions on importation of shrimp when countries failed to use turtle-excluder devices. The case established the precedent that process standards can be mandated in regulations to achieve an environmental goal. This precedent provides a small but significant exception to the product-process doctrine, which deems any regulation affecting trade based on how a product is produced to be out of compliance with the WTO rules. In the shrimp/turtle case, the WTO Appellate Body concluded instead that the objective of the US law was legitimate under GATT Article XX and, ultimately, that US implementation of its policy was justified because of its serious and ongoing efforts to minimize negative trade effects.

Where the greatest difficulties arise for WTO dispute resolution is in cases such as beef hormones in which strongly held differences of views among countries have not been reconciled by other means. That the most contentious of these cases have involved issues of risk, where one might expect scientific evidence to provide a basis for resolution, suggests the practical limits of science in securing regulatory convergence. Unfortunately, too much reliance on the WTO's dispute resolution process to address these disagreements will create problems for the acceptance of its rulings, as may soon become evident for decisions related to genetically modified foods.

When rulings for the complainant in such difficult cases lead to retaliatory tariffs because the respondent fails to change its policy or offer acceptable compensation, the trade system suffers, even if the validity of WTO procedures is upheld. Small developing countries in particular have only a limited ability to use the threat of sanctioned new tariffs to induce compliance by a developed country with a WTO ruling. And whenever retaliatory tariffs are imposed, they have negative economic effects. Thus excessive use of the dispute settlement process in highly contested cases could prove damaging to the WTO and to the liberalization of world agricultural markets.

The Doha Round

One alternative to resolving disputes through panel and Appellate Body rulings is to seek consensus about international trade rules in the Doha Round. Although neither the SPS agreement nor the TBT agreement has been opened for renegotiation in this round, international disciplines that apply to food regulations are nonetheless being addressed in several WTO negotiating venues. The most significant venue is the agriculture negotiating group, which is addressing rules for nontrade concerns raised by WTO members in the initial phases of the negotiations, including food safety, food labeling, and animal welfare. Another venue is the trade and environment negotiating group, which is examining the WTO status of trade measures that might be taken under any of the multilateral environmental agreements (MEAs), including the Biosafety Protocol of 2000, which authorizes potentially WTO noncompliant use of the precautionary principle in risk management. Finally, the Doha Declaration asks the WTO Trade and Environment Committee and the TRIPS Council to continue their work on environmental labeling and GIs, respectively, which are also germane to trade in agricultural and food products.

It is unclear how far these negotiating initiatives will proceed, given the breakdown of negotiations at the September 2003 WTO ministerial meeting in Cancún. Some initiatives that have their origin in the Uruguay Round commitments, such as the development of rules for a central registry for wine and spirits, are on firmer negotiating ground than others. As trade ministers reexamine their national priorities in order to help identify modalities that can serve as a basis for moving the negotiations forward, more specific commercial interests may displace systemic issues related to food regulation in the negotiations. The European Union's efforts at Cancún to secure multilateral GI protection for 41 European products, for example, could be interpreted as a shift in interest from the abstract to the concrete in view of the lack of consensus on food regulation issues. The Cancún ministerial draft text for agriculture reveals clearly that little progress had been made in resolving questions about food regulation, noting only that "certain non-trade concerns" and GIs are "issues of interest but not agreed."

It would be constructive to resolve several of the more contentious issues related to food regulation in negotiations rather than in divisive and possibly damaging dispute settlement cases, but such negotiations do not necessarily have to be part of the Doha Round. In fact, issues that hinge on the interpretation of existing WTO texts are arguably better addressed by the WTO committees created to implement the agreements, and on an independent timetable that allows for further study of the effects of some measures in global food markets.

The case for additional clarity about the existing legal obligations is strong. Simply dismissing as protectionist any initiative to discuss risk management principles, the regulation of production and processing methods, or labeling regimes not only hardens opposition to further trade liberalization among some constituency groups but also squanders an important opportunity to examine how trade can contribute to providing consumers with desired products in the most cost-effective manner. Refusal to engage in this debate will not forestall consumers' interests in certain product attributes; those who wish to export to some markets have already found that the requirements of private firms exceed those found in WTO negotiating proposals. Trade reality can precede trade policy in this respect. Indeed, the recent rise in trade of high-value raw and processed food products arises partly from consumers' preferences for a wide range of attributes.

Progress on these issues will depend on abandoning the polarizing debate over whether certain objectives are legitimate and focusing instead on the requirement that a policy be the least trade-restrictive option for achieving a stated objective. A useful first step for those who propose increased regulation would be to identify, for example, how regulations governing process and production methods (PPMs) can be formulated so that *all* producers have the opportunity to compete in markets. Those who favor less regulation would likewise be challenged to offer explanations and examples of when and how the market, or the market in tandem with limited government oversight, provides optimal solutions to matching product availability with consumer preferences. Ideally, the discussions would lead to a consensus that would reduce, in part, the uncertainty over the interpretation of WTO rules that is exacerbating current trade frictions between agricultural importers and exporters.

As the Doha Round progresses, some of the decisions that will contribute most to improvements in the global food regulatory framework will be discussed as modifications to the Agreement on Agriculture. These decisions will not be about food regulations directly but about strengthened disciplines on agricultural support policies, export subsidies, tariffs, and other border protection. Disciplines on these policies were first strengthened in the Uruguay Round, and at that time it was argued that the SPS and TBT agreements were necessary in part to dissuade countries from resorting to regulatory compensation as other means of agricultural support and protection were reduced. The Uruguay Round disciplines on domestic and trade policies have left considerable support in place, so the propensity of countries to substitute technical barriers for other support measures has not been fully tested. What is apparent is that high levels of agricultural support and border protection are having adverse effects on the dialogue among countries about agricultural and food regulation. Developing countries in particular are often skeptical of new measures that add to the barriers their exports already face among developed countries.

Equally important, market signals in the major developed countries are distorted by those countries' high levels of agricultural support, which affects food regulatory decisions, particularly those related to the adoption of cost-reducing and output-enhancing new technologies. This distortionary effect has been evident in conflicts over concepts such as a "fourth criterion" for domestic food safety policies or the role of "other legitimate concerns" in regulatory decisions. Specific cases have arisen when countries conclude that innovations such as recombinant bovine somatotropin (rbST), growth hormones, or GM technology are not "needed," in part because these innovations would add to the costs of existing farm support programs. The distortionary effects of agricultural support and protectionist policies on regulatory decisions are arguably as significant an impediment to improving the efficiency of the world food system and to harmonious trade relations as the better-recognized direct effects of these policies on agricultural production. An agreement in the Doha Round to substantially reduce agricultural support and protection would lessen tensions and mistrust surrounding regulatory decisions and create the policy environment needed for a more rational discussion of legitimate food regulations.

Recommendations for Improving Regulation

The failure of the Cancún ministerial conference leaves the fate of the Doha Round uncertain. But whatever the eventual outcome of the round, the volume of food regulation is likely to expand over the coming years, and the number of international disputes over food regulations is likely to increase. So far, the mechanisms in place—negotiated WTO agreements, informal conflict resolution through the WTO committees, and formal dispute resolution—have proven useful. There is no doubt at this point that the WTO rules remain necessary. Disingenuous use of regulatory measures is still evident in agricultural markets, and, even though the extent of their incidence and impact has not been fully quantified, these abuses need to be disciplined. Contrary to the predictions of some consumer and environmental advocates, the WTO disciplines have not resulted in the "downward harmonization" of regulations. No credible evidence has emerged to indicate that WTO rules have prevented countries from achieving legitimate regulatory objectives, even when very trade-restrictive measures have been adopted.

Because the current global regulatory framework, in deference to national sovereignty, still allows countries to adopt measures whose global or even national costs outweigh their national benefits, there is scope for enhancing the efficiency of the global food system. One conceptual approach is to envision that national governments entrust regulatory functions to a single global institution. If such a body were to promulgate uniform regulations, then the global food system would resemble one large national market. Such a solution would have some benefits in terms of reducing regulatory incompatibilities and transactions costs, but would run up against insuperable practical, political, and administrative problems. And globally uniform regulations would be ill-suited to remedying most market failures, as the analysis throughout this book has indicated.

A more useful concept might be a global institution able to tailor regulations in a way that would maximize the net benefits of the global food system. Presumably such an institution would use a mix of regulations and voluntary standards and choose an appropriate level of regulatory coordination and diversity based on full assessment of the costs and benefits. Imagining such a global food regulatory agency provides, at the least, a yardstick against which to judge the efficiency of more feasible alternatives. One could calculate, with the requisite information and resources, what such an agency would do to combat FMD, for example, or how it might optimally quarantine an isolated case of BSE. One could also ask of such a hypothetical institution how standards for food quality might best be set so that they do not tax poorer consumers who value lower prices and who trust the food industry to follow safe practices as laid down by regulators. Or one could ask how best to minimize the negative impacts of the political capture of regulatory agencies. In short, one could address the broad challenges of how to devise regulation that is subject to optimal coordination and yet respects countries' diverse situations and sensitivities, and that is supported politically and yet is not suborned to special interests.

In the absence of such a global food agency, the challenges of achieving a balance between harmonization and diversity and between political support and political capture must be faced within the existing institutions. What follows are some recommendations that, if pursued, could improve national and multilateral food regulation in order to promote efficiency within the global food system and at the same time retain consumer confidence and guard against capture of regulatory decisions by narrow interest groups.

Recommendations at the National Level

The merit of economic assessments of regulations has been emphasized throughout this book. This element of the food regulatory framework is still underdeveloped, however. The risk management provisions of the SPS agreement, for example, require regulators to use means that are no more trade-restrictive than necessary for achieving sanitary and phytosanitary goals, and to avoid arbitrary variation in the levels of risk reduction achieved by their policies if such variation creates a disguised restriction on trade. However, the SPS agreement does not elaborate further on risk management principles, which leaves several public policy issues and trade disputes unresolved. Likewise, the TBT agreement provides only limited guidance on which measures are desirable to adopt beyond the requirement that they have some rationale in terms of one or another legitimate goal and that they are not more trade-restrictive than necessary given that rationale. The problem, however, is that national regulatory options taken under these proscriptions are still likely to be contentious if they severely limit market access to achieve incremental health, safety, or other benefits. It remains a challenge for national regulators to build on the legal criteria of the SPS and TBT agreements to undertake the benefit-cost analysis that would give a more defensible basis for import protocols.

Toward this end, developed countries should adopt an "agreements plus" approach to both risk-reducing and quality regulations by balancing the benefits of regulation against all costs, including the costs of forgone trade. A change from the narrow risk analysis perspective to the benefit-cost perspective for SPS measures would be a constructive move toward a beneficial opening up of markets and would reduce the scope for trade disputes. Plant, animal, and human health and safety would not be sacrificed for trade, but trade would be taken into account as an integral part of the commercial environment that regulations affect. Countries should view trade as an activity that provides them with an expanded range of safe agricultural and food products at lowest cost, and regulations as a necessary way of ensuring the safety of food regardless of where it is produced.

Recognition of the benefits of imports would also provide a rationalization for public investment in monitoring and inspection services at a time when the pressures to downsize public agencies are strong. Consumer opposition to trade could be exacerbated by reduced oversight of imports, and it is not in the interests of importing or exporting countries to reduce the effectiveness of inspection services. This is all the more true since the terrorist attacks in the United States of September 11, 2001—countries must now guard against biosecurity threats, but without creating prejudice against legitimate trade. When governments regulate agricultural and food markets, they should do so with confidence and credibility. Stricter enforcement of existing and well-justified regulations, as opposed to indifferent enforcement of additional dubious regulations, is preferred. But such an approach to regulation is not always the one that receives the most vocal public support.

The increasing use of process standards in food regulation noted throughout this book creates both opportunities and challenges for both developed and developing countries in the global food system. In animal and plant health, the use of process standards in systems approaches to risk management is replacing more trade-restrictive measures such as bans. Yet the use of process standards in the regulation of food safety— attributable to a long tradition of reliance on inspection, the relatively recent appearance of feasible testing technologies, and the nature of some food-borne hazards—often impedes trade between developed countries with equally rigorous measures. Any efforts that will lead to the substitution of product for process standards should be encouraged, because process standards are more liable to subjectivity in conformity assessment and thus are more vulnerable to regulatory capture. The wider use of product standards in the regulation of food quality is also to be encouraged. For genetically modified products, a move to label GM products based on detectable product content rather than the production process might minimize labeling costs and help to defuse an international controversy.

Nonetheless, it also must be recognized that process standards are here to stay. The regulation of some quality attributes of foods, such as organic, dolphin-safe, or free-range, will always require process standards. Greater reliance on process standards places more responsibility on the regulatory infrastructure of the exporting country than on border inspection in the importing country. This trend in quality regulation implies the need for further exploration of the potential for using private, third-party certification services in the food sector, especially within countries lacking satisfactory public certification infrastructure. In other situations, joint private–public initiatives in quality assurance may be a way to achieve welfare-enhancing trade. A serious commitment by developed countries to explore such options could substantially reduce developing-country opposition to regulation in developed countries that accommodates the interests of consumer and environmental advocates.

The pledge to examine alternative certification options should be but one manifestation of a broader commitment by national food quality regulators to open and contestable markets that genuinely serve consumer interests. Regulatory proposals that advance measures not coincidentally favorable toward domestic production circumstances could help dispel suspicion that consumer concerns are addressed only when it is politically expedient to do so. In many instances, voluntary labeling is sufficient for achieving the public policy goal of informed choice, but mandatory labeling may sometimes be deemed necessary. Whether labeling policies be voluntary or mandatory, consumers are ill-served unless they are designed in a way that maintains competition in markets.

One policy prescription that is officially endorsed by the WTO and other multilateral institutions is the recommendation that countries adopt international standards. However, international standards should be adopted only if they increase net national welfare, not solely to provide the basis for an export-led growth strategy whose success depends on the adoption of these standards by others. Optimal levels of domestic food safety regulation, for example, will vary with national incomes and other characteristics among countries. Developing countries may not wish to, or be in a position to, adopt international standards for domestic markets. To insist that they do so could impose heavy costs on low-income consumers. The creation of export-oriented production enclaves that meet the standards of developed countries may benefit developing countries more than domestic adoption of an international standard, especially if that standard has not been widely adopted by developed countries. National governments and private firms operating in developing countries can facilitate this approach to ensuring broader participation in the global food system.

Recommendations at the International Level

More transparency in food regulations has been one of the successes of the WTO agreements. Yet a case can be made for even greater transparency, with notifications being clearer about how proposed measures might affect trade. There is also a case for creating an additional transparency mechanism to resolve disputes that surface when bureaucratic intransigence prevents resolution of issues over small differences. One possibility might be to allow exporting countries to ask the international standards organizations to convene a panel of experts to review the technical merits of disputed measures. The rationale for specific elements of some regulatory regimes is so weak that the prospect of such a peer review could prompt negotiated solutions without recourse to a WTO complaint or formal dispute settlement panel.

Besides convening experts to reconcile differences in regulations, the international standards organizations could take on more ambitious tasks to improve the global food system. National governments have on occasion vested international organizations with the mandate and the resources to eradicate particular human diseases. This model could be applicable to the eradication of certain animal or plant pests or diseases. The prospect for global eradication of FMD may seem remote, but further examination of similar cases is warranted. Existing international standards institutions could be asked to estimate the cost of global eradication of a disease that limits export potential and disrupts imports. In other words, animal and plant pests and diseases could be addressed as common problems for the global economy rather than as a local disadvantage that occasionally spills over from one country to another. At a minimum, international efforts should be increased to achieve regional pest and disease eradication goals.

Proposals to expand the existing mandates of the international standards organizations may raise concerns that these organizations would be diverted from their core activity of promulgating standards. The dissemination of information at the multilateral level in the form of international standards can be important to national regulators in several ways. Such standards can promote scientific approaches to regulation and educate developing countries about innovations in risk mitigation. International standards also benefit the trade system. They can provide the basis for disciplining an egregiously protectionist measure, and can also be useful in relieving countries of the obligation to defend their standards to others.

However, the normative basis for harmonization is not overwhelming, and there is little evidence to indicate that international standards in foods have succeeded notably in opening up trade. Therefore, it must be concluded that international standards have improved the functioning of food markets, but more by improving the quality of regulation, which mostly benefits consumers, than by reducing the transactions costs of exporting to specific markets, which delivers more benefits to exporters. Expectations about what international standards can contribute to the world trade system may therefore have to be adjusted downward, even as steps are taken to increase the participation of developing countries in the activities of these organizations. International standards may ultimately have only modest impacts on the specific regulations of the major countries.

Even if developing countries choose to allocate more resources to meeting the requirements of major import markets rather than to adopting international standards, their regulatory infrastructure and production conditions will often be lacking. Meeting new requirements can be an uphill task for developing-country exporters, even within an export production enclave. As the complexity of the standards they face increases, the disparity can be expected to widen. In view of these difficulties, WTO members, when launching the Doha Round, agreed to undertake several initiatives to help developing countries. For example, members agreed to give developing countries more time to comply with new import requirements, as long as staggered implementation allows the importing country to achieve its overall health or product quality objectives.

In the area of food regulation, the approach of offering special and differential treatment to developing countries under the GATT/WTO is highly questionable. In seeking greater exemptions from importers' standards, developing countries would be branding their products inferior or unsafe. For SPS regulations, any such allowances are especially pernicious to the interests of developing countries. Fundamentally, special and differential treatment runs counter to the science-based foundation of the SPS agreement. Even in the unlikely event that regulators were to tolerate such positive discrimination, it is unlikely that producers or consumers in the importing countries would allow anything except the most trivial concessions. Special and differential treatment does not further the goal of the integration of developing countries into the global food system. Reputation matters in agricultural and food markets.

Technical assistance is the better remedy for the challenges faced by developing countries. Given the limited effects of harmonization, the difficulty in reaching equivalence agreements to expand market access, and the increasing importance of process attributes in consumer demand for foods, technical assistance directed at conformity assessment services to certify compliance is likely to yield the highest payoff for developing countries and therefore should be a priority within the global food system. Technical assistance to increase participation in international standards organizations or to increase the presence of developing countries in the WTO is likely to have a lower payoff both for the country concerned and for global trade.

Some developing countries believe strengthened and expanded protection for geographical indications serve their interests, although European countries are primarily responsible for the prominence of this issue in the Doha Round negotiations. At present, WTO members are obliged to establish the legal infrastructure necessary to protect GIs. But new questions have been raised: Should countries be obliged to afford global protection to GIs for wines and spirits that are included in a central registry? Should countries provide greater protection to products other than wine and spirits? In principle, the protection of commercial identity can be welfare enhancing, but the protection of intellectual property in the form of GIs has a lesser claim on the support of the international community than the protection of intellectual property through patents, which are widely thought to further innovation and growth. A multilateral commitment is needed to further study of the impact of the GI proposals on the global food system, as has been undertaken for standard trade policies. From a negotiating perspective, it might be possible to persuade those countries demanding strengthened GI protection to sharply reduce trade barriers. Rents associated with consumer familiarity with GI-protected goods would then not merely be added to those afforded by tariffs and other measures. Producers and consumers of undifferentiated products in the global food system would also reap benefits from the negotiation of such an agreement.

Seizing the Opportunities from Trade

Much remains to be done by national governments and international institutions to improve the global regulatory framework for agricultural and food markets. The debate on the international effects of food regulation has been framed largely by the WTO rules. From a broader perspective, governments should adopt the policy options that provide the greatest expected benefits relative to costs, and should not be satisfied merely with legally defensible measures. However, understanding what is legally possible is important in judging the costs and benefits of regulation. To that end, ongoing discussions in the WTO will improve governance in this area of public policy. These discussions alone, however, are unlikely to provide sufficient guidance. Seizing the opportunities that trade provides for a diverse, safe, and economical global food supply requires overcoming the shortcomings stemming from too narrow a focus on the legal interpretation of the relevant WTO agreements.

The public would be better served if governments themselves undertake comprehensive evaluations of regulatory decisions, even if not required to do so by international commitments. Indeed, they should do so even for risk-related measures, where the justification for government regulation is strongest. For quality goals, there appears to be too little recognition of the incentives offered by the market for firms to voluntarily provide information. Governments should adopt approaches to complement market incentives that encourage producers to compete for market shares of sales to attribute-conscious consumers. Poorly designed policies, by contrast, stifle innovation and competition by fostering false product differentiation that stigmatizes foreign products.

In short, what is needed is a constructive shift in the current policy debates. The emphasis should move from viewing expanded trade as a threat to providing consumers with products that have desired attributes, to viewing expanded trade as a resource-efficient means of achieving this objective. Appropriate national regulation within an effective framework of international oversight is the key to securing open food markets that contribute to higher standards of living.

References

Akerlof, G.A. 1970. The Market for "Lemons": Quality Uncertainty and the Market Mechanism. *Quarterly Journal of Economics* 84: 488–500.

Antle, John. 1996. Efficient Food Safety Regulation in the Food Manufacturing Sector. *American Journal of Agricultural Economics* 78, no. 5: 1242–47.

Atkinson, Nigel. 1999. The Impact of BSE on the UK Economy. Paper presented at the Symposium on Animal and Human TSEs, Instituto Interamericano de Cooperación para la Agricultura, Buenos Aires.

AVIS. 2003. Foot and mouth disease (FMD). http://aleffgroup.com/avisfmd/.

Barnett P.V., A.R. Samuel, and R.J. Statham. 2001. The Suitability of the "Emergency" Foot-and-Mouth Disease Antigens Held by the International Vaccine Bank Within a Global Context. *Vaccine* 19: 2107–17.

Becker, Geoffrey. 1999. U.S.-European Agricultural Trade: The Veterinary Equivalence Agreement. Report RS20242. Congressional Research Service, July 26.

Beghin, John C., and Jean-Christophe Bureau. 2001. *Quantification of Sanitary, Phytosanitary, and Technical Barriers to Trade for Trade Policy Analysis*. Working Paper 01-WP 291. Ames, IA: Center for Agricultural and Rural Development, Iowa State University.

Bernstein, Jason, Jean C. Buzby, and Kenneth H. Mathews Jr. 2003. International Trade of Meat and Poultry Products and Food Safety Issues. In *International Trade and Food Safety*, ed. J. Buzby. Agricultural Economic Report 828. Washington: Economic Research Service, US Department of Agriculture.

Brown, Cheryl, Lori Lynch, and David Zilberman. 2002. The Economics of Controlling Insect-Transmitted Diseases. *American Journal of Agricultural Economics* 84, no. 2: 279–91.

Brown, David W.G. 2001. Foot and Mouth Disease in Human Beings. *The Lancet* 357 (May 12): 1463.

Caswell, Julie. 1997. *Uses of Food Labelling Regulations*. OCDE/GD(97)150. Paris: Directorate for Food, Agriculture and Fisheries, OECD.

Caswell, Julie A., Maury Bredahl, and Niel Hooker. 1998. How Quality Management Metasystems Are Affecting the Food Industry. *Review of Agricultural Economics* 10: 547–57.

Caswell, Julie, and E. Mojduszka. 1996. Using Informational Labeling to Influence the

Market for Quality in Food Products. *American Journal of Agricultural Economics* 78, no. 5: 1248–53.

Caswell, Julie, and Daniel Padberg. 1992. Toward a More Comprehensive Theory of Food Labels. *American Journal of Agricultural Economics* 74, no. 2: 460–68.

Codex Alimentarius Commission. 1999a. Report of the 23rd Session Food and Agricultural Organization and World Health Organization, ALINORM 99/37. 1999, Rome. www.codexalimentarius.net/archives.asp.

Codex Alimentarius Commission. 1999b. Understanding the Codex Alimentarius. Food and Agricultural Organization and World Health Organization, Rome. www.fao.org/docrep/w9114e/W9114e00.htm.

Codex Alimentarius Commission. 2001a. Procedural Manual. 12th ed. Food and Agricultural Organization and World Health Organization, Rome. www.fao.org/DOCREP/005/Y2200E/Y2200E00.HTM.

Codex Alimentarius Commission. 2001b. *Report of the Sixteenth Session of the Codex Committee on General Principles.* ALINORM 01/33A. Geneva: Codex.

Codex Alimentarius Commission. 2001c. *Report of the Twenty-Ninth Session of the Codex Committee on Food Labelling.* ALINORM 01/22A. Geneva: Codex.

Cohen, Joshua, Keith Duggar, George M. Gray, Silvia Kreindel, Hatim Abdelrahman, Tsegaye Habtemariam, David Oryang, and Berhanu Tameru. 2001. Evaluation of the Potential for Bovine Spongiform Encephalopathy in the United States. Harvard School of Public Health Center for Risk Analysis and Tuskegee University Center for Computational Epidemiology. www.aphis.usda.gov/lpa/issues/bse/bse-riskassmt.html (November).

Council for Agricultural Science and Technology (CAST). 1994. *Foodborne Pathogens: Risks and Consequences.* Ames, IA: CAST.

Crutchfield, S.R., Jean C. Buzby, Tanya Roberts, M. Ollinger, and C.-T. Jordan Lin. 1997. *An Economic Assessment of Food Safety Regulations: The New Approach to Meat and Poultry Inspection.* Agricultural Economic Report 755. Washington: Economic Research Service, US Department of Agriculture.

Darby, Michael R., and Edi Karni. 1973. Free Competition and the Optimal Amount of Fraud. *Journal of Law and Economics* 16, no. 1: 67–68.

DEFRA (UK Department for Environment, Food and Rural Affairs). 2000. The Inquiry into BSE and variant CJD in the United Kingdom. www.bseinquiry.gov.uk/report/index.htm.

DEFRA (UK Department for Environment, Food and Rural Affairs). 2003. Foot and Mouth Disease. www.defra.gov.uk/footandmouth/.

Dimitri, Carolyn. 2003. Agricultural Marketing Institutions: A Response to Quality Disputes. *Journal of Agricultural and Food Industrial Organization* 1, no. 1, article 17.

Dimitri, C., and Barry Krissoff. 2001. Quality Standards for Agricultural Commodities: Private and Public Sector Roles. US Department of Agriculture, Economic Research Service. Photocopy.

Donaldson, A.I., R.P. Kitching, and P.V. Barnett. 2000. Bovine Spongiform Encephalopathy. *OIE Manual of Standards for Diagnostic Tests and Vaccines.* www.oie.int/eng/normes/mmanual/A_00060.htm.

Ekboir, J.M. 1999. *Potential Impact of Foot-and-Mouth Disease in California: The Role and Contribution of Animal Health Surveillance and Monitoring Services.* Davis: Agri-cultural Issues Center, University of California, Davis.

European Commission. 2002. Commission Adopts First Report on Irradiated Foods. Press Release IP/02/1462, October 11.

European Court of Justice. 2003. Case C-108/01. *Consorzio del Prosciutto di Parma and Salumificio S. Rita SpA v. Asda Stores Ltd. and Hygrade Foods Ltd.* http//curia.eu.int/en/content/juris/index.htm (May 20).

FAO (Food and Agriculture Organization). 2001. Economic Impacts of Transboundary Plant Pests and Animal Diseases. *The State of Food and Agriculture.* Rome: FAO.

Federal Register. 1991. Regulatory Impact Assessment for Proposed Rules to Amend the Food Labeling Regulations. 56 FR 229, 60856–78.

Food Marketing Institute. 2000. Comment on Country of Origin Labeling. Mandatory Country of Origin Labeling of Imported Fresh Muscle Cuts of Beef and Lamb. Communication to Congress, Food Safety and Inspection Service, US Department of Agriculture, January.

FSIS (Food Safety and Inspection Service, USDA). 1995. *Focus on Chicken*. Consumer Education and Information. Washington: US Department of Agriculture.

FSIS (Food Safety and Inspection Service, USDA). 2000. Mandatory Country of Origin Labeling of Imported Fresh Muscle Cuts of Beef and Lamb. Communication to Congress, Food Safety and Inspection Service, US Department of Agriculture, January.

GAO (General Accounting Office). 1999. *Food Safety: The Agricultural Use of Antibiotics and Its Implications for Human Health*. GAO/RCED-99-74. Washington: GAO.

Garner, M.G., and M.B. Lack. 1995. An Evaluation of Alternate Control Strategies for Foot and Mouth Disease in Australia: A Regional Approach. *Preventive Veterinary Medicine* 23: 9–32.

Gascoine, Digby. 1999. Harmonization, Mutual Recognition and Equivalence: How and What Is Attainable. Paper presented at the WHO/FAO Conference on International Food Trade Beyond 2000, Melbourne, Australia, October.

Golan, Elise, Fred Koehler, and Lorraine Mitchell (with contributions from Catherine Greene and Amber Jessup). 2000. *The Economics of Food Labeling*. Agricultural Economic Report 793. Washington: Economic Research Service, US Department of Agriculture.

Golan, Elise, Barry Krissoff, Fred Kuchler, Ken Nelson, Greg Price, and Linda Calvin. 2003. Traceability in the U.S. Food Supply: Dead End or Superhighway? *Choices* (2nd quarter). www.choicesmagazine.org/archives/2003/q2/2003-2-04.htm.

Grant, Wyn. 1999. Biotechnology: A Source of Tensions in the U.S.-EU Trade Relations. Department of Political Science, University of Warwick, UK. Photocopy.

Hammonds, Tim. 2003. Retailer Expectations for Country-of-Origin Labeling. Paper presented at the conference Emerging Roles for Food Labels: Inform, Protect, Persuade. American Agricultural Economic Association, Washington (March 20–21).

Health Canada. 2003. Nutrition Labelling. www.hc-sc.gc.ca/hpfb-dgpsa/onpp-bppn/labelling-etiquetage/index_e.html.

Henson, Spencer J., R.J. Loader, Alan Swinbank, Maury Bredahl, and N. Lux. 2000. Impact of Sanitary and Phytosanitary Measures on Developing Countries. Department of Agricultural and Food Economics, University of Reading.

Henson, Spencer J., and Mario Mazzocchi. 2002. Impact of Bovine Spongiform Encephalopathy on Agribusiness in the United Kingdom: Results of an Event Study on Equity Prices. *American Journal of Agricultural Economics* 84, no. 2: 370–86.

Heumeuller, Dirk, and Tim Josling. 2001. Trade Restrictions on Genetically Engineered Foods: The Application of the TBT Agreement. Paper presented at the Fifth International Conference on Biotechnology, Science and Modern Agriculture: A New Industry at the Dawn of the Century, Ravello, Italy (June 15–18).

Hill, A.F., M. Desbruslais, S. Joiner, K.C.L. Sidle, I. Gowland, J. Collinge, L.J. Doey, and P. Lantos. 1997. The Same Prion Strain Causes vCJD and BSE. *Nature* 389: 448–50.

Hoeckman, Bernard, and Michael Leidy. 1993. Environmental Policy Formation in a Trading Economy: A Public Choice Perspective. In *The Greening of World Trade Issues*, ed. Kym Anderson and Richard Blackhurst. London: Harvester Wheatsheaf.

Huang, S. 2000. Taiwan's Hog Industry—3 Years after Disease Outbreak. *Agricultural Outlook* (October): 20–23.

Hudec, Robert. 1996. GATT Legal Restraints on the Use of Trade Measures Against Foreign Environmental Practices. In *Fair Trade and Harmonization: Prerequisites for Free Trade?* Vol. 2, *Legal Analysis*, ed. Jagdish Bhagwati and Robert Hudec. Cambridge, MA: MIT Press.

Hudec, Robert. 2001. The Product-Process Doctrine in GATT/WTO Jurisprudence. In *New Directions in International Economic Law*, ed. Marco Bronckers and Reinhard Quick. The Hague: Kluwer Law International.

IISD and UNEP (International Institute for Sustainable Development and United Nations Environment Programme). 2000. *Environment and Trade, A Handbook*. Geneva: IISD and UNEP.

Ippolito, Pauline, and Alan Mathios. 1990. The Regulation of Science-Based Claims in Advertising. *Journal of Consumer Policy* 13: 413–45.

James, S., and Kym Anderson. 1998. On the Need for More Economic Assessment of Quarantine Policies. *Australian Journal of Agricultural and Resource Economics* 42, no. 4 (December): 425–44.

Jessup, Amber. 2000. Nutrition Labeling. In *The Economics of Food Labeling*, ed. E. Golan, F. Kuchler, and L. Mitchell, with contributions from A. Jessup and C. Greene. Agricultural Economic Report 793. Washington: Economic Research Service, US Department of Agriculture.

Johnson, Robbin. 1996. APEC and the Global Food System. Paper presented at *Toward a Pacific Rim Food System: Forum on US Agriculture and Food Trade Policy in APEC*. National Center for APEC, Washington State University (April).

Josling, Tim. 1998. *Agricultural Trade Policy: Completing the Reform*. Washington: Institute for International Economics.

Josling, Tim, Donna Roberts, and Ayesha Hassan. 1999. The Beef-Hormone Dispute and Its Implications for Trade Policy. European Forum Working Paper. Stanford University, September.

Kramer, Carol S. 1989. Food Safety and International Trade: The US-EC Meat and Hormone Controversies. In *The Political Economy of US Agriculture*, ed. Carol S. Kramer. Washington: National Center for Food and Agricultural Policy, Resources for the Future.

Krissoff, Barry, Mary Bohman, and Julie A. Caswell, eds. 2002. *Global Food Trade and Consumer Demand for Quality*. New York: Kluwer Academic/Plenum Publishers.

Lohr, Luanne. 2001. Factors Affecting International Demand and Trade in Organic Food Products. In *Changing Structure of Global Food Consumption and Trade*, ed. Anita Regmi. Agriculture and Trade Report WRS-01-1. Washington: Economic Research Service, US Department of Agriculture.

Lowles, I., R. Hill, V. Auld, H. Stewart, and C. Colhoun. 2002. Monitoring the Pollution from a Pyre Used to Destroy Animal Carcasses During the Outbreak of Foot and Mouth Disease in Cumbria, United Kingdom. *Atmospheric Environment* 36, no. 17: 2901–05.

MacDonald, James, and Stephen Crutchfield. 1996. Modeling the Costs of Food Safety Regulation. *American Journal of Agricultural Economics* 78, no. 5: 1285–90.

Magat, Wesley, and W. Kip Viscusi. 1992. Informational Approaches to Regulation. Cambridge, MA: MIT Press.

Marshall, M., M. Boland, D. Comforte, and D. Cesar. 2002. A Case Study of Beef Production and Exports in Uruguay. In *Global Food Trade and Consumer Demand for Quality*, ed. Barry Krissoff, Mary Bohman, and Julie A. Caswell. New York: Kluwer Academic/Plenum Publishers.

Maskus, Keith E. 2000. *Intellectual Property Rights in the Global Economy*. Washington: Institute for International Economics.

Maskus, Keith E., and John S. Wilson, eds. 2001. *Quantifying the Impact of Technical Barriers to Trade: Can It Be Done?* Ann Arbor: University of Michigan Press.

Mathews, Kenneth, Jr. 2001. Dissecting the Challenges of Mad Cow and Foot-and-Mouth Disease. *Agricultural Outlook* (August): 4-6.

McNeil, Dale. 1998. The First Case Under the WTO's Sanitary and Phytosanitary Agreement: The European Union's Hormone Ban. *Virginia Journal of International Law* 39: 89–134.

Meltzer, E. 2001. Geographical Indications—Background Information. US Patent and Trademark Office. Photocopy.

Mitchell, Lorraine. 2001. Impact of Consumer Demand for Animal Welfare on Global Trade. In *Changing Structure of Global Food Consumption and Trade*, ed. Anita Regmi. Agriculture and Trade Report WRS-01-1. Washington: Economic Research Service, US Department of Agriculture.

Motaal, Doaa Abdel. 2002. The Agreement on Technical Barriers to Trade, the Committee on Trade and Environment, and Eco-labelling. In *Trade, Environment and the Millennium*, ed. Gary Sampson and W. Bradnee Chambers. New York: United Nations University Press.

Moyer, H. Wayne, and Tim Josling. 2002. *Agricultural Policy Reform: Politics and Process in the EU and the US in the 1990s*. Aldershot, UK: Ashgate Press.

Narang, H. 1996. The Nature of the Scrapie Agent: The Virus Theory. *Proceedings of the Society for Experimental Biology and Medicine* 212, no. 3: 208–24.

New Zealand Ministry of Agriculture and Forestry. 2000. *Import Risk Analysis: Chicken Meat and Chicken Meat Products*. Wellington, NZ: Biosecurity Authority.

Noah, L. 1994. The Imperative to Warn: Disentangling the "Right to Know" from the "Need to Know" about Consumer Product Hazards. *Yale Journal on Regulation* 11, no. 2: 293-400.

OECD (Organization for Economic Cooperation and Development). 1997. *Regulatory Reform and the Agro-Food Sector*. OECD Report on Regulatory Reform. Vol. 1, *Sectoral Studies*. Paris: OECD.

OECD (Organization for Economic Cooperation and Development). 1999. *Food Safety and Quality: Trade Considerations*. Paris: OECD.

OECD (Organization for Economic Cooperation and Development). 2000. *Appellations of Origin and Geographical Indications in OECD Member Countries: Economic and Legal Implications*. COM/AGR/APM/TD/WP(2000)15. Paris: OECD.

OECD (Organization for Economic Cooperation and Development). 2002. *A Survey of Issues and Concerns Raised in the WTO's SPS Committee*. COM/TP/AGR/WP/(2002)21. Paris: OECD.

OECD (Organization for Economic Cooperation and Development). 2003. *Agricultural Policies in OECD Countries: Monitoring and Evaluation 2002*. Paris: OECD.

OIE (L'Office International des Epizooties). 2003a. *Bovine spongiform encephalopathy* (BSE). www.oie.int/eng/info/en_esb.htm.

OIE (L'Office International des Epizooties). 2003b. Foot and Mouth Disease. www.oie.int/eng/info/en_fmd.htm.

OIE (L'Office International des Epizooties). 2003c. Handistatus II. www.oie.int/hs2/report.asp.

Orden, David, Timothy Josling, and Donna Roberts. 2002. Product Differentiation, Sanitary Barriers, and Arbitrage in World Poultry Markets. In *Global Food Trade and Consumer Demand for Quality*, ed. Barry Krissoff, Mary Bohman, and Julie Caswell. New York: Kluwer Academic/Plenum Publishers.

Orden, David, Clare Narrod, and Joseph W. Glauber. 2001. Least Trade-Restrictive SPS Policies: An Analytic Framework Is There but Questions Remain. In *The Economics of Quarantine and the SPS Agreement*, ed. Kym Anderson, Cheryl McRae, and David Wilson. Adelaide, Australia: Centre for International Economic Studies.

Orden, David, Robert Paarlberg, and Terry Roe. 1999. *Policy Reform in American Agriculture: Analysis and Prognosis*. Chicago: University of Chicago Press.

Orden, David, and Donna Roberts, eds. 1997. *Understanding Technical Barriers to Agricultural Trade*. St. Paul: International Agricultural Trade Research Consortium, Department of Applied Economics, University of Minnesota.

Orden, David, and Eduardo Romano. 1996. The Avocado Dispute and Other Technical Barriers to Agricultural Trade Under NAFTA. Paper presented at the conference on NAFTA and Agriculture: Is the Experiment Working? San Antonio, Texas (November).

Otsuki, Tsunehiro, John S. Wilson, and Mirvat Sewadeh. 2001. What Price Precaution? European Harmonisation of Aflatoxin Regulations and African Groundnut Exports. *European Review of Agricultural Economics* 28, no. 2: 263–83.

Paarlberg, Philip L., and John G. Lee. 1998. Import Restrictions in the Presence of a Health Risk: An Illustration Using FMD. *American Journal of Agricultural Economics* 80: 175–83.

Paarlberg, Philip L., and John G. Lee. 2001. Import Rules for Foot-and-Mouth Disease Contaminated Beef. In *Agricultural Globalization, Trade and the Environment*, ed. C. Moss, G. Rausser, A. Schmitz, T. Taylor, and D. Zilberman. New York: Kluwer Academic Publishers.

Paarlberg, Robert. 2002. The Restricted Global Uptake of GM Crops: The Trade Rules Connection. Department of Political Science, Wellesley College. Photocopy.

Patterson, Lee Ann, and Tim Josling. 2001. Biotechnology Regulatory Policy in the United States and the European Union: Source of Transatlantic Trade Conflict or Opportunity for Cooperation? Paper presented at the Western Economic Association International Conference, San Francisco (July).

Phillips, P., and Josling, Timothy. 2002. GM Foods, Labeling, and the WTO. Paper presented to the IATRC Annual Conference, Monterey, California (December 16).

Pollack, Mark A., and Gregory C. Shaffer. 2001. The Challenge of Reconciling Regulatory Differences: Food Safety and GMOs in the Transatlantic Relationship. In *Transatlantic Governance in the Global Economy*, ed. Mark A. Pollack and Gregory C. Shaffer. Lanham, MD: Rowman and Littlefield.

President of the United States. 1994. Message from the President of the United States Transmitting the Uruguay Round Trade Agreements to the Second Session of the 103rd Congress, Texts of Agreements Implementing Bill, Statement of Administrative Action and Required Supporting Statements, House Document 103-316. Vol. 1: 742–63.

Roberts, Donna. 1998. Preliminary Assessment of the Effects of the WTO Agreement on Sanitary and Phytosanitary Trade Regulations. *Journal of International Economic Law* 1, no. 3: 377–405.

Roberts, Donna. 2000. Sanitary and Phytosanitary Risk Management in the Post-Uruguay Round Era: An Economic Perspective. In *Incorporating Science, Economic, and Sociology in Developing Sanitary and Phytosanitary Standards in International Trade, Proceedings of a Conference*. Washington: National Academy Press.

Roberts, Donna, and Kate DeRemer. 1997. *Overview of Foreign Technical Barriers to US Agricultural Exports*. Technical Bulletin 9705. Washington: Economic Research Service, US Department of Agriculture.

Roberts, Donna, Timothy E. Josling, and David Orden. 1999. *A Framework for Analyzing Technical Trade Barriers in Agricultural Markets*. Technical Bulletin 1876. Washington: Economic Research Service, US Department of Agriculture.

Roberts, Donna, and David Orden. 1996. Determinants of Technical Barriers to Trade: The Case of U.S. Phytosanitary Restrictions on Mexican Avocados, 1972–1995. In *Understanding Technical Barriers to Agricultural Trade*, ed. David Orden and Donna Roberts. St. Paul: International Agricultural Trade Research Consortium, Department of Applied Economics, University of Minnesota.

Roberts, Donna, David Orden, and Timothy Josling. 1999. WTO Disciplines on Sanitary and Phytosanitary Barriers to Agricultural Trade: Progress, Prospects, and Implications for Developing Countries. Paper presented at the World Bank Conference on Agriculture and the New Trade Agenda from a Developing Country Perspective, Geneva (October).

Roberts, Donna, and Laurian Unnevehr. 2002. Trends in Food Safety Regulation and Their Impact on Trade Disputes. In *International Trade and Food Safety*, ed. J. Buzby. Agricultural Economic Report 828. Washington: Economic Research Service, US Department of Agriculture.

Roberts, Donna, L. Unnevehr, J. Caswell, I. Sheldon, J. Wilson, T. Otsuki, and D. Orden. 2001. Agriculture in the WTO: The Role of Product Attributes in the Agricultural Negotiations. International Agricultural Trade Research Consortium, Commissioned Paper no. 17. http://iatrcweb.org/Publications/commiss.html (May).

Romano, Eduardo. 1998. Two Essays on Sanitary and Phytosanitary Barriers Affecting Agricultural Trade Between Mexico and the United States. Ph.D. dissertation, Virginia Polytechnic Institute and State University.

Samuel, A.R., and Nick J. Knowles. 2001. Foot and Mouth Disease Virus: Cause of the Recent Crisis for the UK Livestock Industry. *Trends in Genetics* 17 (August): 8.

Scott, M.R., R. Will, J. Ironside, H.-O.B. Nguyen, P. Tremblay, S.J. DeArmond, and S.B. Prusiner. 1999. Compelling Transgenetic Evidence for Transmission of Bovine Spongiform Encephalopathy Prions to Humans. *Proceedings of National Academy of Sciences* 96: 15137–42.

Scudamore, Jim. 2002. Measures Related to the Eradication of FMD in Great Britain. http://cmlag.fgov.be/eng/CVOs-abstract.pdf.

Snape, Richard, and David Orden. 2001. Integrating Import Risk and Trade Benefit Analysis. In *The Economics of Quarantine and the SPS Agreement*, ed. Kym Anderson, Cheryl McRae, and David Wilson. Adelaide, Australia: Centre for International Economic Studies.

Snyder, Louis L. 1945. The American-German Pork Dispute, 1879–1891. *Journal of Modern History* 17: 16–28.

Stanton, Gretchen. 1997. Implications of the WTO Agreement on Sanitary and Phytosanitary Measures. In *Understanding Technical Barriers to Agricultural Trade*, ed. David Orden and Donna Roberts. St. Paul: International Agricultural Trade Research Consortium, Department of Applied Economics, University of Minnesota.

Sumner, Daniel, and Hyunok Lee. 1997. Sanitary and Phytosanitary Trade Barriers and Empirical Trade Modeling. In *Understanding Technical Barriers to Agricultural Trade*, ed. David Orden and Donna Roberts. St. Paul: International Agricultural Trade Research Consortium, Department of Applied Economics, University of Minnesota.

Sykes, Alan O. 1995. *Product Standards for Internationally Integrated Goods Markets*. Washington: Brookings Institution.

Tait, Joyce, and Les Levidow. 1992. Proactive and Reactive Approaches to Risk Regulation: The Case of Biotechnology. *Futures* (April): 219–31.

Takahashi, Hiroshi. 1999. Reform of the Food Labelling and Food Standard System in Japan: The Revision of the JAS Law. Extract, *News and Views from Japan*. Japanese Mission to the European Union. www.eu.emb-japan.go.jp/interest/jaslaw.htm (May).

Thilmany, Dawn, and Christopher Barrett. 1996. Regulatory Barriers in an Integrating World Food Market. *Review of Agricultural Economics* 19, no. 1: 91–107.

Thornsbury, Suzanne. 1998. The Impact of Market and Political Economy Forces on Technical Barriers to U.S. Agricultural Exports. Ph.D. dissertation, Virginia Polytechnic Institute and State University.

Thornsbury, Suzanne, Donna Roberts, Kate DeRemer, and David Orden. 1999. A First Step in Understanding Technical Barriers to Agricultural Trade. In *Food Security, Diversification and Resource Management: Refocusing the Role of Agriculture?* ed. George H. Peters and Joachim von Braun. Aldershot, UK: Ashgate Press.

UNDP-FAO (United Nations Development Program–Food and Agriculture Organization). 1998. Regional Network Inter-Country Cooperation on Preharvest Technology and Quality Control of Food Grains (REGNET) and the ASEAN Grain Postharvest Program. Bangkok, Thailand.

Unnevehr, Laurian J., and Helen H. Jensen. 1999. The Economic Implications of Using HACCP as a Food Safety Regulatory Standard. *Food Policy* 24: 625–35.

Unnevehr, Laurian J., and Gerald C. Nelson. 2002. Balancing the Costs and Benefits of Labeling and Traceability for GMOs. Paper presented at the Workshop on Labeling Products of Food Biotechnology: Panacea or Hidden Trade Barrier? The European Forum, Institute for International Studies, Stanford University (June 28).

USDA (US Department of Agriculture). 1997a. Foot and Mouth Disease Spreads Chaos in Pork Markets. Livestock and Poultry, World Markets and Trade. www. fas.usda.gov/ dlp2/circular/1997/97-10LP/taiwanfmd.htm (October).

USDA (US Department of Agriculture). 1997b. Importation of Hass Avocado Fruit Grown in Michoacan, Mexico. *Federal Register*. 7 CFR Part 319, Docket 94-116-5, February 5.

USDA (US Department of Agriculture). 1998. 1998 Foreign Country of Origin Labeling Survey. Foreign Agricultural Service, Food Safety and Technical Services Division, Washington.

USDA (US Department of Agriculture). 2001a. FMD Shatters Argentine and Uruguayan Hopes for Increased Beef Exports. International Agricultural Trade Report, Dairy, Livestock and Poultry Market, June 8.

USDA (US Department of Agriculture). 2001b. Mexican Hass Avocado Import Program: Final Rule. *Federal Register* 7 CFR Part 319, Docket 00-003-4, November 1, 55530–52.

USDA (US Department of Agriculture). 2001c. Trade Impact of FMD-Related Import Restrictions on Argentine Products. www.usda.gov/special/fmd/fmdimpactargentina.htm.

USDA (US Department of Agriculture). 2001d. Trade Impact of FMD-Related Import Restrictions on EU Products. www.usda.gov/special/fmdimpact.htm.

USDA (US Department of Agriculture). 2002. Database of Notifications to the Sanitary and Phytosanitary Committee and Technical Barriers to Trade Committee of the World Trade Organization, Foreign Agricultural Service, Division of Food Safety and Technical Services (accessed in October).

USDA (US Department of Agriculture). 2003. Importation of "Hass" Avocado Fruit (*Persea Americana* cv. Hass) from Mexico: A Risk Assessment. June.

USDA/FSIS (US Department of Agriculture, Food Safety and Inspection Service). 1996. Pathogen Reduction: Hazard Analysis and Critical Control Points (HACCP) Systems; Final Rule. May 17.

USDA/FSIS (US Department of Agriculture, Food Safety and Inspection Service). 2002. Current Thinking on Measures That Could Be Implemented to Minimize Human Exposure to Materials That Could Potentially Contain the Bovine Spongiform Encephalopathy Agent. www.fsis.usda.gov/oa/topics/BSE_thinking.htm (January 15).

USFDA (US Food and Drug Administration). 2000. *Foodborne Pathogenic Microorganisms and Natural Toxins Handbook.* Washington: FDA.

Veggeland, Frode, and Svein Ole Borgen. 2002. Changing the Codex: The Role of International Institutions. Norwegian Agricultural Economics Research Institute, Oslo (January).

Victor, David G. 1998. Risk Management and the World Trading System: Regulating International Trade Distortions Caused by National Sanitary and Phytosanitary Policies. In *Incorporating Science, Economic, and Sociology in Developing Sanitary and Phytosanitary Standards in International Trade.* Proceedings of a Conference. Washington: National Academy Press.

Victor, David G., and C. Ford Runge. 2002. Farming the Genetic Frontier. *Foreign Affairs* 81, no. 3 (May/June): 107–21.

Vogel, David. 2001. The Regulation of GMOs in Europe and the United States: A Case-Study of Contemporary European Regulatory Politics. New York: Council on Foreign Relations.

Watal, Jayashree. 2000. *Intellectual Property Rights in the World Trade Organization: The Way Forward for Developing Countries.* Oxford: Oxford University Press.

Wilesmith, J.W., G.A.H. Wells, M.P. Cranwell, and J.B.M. Ryan. 1988. Bovine Spongiform Encephalopathy: Epidemiological Studies. *Veterinary Record* 123: 638–44.

Wilson, John S. 1995. *Standards and APEC: An Action Agenda.* Washington: Institute for International Economics.

Wilson, John S., and Tsunehiro Otsuki. 2002. *To Spray or Not to Spray: Pesticides, Banana Exports and Food Safety.* Washington: World Bank Development Research Group.

World Food Chemical News. 1998. Survey Shows Consumers Support Country-of-Origin Labeling for Meat. December 9, 22.

World Food Chemical News. 2000. U.S. Congress Debates Country-of-Origin Labeling for Beef. October 11, 19.

World Food Chemical News. 2001a. Quarantine Laws Cited as Way to Gain Market Access. September.

World Food Chemical News. 2001b. Groups Seek Harmonization of U.S. and Canadian Nutrition Labels. September 24, 8.

World Food Chemical News. 2002a. Country of Origin Labeling—Momentum Growing. April 29, 9.

World Food Chemical News. 2002b. EU Advocate General Proposes Limits on Geographical Names. May 6, 21.

WTO (World Trade Organization). 1996. Recommended Notification Procedures. Committee on Sanitary and Phytosanitary Measures, G/SPS/7, June 11.

WTO (World Trade Organization). 1997a. EC Measures Concerning Meat and Meat Products (Hormones). Complaint by the United States, Report of the Panel, WT/DS26/R/USA, August 18.

WTO (World Trade Organization). 1997b. Overview of Existing International Notification and Registration Systems for Geographical Indications Relating to Wines and Spirits. IP/C/W/85, November 17.

WTO (World Trade Organization). 1998a. EU Measures Concerning Meat and Meat Products (Hormones). Arbitration under Article 21.3 (c) of the Dispute Settlement Understanding, WT/DS26/15 and WT/DS48/13, May 27.

WTO (World Trade Organization). 1998b. European Council Regulation No. 1139/98. Compulsory Indication of the Labeling of Certain Foodstuffs Produced from Genetically Modified Organisms. Committee on Technical Barriers to Trade, G/TBT/W/94, October 16.

WTO (World Trade Organization). 1998c. The WTO SPS Agreement and Developing Countries. Committee on Sanitary and Phytosanitary Measures, G/SPS/W/93, November 5.

WTO (World Trade Organization). 1999a. European Communities—Protection of Trademarks and Geographical Indications for Agricultural Products and Foodstuffs. Request for Consultations by the United States, June 7.

WTO (World Trade Organization). 1999b. Notification—Japan. Committee on Technical Barriers to Trade, G/TBT/Notif.99/668, December 23.

WTO (World Trade Organization). 1999c. Overview of Existing International Notification and Registration Systems for Geographical Indications Relating to Products Other Than Wine and Spirits, IP/C/W/85/Add.1, July 2.

WTO (World Trade Organization). 1999d. Response from the European Commission to Comments by the United States and Canada Concerning Notification 97.766. Committee on Technical Barriers to Trade, G/TBT/W/104, February 12.

WTO (World Trade Organization). 1999e. Summary of the Meeting Held on 7–8 July, 1999, Sanitary and Phytosanitary Committee, G/SPS/R/15, October 29.

WTO (World Trade Organization). 2000a. Equivalence: Submission from the United States. Committee on Sanitary and Phytosanitary Measures, G/SPS/GEN/212, November 7.

WTO (World Trade Organization). 2000b. Notification—Chile, Committee on Sanitary and Phytosanitary Measures. Committee on Sanitary and Phytosanitary Measures, G/SPS/N/CHL/56, February 11.

WTO (World Trade Organization). 2000c. Second Triennial Review of the Operation of the Implementation of the Agreement on Technical Barriers to Trade. Committee on Technical Barriers to Trade, G/TBT/9, November 13.

WTO (World Trade Organization). 2001a. Decision on the Implementation of Article 4 of the Agreement on the Application of Sanitary and Phytosanitary Measures, G/SPS/19, October 26.

WTO (World Trade Organization). 2001b. Equivalence: Note by the Secretariat. Committee on Sanitary and Phytosanitary Measures, G/SPS/W/111, July 4.

WTO (World Trade Organization). 2001c. European Communities—Measures Affecting

Asbestos and Asbestos-Containing Products. Report of the Appellate Body, WT/DS135/AB/R, March 12.

WTO (World Trade Organization). 2001d. Experience with Recognition of Equivalence: Statement by Thailand. Committee on Sanitary and Phytosanitary Measures, G/SPS/GEN/242, April 6.

WTO (World Trade Organization). 2001e. Implementation-Related Issues and Concerns—Decision of 14 November, WT/MIN(01)/17, November 20.

WTO (World Trade Organization). 2001f. Marking and Labelling Requirements: Submission from Switzerland. Committee on Technical Barriers to Trade, G/TBT/W/162, June 19.

WTO (World Trade Organization). 2001g. Minutes of the Meeting Held on 9 October, Committee on Technical Barriers to Trade. Committee on Technical Barriers to Trade, G/TBT/M/25, November 11.

WTO (World Trade Organization). 2002a. European Communities—Trade Description of Sardines. Report of the Appellate Body, WT/DS231/AB/R/, September 26.

WTO (World Trade Organization). 2002b. European Communities—Trade Description of Sardines. Report of the Panel, WT/DS231/R, May 29.

WTO (World Trade Organization). 2002c. Labelling and Requirements of the Agreement on Technical Barriers to Trade: Framework for Informal, Structured Discussions—Communication from Canada. Committee on Technical Barriers to Trade, G/TBT/W/174, March 12.

WTO (World Trade Organization). 2002d. A Practical Example of Implementation of the Principle of Equivalence: Submission of the European Communities, G/SPS/GEN/304, March 12.

WTO (World Trade Organization). 2002e. Seventh Annual Review of the Implementation and Operation of the Agreement, G/TBT/11, February 18.

WTO (World Trade Organization). 2002f. Specific Trade Concerns. Note by the Secretariat. Committee on Sanitary and Phytosanitary Measures, G/SPS/GEN/204/Rev.2, January 16.

WTO (World Trade Organization). 2002g. Specific Trade Concerns Related to Labelling Brought to the Attention of the Committee Since 1995—Note by the Secretariat. Committee on Technical Barriers to Trade, G/TBT/W/184, October 4.

WTO (World Trade Organization). 2002h. Summaries of the Meetings of the Committee on Sanitary and Phytosanitary Measures. Committee on Sanitary and Phytosanitary Measures, G/SPS/R series, 1995–2001.

WTO (World Trade Organization). 2003a. Update of WTO Dispute Settlement Cases. WT/DS/OV/10, January 22.

WTO (World Trade Organization). 2003b. Minutes of the Meeting Held on 25–27 November and 29 November and 20 December, 2002. Council for Trade-Related Aspects of Intellectual Property Rights, IP/C/W/38, May 2.

WTO (World Trade Organization). 2003c. Japan—Measures Affecting the Importation of Apples, WT/DS245/R, July 15.

Zago, A.M., and Daniel Pick. 2002. A Welfare Analysis of European Products with Geographical Indications and Products with Designations of Origin. In *Global Food Trade and Consumer Demand for Quality*, ed. Barry Krissoff, Mary Bohman, and Julie Caswell. New York: Kluwer Academic/Plenum Publishing.

Acronyms

ADI	Acceptable Daily Intake
ANZFA	Australia New Zealand Food Authority
ANZFSC	Australia New Zealand Food Standards Councils
APEC	Asia Pacific Economic Cooperation (forum)
BSE	bovine spongiform encephalopathy (mad cow disease)
CAP	Common Agricultural Policy (EU)
CBD	Convention on Biological Diversity
CCRVDF	Codex Committee on Residues of Veterinary Drugs in Foods
CITES	Convention on International Trade in Endangered Species of Wild Fauna and Flora
CCFAC	Codex Committee on Food Additives and Contaminants
CCFL	Codex Committee on Food Labeling
Codex	Codex Alimentarius Commission
DHHS	US Department of Health and Human Services
DSU	Dispute Settlement Understanding
EC	European Communities
EPPO	European Plant Protection Organization
FAO	Food and Agriculture Organization
FDA	US Food and Drug Administration
FMD	foot-and-mouth disease
FSIS	Food Safety and Inspection Service (USDA)
GAO	US General Accounting Office
GATT	General Agreement on Tariffs and Trade
GI	geographical indications
GM	genetically modified

GMO	genetically modified organism
HACCP	Hazard Analysis and Critical Control Point
IDF	International Dairy Federation
IFOAM	International Federation of Organic Agriculture Movements
IPPC	International Plant Protection Convention
ISO	International Organization for Standardization
JECFA	Joint FAO/WHO Expert Committee on Food Additives
JMPR	Joint FAO/WHO Meeting on Pesticide Residues
LCA	life-cycle analysis
LMOs	living modified organisms
MBM	meat and bonemeal
MEAs	multilateral environmental agreements
MRL	maximum residue level
NAFTA	North American Free Trade Agreement
NLEA	Nutrition Labeling and Education Act of 1990 (US)
npr-PPMs	non-product-related process and production methods
OECD	Organization for Economic Cooperation and Development
OIE	L'Office International des Epizooties
PAHs	polycyclic aromatic hydrocarbons
%DV	percent daily value
PM	particulate matter
PPM	process and production method
rbST	recombinant bovine somatotropin
rDNA	recombinant DNA
RPPC	regional plant protection convention
SO_2	sulfur dioxide
SPS	sanitary and phytosanitary
SRM	specified risk material
TBT	technical barriers to trade
TE	traditional expression
TED	turtle excluder device
TRIPS	Trade-Related Aspects of Intellectual Property Rights
TRQ	tariff rate quota
TSE	transmissible spongiform encephalopathy
UNCTAD	United Nations Conference on Trade and Development
UN/ECE	United Nations Economic Commission for Europe
URAA	Uruguay Round Agreement on Agriculture
USDA	US Department of Agriculture
vCJD	variant Creutzfeldt-Jakob disease
WB	World Bank
WHO	World Health Organization
WIPO	World Intellectual Property Organization
WTO	World Trade Organization

Index

cost-benefit analysis *(Cont.)*
 as policy, 29–31, 29*f*
 of SPS measures, 201
 and trade opportunities, 205
 in US-Mexico avocado dispute, 85–86
costs
 compliance, 27, 62, 148
 of foodborne illness, 105
 of informational remedies, 24
 of labeling, 62, 128, 129, 131, 143, 145–46,
 147, 148
 private, 188
 and scope of regulations, 21
 of technical standards, 23
 of verification, 27, 192
Council of Europe Convention for the
 Protection of Animals for Slaughter,
 178*n*
Council of Europe Convention for the
 Protection of Animals Kept for Farming
 Purposes, 178*n*
counter-notifications
 addressing pest and disease control, 81–82
 BSE-related, 97
 definition of, 60*n*
 FMD-related, 92, 99
 under SPS agreement, 59–63, 61*t*
 under TBT agreement, 59–63, 61*t*, 157, 158*t*
country-of-origin labeling, 10, 16, 19, 54, 62,
 129*n*, 132, 140–44, 191–92
 for products of mixed origin, 142
 requirements for, 141, 141*t*
 trade effects of, 143–44, 148, 153, 189
 by US states, 142*n*
credence characteristics, 15–16, 129, 151, 175
 definition of, 129
Creutzfeldt-Jakob disease, 82, 92, 94–98, 189
Cuba, 134
Czech Republic, 108–109, 133, 135

dairy products, 53–54, 61*n*, 110–11, 133. *See
 also* milk production
 equivalence determinations, 49, 49*n*
 pathogens in, 107–108
database, global plant pest and information
 system, 79
decision making
 consumer, 27, 127
 risk-related, 28
Decision on the Implementation of Article 4,
 50*n*
definitional standards, 136–37, 147–48
Delaney Clause, 162*n*
demand
 consumer, importance of, 14
 regulations affecting, 27
Denmark, 116
Department of Agriculture (USDA), 83–87, 91,
 96, 103*n*–104*n*, 119*n*, 141, 142

Department of Health and Human Services
 (DHHS), 124, 124*n*
developed countries. *See also specific country*
 agricultural support issues, 198–99
 animal welfare issues in, 176
 counter-notifications by, 61–62, 61*t*
 geographical indications protection in,
 147
 organic foods in, 170
 and process attribute regulation, 183, 190
 WTO dispute cases, 63
developing countries. *See also specific country*
 animal welfare issues in, 176
 counter-notifications by, 61–62, 61*t*
 and Doha Round trade negotiations,
 198–99
 equivalence issues, 50
 food safety regulation in, 103–104, 106,
 125–26, 190
 and genetically modified food dispute, 169
 geographical indication protection, 134–36,
 147, 205
 and international regulation, 3, 202–204
 and process attribute regulation, 183, 190
 and regionalization provisions, 51
 technical and financial assistance to, 75,
 204–205
 WTO dispute cases, 63
Diamond *vs.* Chakrabarty, 163*n*
disclosure requirements, mandatory, 23, 148
discriminatory applications, of food safety
 regulations, 108, 110, 189
disease-causing organisms, 1–2, 107, 107*b*. *See
 also specific organism*
disease control. *See* pest and disease control
dispute settlement process
 GATT, 36–39
 WTO, 8, 38–39, 53, 55, 151
 cases under, 63–74, 64*t*–68*t*, 97, 100, 140
 informal, 59
 lessons from, 195–96
Doha Development Agenda, 6, 8, 74–76
Doha Ministerial Declaration, 58, 76
Doha Round, 6, 187, 197–99
 aid to developing countries, 204
 animal welfare issues under, 175, 179
 geographical indications protection under,
 132, 134, 135–36, 149
dolphin-safe tuna, labeling scheme for, 62–63,
 74, 74*n*, 156, 157, 157*n*, 180
domestic producers, misuse of safety
 regulations to protect, 108, 110
domestic products
 differentiation from foreign products, 132
 support for country-of-origin labeling, 140
domestic regulation, 5
domestic supply function, 27
downward harmonization, 199
drug residues, 122–25. *See also* antibiotics
drug resistance, 124, 124*n*

trade effects of, 153
versus trademarks, 135, 147
geographical pattern, of disease outbreaks, 78–79, 88
Germany, 116
  milk production standards, 44n
  organic foods in, 170n, 171n
  pork import ban, 31n, 103n
ginseng, 132, 140
global framework, 11, 35–76, 101, 106, 199–200. *See also* multilateral governance
  justifications for, 185–86
  for pest and disease control, 15, 99
  recommendations for, 203–205
global good dimension, in food safety regulation, 106
globalization, of food supply, 3–7
glyphosate-resistant (GR) soybeans, 162
GM foods. *See* genetically modified foods
GMOs. *See* genetically modified organisms (GMOs)
goals, 17, 18–19, 18t, 187
  quality, 151, 152
  social, labeling and, 63, 127, 147
government. *See also* national regulation
  role in food regulation, 185, 206
  role in labeling regimes, 147, 152
  role in process attribute regulations, 181–82
  role in regulating quality, 127
government information services, 130, 131
government penalties, 14
"green box," 180n
Green Party, 171n
Greenpeace, 176n, 178n
Grocery Manufacturers of America, 146
groundnuts, 111–14
growth hormones, 102, 105, 114, 115, 199. *See also* beef growth hormone dispute; *specific hormone*
growth promoters, 114. *See also* antibiotics; *specific substance*

ham, 135n, 137n
harmonization. *See also* global framework; multilateral governance
  downward, 199
  in genetically modified product regulation, 154
  of labeling regimes, 132, 146, 149
  normative basis for, 204
  under SPS agreement, 40, 45–46
  trade impact of, 45, 199, 204
  WTO promotion of, 193–94
Hass avocados, 9, 82–87, 99, 189
Hazard Analysis and Critical Control Point (HACCP), 103, 103n, 190
health and safety issues, 8–9. *See also* human health hazards; *specific issue*
health features, and purchasing decisions, 127

Health of Animals Act of 1990 (Canada), 124, 178
hedonistic attributes, 127
Honduras, 108
"horizontal" regulations, 20
hormones. *See* beef growth hormone dispute; growth hormones
Humane Slaughter Act of 1958 (US), 176
human health hazards, 101–26
  classification of, 101–102, 105
  consumer reactions to, 105
  entering after point of sale, 106n
  management of, in trade system, 125–26
  not tied to animal diseases, 9–10
  and nutritional labeling, 145
Hungary, 124, 133, 134

identity standards. *See* standards of identity
IDF. *See* International Dairy Federation (IDF)
IFOAM. *See* International Federation of Organic Agriculture Movements (IFOAM)
import bans, 21–22, 27, 28, 31
  addressing pest and disease control, 81
  and food safety regulation, 104
  partial, 22
  seasonal, 22, 86–87
  trade-restrictive, 23
import standards, for food-borne pathogens, 108–11
India, 63, 73, 124, 134, 196
infectious bursal disease, 47, 47n
information
  credibility of, 128–29
  detrimental to sales, disclosure of, 129, 129n
  nutritional (*See* nutritional labeling)
  provision of, 203–204
    and process attribute labeling, 156
  public *versus* private, 128–31, 152
informational remedies, 22b, 23–24, 27, 31, 128. *See also* labeling
information exchange mechanisms
  under SPS agreement, 41
  under TBT agreement, 53
information failures, 9, 192
  market failures stemming from, 129, 129n
information services
  government, 130, 131
  private sector, 181
inspection systems. *See also* verification
  meat, 103n
  and process attributes, 152–53, 156
instruments, used in food regulations, 21–25, 22b
intellectual property. *See also* trade-related aspects of intellectual property (TRIPS)
  and biotechnology, 154n
  geographical indications as form of, 16, 205
  types of instruments, 56

interest groups, 13
    consumer, 2
    and genetically modified foods, 19, 181
    political pressures exerted by, 5
    producer, 2
    and regulatory capture, 32, 186
International Agreement on Olive Oil and
        Table Olives, 133, 134t
International Animal Health Code, 42, 78
International Aquatic Animal Health Code, 42
International Convention for the Use of
        Appellations d'Origine and Denominations
        of Cheeses, 133, 134t
international coordination. *See* global
        framework; multilateral governance
International Dairy Federation (IDF), 53, 54
International Federation of Organic
        Agriculture Movements (IFOAM),
        172–73
International Organization for Standardization
        (ISO), 53–54
International Plant Protection Convention
        (IPPC), 41, 79, 81, 189
international standards organizations. *See also*
        regulatory institutions; *specific
        organization*
    role of, 203–205
Ireland, 116, 117
irradiation, food, 109n
ISO. *See* International Organization for
        Standardization (ISO)
Israel, 124, 134, 173n
Italy, 23n, 116, 133, 135n

Japan
    animal welfare in, 174, 176
    antibiotic regulations, 124n
    FMD measures, 99
    labeling regimes, 62, 132, 143
    organic foods, 157, 170–72, 170n, 172
    ski standards dispute, 36n
    tomato import ban, 44
    varietal testing case, 46n, 63, 70t–71t, 72
    WTO dispute cases, 63, 68, 68n, 70t–71t, 72
Joint FAO/WHO Expert Committee on Food
        Additives (JECFA), 43, 44n, 111, 118,
        123n
Joint FAO/WHO Meeting on Pesticide
        Residues (JMPR), 43
judicial redress. *See* legal system
juice, 129n

labeling, 10, 11, 127–49
    alternative regimes for, 130, 131t
    animal welfare, 156, 156t, 175
    certification of, 148
    costs of, 62, 128, 129, 131, 143, 147, 148
    and counter-notifications, 62

country-of-origin (*See* country-of-origin
        labeling)
    for dolphin-safe tuna, 62–63, 74, 74n, 156,
        157, 157n, 180
    eco-, 11, 54, 62, 76, 166n, 197
    of genetically modified foods, 54, 62, 153,
        157, 159–60, 161, 161n, 195
        debate over, 163–69
    geographical indications, 130, 131–32, 131t
    mandatory, 130, 131t, 202
    multilateral governance of, 132, 149, 156–60
    nutritional (*See* nutritional labeling)
    of organic foods, 156, 156t, 157, 171, 183
    private sector role in, 152
    process, 19, 24, 76, 155–56, 156t, 195
    public sector role in, 127, 152
    regulation of, 23–24
    and social goals, 63, 127, 147
    under TBT agreement, 54–56, 62
    trade effects of, 128, 146–49, 153
Lamming Report, 117
Law Concerning Standardization and Proper
        Labeling of Agricultural and Forestry
        Products (Japan), 143, 172
Law Concerning the Protection and Control
        of Animals (Japan), 176
legal system, 13, 14, 17, 37, 38f, 197–98,
        205–206
    and geographical indications, 135n, 205
    and labeling regimes, 149
    pre-Uruguay Round, 36–37, 38f
"lemon" problem, 129
life-cycle analysis (LCA), 166n, 171, 181
like products, national treatment for, 36, 55n,
        138–39, 153, 166, 181
Lisbon Agreement, 57, 133–34, 134t
List A diseases, 78, 88
List B diseases, 78, 94
Listeria monocytogenes, 46, 107b
livestock diseases. *See* pest and disease
        control; *specific disease*
living modified organisms (LMOs), 159
locality of production, 10
L'Office International des Epizooties (OIE), 41,
        47n, 78, 82, 88–89, 92, 94, 96–97, 189
Luxembourg, 116

Maastricht Treaty, 178n
mad cow disease. *See* bovine spongiform
        encephalopathy (BSE)
maize. *See* corn
Malaysia, 63, 73, 196
"manmade " food safety risks, 101–102, 105
Marine Mammal Protection Act (US), 180
market efficiency, regulations enhancing,
        14–16, 206
market failures, 8
    stemming from information failures, 129,
        129n

regulation of, 151, 156–60, 181–83, 202
TBT Committee discussions on, 157–58,
    158t
trade disputes regarding, 151, 152–55
verification of, 152–53, 156, 192, 202
process-oriented groups, 2
process standards, 22–23, 201–202
    addressing pest and disease control, 81
    equivalence of, 48, 49
    in health and food safety, 24, 190
    and pest control, 99
    and political economy capture, 32
producers
    market incentives to encourage, 206
    regulatory capture by, 31–32, 186, 188
    risk reduction by, 188
product bans, 28
product differentiation
    based on production methods (*see* process
        attributes)
    domestic from foreign, 132
    quality-related, consumer demand for, 188
production, locality of, 10
production methods, product differentiation
    based on. *See* process attributes
productivity-enhancing technology, 102, 105,
    191. *See also specific technology*
    health effects of, 114–26
product names, and trademark law, 57
product-process doctrine, 74
product standards, 22–23, 202. *See also* quality
progesterone, 117
protection. *See also* overprotection;
    underprotection
    optimal level of, 30–31
    social meaning of, 30
protectionism, 11, 36, 188
protectionist capture, 153
public certification infrastructure, 202
public good element, 18, 45, 125–26
public goods, provision of, 14–15, 187
public sector
    role in labeling, 147, 152
    role in process attribute regulations, 181–82
    role in regulating quality, 127, 201–202
Punta del Este Ministerial Declaration, 37
purchasing decisions, 15–16, 27, 127

quality attributes, 10–11, 55
    and consumer preference, 127
    disputes over, 32
    and pricing, 129
quality goals
    regulation of process attributes to achieve,
        151
    versus risk, 152
quality regulation, 8–9, 10, 18, 127–49, 187–88
    international standards for, 148, 202
    in practice, 131–146

quality-related measures, 191–93
quantitative restrictions, 21–22, 22b
quarantine restrictions, 31

recombinant bovine somatotropin (rbST),
    43–44, 44n, 119n, 199
recombinant DNA (rDNA), 163
regionalization, 41, 51, 194–95
regional plant protection conventions
    (RPPCs), 79
regulatory capture, 31–32, 102, 186
regulatory institutions, 17. *See also specific
    institution*
    international differences in, 17, 185–86
    for pest and disease control, 98
    under SPS agreement, 41–44
    use of information remedies by, 130
regulatory measures
    abuse of, 199
    categorization of, 10
    mandatory, 14, 202
rendering process, for animal feed, 92–93, 99
rent-seeking, 31, 205
Report of the Working Party on Border Tax
    Adjustments, 55n
resource constraints, 3
retaliation, in beef hormone case, 118–19,
    122
rhododendrons, 44
rice, 131, 132, 134
Rio Declaration. *See* Convention on Biological
    Diversity (CBD)
risk, 11
    communication of, 18, 127
    versus quality goals, 152
    trade conflicts over, 32–33
risk assessment, 18
    and appropriate degrees of caution, 25–26
    as basis for regulations, 69, 73, 104, 125,
        186, 189–90
    in beef hormone case, 120–21
    and pest and disease control, 78, 81
risk avoidance, levels of, 25–26, 47–48, 47n
risk-based rule, 29–31, 29f
risk management, 8, 9, 15, 18, 187, 200
    in agricultural trade, 98–100, 188
    precautionary principle of, 25–26, 69, 76,
        197
    science and economics in, 28–31, 40–41,
        46–48, 87
    systems approach to, 23, 83, 84t, 87, 99,
        189
risk-reducing measures, 188–91
    disputes over, 189
Roquefort cheese, 110–11, 137n
Roundup-ready soybeans, 153
RPPCs. *See* regional plant protection
    conventions (RPPCs)
Russia, 110n

United States *(Cont.)*
  Statement of Administrative Action, 47
  tomato exports, 44
  varietal testing case, 46*n*, 63, 70*t*–71*t*, 72
  veterinary equivalence agreement with EU, 190, 194
  WTO dispute cases, 63, 69, 73–74
United States Country of Origin Labeling (US COOL), 142
Uruguay, 90, 99
Uruguay Round, 6, 35, 35*n*, 75
  Agreement on Agriculture (URAA), 35, 62*n*, 125, 180*n*, 198
  beef hormone dispute in, 119–20
  labeling requirements, 128, 157
  legal system for food regulation since, 37, 38*f*

vaccination, against animal diseases, 88–91
varietal testing, 46*n*, 63, 70*t*–71*t*, 72
vCJD. *See* Creutzfeldt-Jakob disease
veal boycott, 116
Venezuela, 138, 139
verification, 11, 20, 23, 24–25, 187. *See also* enforcement; notifications
  costs of, 27, 192
  of labeling, 148
  of maximum residue limits, 123
  of organic foods, 19, 155, 169, 172–73, 173*n*, 183
  and pricing, 156
  of process attributes, 152–53, 156, 192, 202
  public investment in, 201–202
  traceability issues in, 151
  trade-restrictive, 23
"vertical" regulations, 20
vertification, alternative options for, 202
veterinary drugs, 122–25. *See also* antibiotics; growth promoters
veterinary equivalence agreement (US-EU), 190, 194
Vietnam, 140
voluntary claims, 23, 181, 187–88, 192
  labeling regime regulating, 130, 131*t*

watermelons, 51
welfare-enhancing regulations, 32–33
wheat, transgenic, 182
wines and spirits, 131, 133, 134, 135, 167, 197
  geographical indications for, 57, 58, 76, 205
Working Group on Anabolic Agents in Animal Production (EC), 117

World Bank (WB), 75*n*, 113, 115
World Health Organization (WHO), 39, 43, 53*n*
World Intellectual Property Organization (WIPO), 57, 134
World Trade Center attack (9/11), 3
World Trade Organization (WTO), 5–6. *See also* Doha Round
  Agreement on Agriculture, 35, 62*n*, 125, 180*n*, 198
  aid to developing countries, 204
  animal welfare issues under, 179–81
  and Biosafety Protocol, 159
  Cancún ministerial meeting (September 2003), 197
  dispute mechanisms, 8, 38–39, 53, 55, 151
    cases under, 63–74, 64*t*–68*t*, 97, 100, 140
    informal, 59
    lessons from, 195–96
  food safety disputes in, 111–13
  genetically modified food regulations, 161, 164–65
  geographical indications protection, 135
  growth hormone dispute, 118–22, 195–96
  labeling issues, 128, 131, 132, 137–40, 143, 148, 164–65
  legal system for food regulations, 37, 38*f*, 205–206
  Marrakesh Agreement Establishing, 35*n*
  notification requirements, 59, 193
  pest and disease control regulations, 97–100
  role in regulatory framework, 8, 193–99, 205–206
  special and differential treatment, 75, 204
  TBT agreement (*See* Technical Barriers to Trade [TBT] Agreement)
  Trade and Environment Committee, 76, 195, 197

yield-enhancing technology, 102, 105. *See also specific technology*
  health effects of, 114–26
yogurt, 134, 136

zero risk level, 47
zero-tolerance standards, 108–109
zoonotic diseases, 9, 102. *See also* bovine spongiform encephalopathy (BSE); *specific disease*
zoosanitary measures, 8*n*

Other Publications from the Institute for International Economics

* = out of print

POLICY ANALYSES IN INTERNATIONAL ECONOMICS Series

U.S. Taxation of International Income: Blueprint for Reform*   Gary Clyde Hufbauer, assisted by Joanna M. van Rooij
October 1992   ISBN 0-88132-134-6

Who's Bashing Whom? Trade Conflict in High-Technology Industries   Laura D'Andrea Tyson
November 1992   ISBN 0-88132-106-0

Korea in the World Economy*   Il SaKong
January 1993   ISBN 0-88132-183-4

Pacific Dynamism and the International Economic System*
C. Fred Bergsten and Marcus Noland, editors
May 1993   ISBN 0-88132-196-6

Economic Consequences of Soviet Disintegration*
John Williamson, editor
May 1993   ISBN 0-88132-190-7

Reconcilable Differences? United States-Japan Economic Conflict*
C. Fred Bergsten and Marcus Noland
June 1993   ISBN 0-88132-129-X

Does Foreign Exchange Intervention Work?
Kathryn M. Dominguez and Jeffrey A. Frankel
September 1993   ISBN 0-88132-104-4

Sizing Up U.S. Export Disincentives*
J. David Richardson
September 1993   ISBN 0-88132-107-9

NAFTA: An Assessment
Gary Clyde Hufbauer and Jeffrey J. Schott/ *rev. ed.*
October 1993   ISBN 0-88132-199-0

Adjusting to Volatile Energy Prices
Philip K. Verleger, Jr.
November 1993   ISBN 0-88132-069-2

The Political Economy of Policy Reform
John Williamson, editor
January 1994   ISBN 0-88132-195-8

Measuring the Costs of Protection in the United States
Gary Clyde Hufbauer and Kimberly Ann Elliott
January 1994   ISBN 0-88132-108-7

The Dynamics of Korean Economic Development*   Cho Soon
March 1994   ISBN 0-88132-162-1

Reviving the European Union*
C. Randall Henning, Eduard Hochreiter, and Gary Clyde Hufbauer, editors
April 1994   ISBN 0-88132-208-3

China in the World Economy   Nicholas R. Lardy
April 1994   ISBN 0-88132-200-8

Greening the GATT: Trade, Environment, and the Future   Daniel C. Esty
July 1994   ISBN 0-88132-205-9

Western Hemisphere Economic Integration*
Gary Clyde Hufbauer and Jeffrey J. Schott
July 1994   ISBN 0-88132-159-1

Currencies and Politics in the United States, Germany, and Japan
C. Randall Henning
September 1994   ISBN 0-88132-127-3

Estimating Equilibrium Exchange Rates
John Williamson, editor
September 1994   ISBN 0-88132-076-5

Managing the World Economy: Fifty Years After Bretton Woods   Peter B. Kenen, editor
September 1994   ISBN 0-88132-212-1

Reciprocity and Retaliation in U.S. Trade Policy
Thomas O. Bayard and Kimberly Ann Elliott
September 1994   ISBN 0-88132-084-6

The Uruguay Round: An Assessment*
Jeffrey J. Schott, assisted by Johanna W. Buurman
November 1994   ISBN 0-88132-206-7

Measuring the Costs of Protection in Japan*
Yoko Sazanami, Shujiro Urata, and Hiroki Kawai
January 1995   ISBN 0-88132-211-3

Foreign Direct Investment in the United States,
3d ed., Edward M. Graham and Paul R. Krugman
January 1995   ISBN 0-88132-204-0

The Political Economy of Korea-United States Cooperation*
C. Fred Bergsten and Il SaKong, editors
February 1995   ISBN 0-88132-213-X

International Debt Reexamined*   William R. Cline
February 1995   ISBN 0-88132-083-8

American Trade Politics, 3d ed., I.M. Destler
April 1995   ISBN 0-88132-215-6

Managing Official Export Credits: The Quest for a Global Regime*   John E. Ray
July 1995   ISBN 0-88132-207-5

Asia Pacific Fusion: Japan's Role in APEC*
Yoichi Funabashi
October 1995   ISBN 0-88132-224-5

Korea-United States Cooperation in the New World Order*
C. Fred Bergsten and Il SaKong, editors
February 1996   ISBN 0-88132-226-1

Why Exports Really Matter!*   ISBN 0-88132-221-0
Why Exports Matter More!*   ISBN 0-88132-229-6
J. David Richardson and Karin Rindal
July 1995; February 1996

Global Corporations and National Governments
Edward M. Graham
May 1996   ISBN 0-88132-111-7

Global Economic Leadership and the Group of Seven   C. Fred Bergsten and C. Randall Henning
May 1996   ISBN 0-88132-218-0

The Trading System After the Uruguay Round*
John Whalley and Colleen Hamilton
July 1996   ISBN 0-88132-131-1

Private Capital Flows to Emerging Markets After the Mexican Crisis*   Guillermo A. Calvo, Morris Goldstein, and Eduard Hochreiter
September 1996   ISBN 0-88132-232-6

The Crawling Band as an Exchange Rate Regime: Lessons from Chile, Colombia, and Israel
John Williamson
September 1996   ISBN 0-88132-231-8

WORKS IN PROGRESS

Transforming the European Economy
Martin Neil Baily and Jacob Kirkegaard
New Regional Arrangements and
the World Economy
C. Fred Bergsten
The Globalization Backlash in Europe and
the United States
C. Fred Bergsten, Pierre Jacquet, and Karl Kaiser
Dollar Adjustment: How Far? Against What?
C. Fred Bergsten and John Williamson, editors
Trade Policy and Global Poverty
William R. Cline
China's Entry into the World Economy
Richard N. Cooper
American Trade Politics, 4th ed.
I.M. Destler
The ILO in the World Economy
Kimberly Ann Elliott
Reforming Economic Sanctions
Kimberly Ann Elliott, Gary C. Hufbauer,
and Jeffrey J. Schott
Cooperation Between the IMF and
the World Bank
Michael Fabricius
Controlling Currency Mismatches in
Emerging Economies
Morris Goldstein and Philip Turner
Future of Chinese Exchange Rates
Morris Goldstein and Nicholas R. Lardy
NAFTA: A Ten-Year Appraisal
Gary C. Hufbauer and Jeffrey J. Schott

New Agricultural Negotiations in
the WTO
Tim Josling and Dale Hathaway
Workers at Risk: Job Loss from Apparel,
Textiles, Footwear, and Furniture
Lori G. Kletzer
Responses to Globalization: US Textile
and Apparel Workers and Firms
Lori Kletzer, James Levinsohn, and
J. David Richardson
The Strategic Implications of China-Taiwan
Economic Relations
Nicholas R. Lardy
Making the Rules: Case Studies on
US Trade Negotiation
Robert Z. Lawrence, Charan Devereaux,
and Michael Watkins
US-Egypt Free Trade Agreement
Robert Z. Lawrence and Ahmed Galal
High Technology and the Globalization
of America
Catherine L. Mann
International Financial Architecture
Michael Mussa
Germany and the World Economy
Adam S. Posen
The Euro at Five: Ready for a Global Role?
Adam S. Posen, editor
Automatic Stabilizers for the Eurozone
Adam S. Posen
Chasing Dirty Money: Progress on
Anti-Money Laundering
Peter Reuter and Edwin M. Truman
Global Forces, American Faces:
US Economic Globalization at the
Grass Roots
J. David Richardson
US-Taiwan FTA Prospects
Daniel H. Rosen and Nicholas R. Lardy
Bail-in or Bailout? Responding to Financial
Crises in Emerging Markets
Nouriel Roubini and Brad Setser
Free Trade Agreements: US Strategies
and Priorities
Jeffrey J. Schott, editor
The Role of Private Capital in Financing
Development
John Williamson

Australia, New Zealand,
and Papua New Guinea
D.A. Information Services
648 Whitehorse Road
Mitcham, Victoria 3132, Australia
tel: 61-3-9210-7777
fax: 61-3-9210-7788
email: service@adadirect.com.au
http://www.dadirect.com.au

United Kingdom and Europe
(including Russia and Turkey)
The Eurospan Group
3 Henrietta Street, Covent Garden
London WC2E 8LU England
tel: 44-20-7240-0856
fax: 44-20-7379-0609
http://www.eurospan.co.uk

Japan and the Republic of Korea
United Publishers Services, Ltd.
KenkyuSha Bldg.
9, Kanda Surugadai 2-Chome
Chiyoda-Ku, Tokyo 101 Japan
tel: 81-3-3291-4541
fax: 81-3-3292-8610
email: saito@ups.co.jp
For trade accounts only.
Individuals will find IIE books in
leading Tokyo bookstores.

Thailand
Asia Books
5 Sukhumvit Rd. Soi 61
Bangkok 10110 Thailand
tel: 662-714-07402 Ext: 221, 222, 223
fax: 662-391-2277
email: purchase@asiabooks.co.th
http://www.asiabooksonline.com

Canada
Renouf Bookstore
5369 Canotek Road, Unit 1
Ottawa, Ontario KlJ 9J3, Canada
tel: 613-745-2665
fax: 613-745-7660
http://www.renoufbooks.com

India, Bangladesh, Nepal, and Sri Lanka
Viva Books Pvt.
Mr. Vinod Vasishtha
4325/3, Ansari Rd.
Daryaganj, New Delhi-110002
India
tel: 91-11-327-9280
fax: 91-11-326-7224
email: vinod.viva@gndel.globalnet.
ems.vsnl.net.in

Southeast Asia (Brunei, Cambodia,
China, Malaysia, Hong Kong, Indonesia,
Laos, Myanmar, the Philippines, Singapore,
Taiwan, and Vietnam)
Hemisphere Publication Services
1 Kallang Pudding Rd. #0403
Golden Wheel Building
Singapore 349316
tel: 65-741-5166
fax: 65-742-9356

Visit our Web site at:
www.iie.com
E-mail orders to:
orders@iie.com